The Common Cause

The Common Cause

Postcolonial Ethics and the Practice of Democracy, 1900–1955

LEELA GANDHI

The University of Chicago Press   Chicago and London

LEELA GANDHI is professor of English at the University of Chicago. She is the founding coeditor of the journal *Postcolonial Studies* and the author, most recently, of *Affective Communities: Anticolonial Thought and the Politics of Friendship*.

The University of Chicago Press, Chicago 60637
The University of Chicago Press, Ltd., London
© 2014 by The University of Chicago
All rights reserved. Published 2014.
Printed in the United States of America

23 22 21 20 19 18 17 16 15 14   1 2 3 4 5

ISBN-13: 978-0-226-01987-1 (cloth)
ISBN-13: 978-0-226-01990-1 (paper)
ISBN-13: 978-0-226-02007-5 (e-book)
DOI: 10.7208/chicago/9780226020075.001.0001

Library of Congress Cataloging-in-Publication Data
Gandhi, Leela, 1966– author.
  The common cause: postcolonial ethics and the practice of democracy, 1900–1955 / Leela Gandhi.
    pages; cm
  Includes bibliographical references and index.
  ISBN 978-0-226-01987-1 (cloth: alk. paper)—ISBN 978-0-226-01990-1 (pbk.: alk. paper)—ISBN 978-0-226-02007-5 (e-book) 1. Democracy—Moral and ethical aspects. 2. Postcolonialism—Moral and ethical aspects. 3. Postcolonialism—India. 4. Anti-imperialist movements—India. I. Title.
  JC423.G36 2014
  172.0954'09041—dc23

                                                                    2013036399

♾ This paper meets the requirements of ANSI/NISO Z39.48–1992 (Permanence of Paper).

For my father, Ramchandra Gandhi

Contents

Acknowledgments

This book has been in process for a long time, and many people and institutions have helped along the way. A sabbatical term from La Trobe University allowed me to work in dispersed archives; another from the University of Chicago, supported by a fellowship at the Franke Institute for the Humanities, yielded invaluable writing time. At the University of Chicago Press, Alan Thomas has been the most encouraging and engaged of editors and interlocutors. I am truly grateful for his direction and advice throughout the writing process.

The project came into view in the rare intellectual environment of the School of Criticism and Theory at Cornell University, where I served a summer term as faculty under the exemplary directorship of Amanda Anderson. I have gained immeasurably from her incisive and generous input over time, and from her ongoing work on political ethos and on the transnational histories of liberalism. My gratitude extends as well to the SCT community of participants, staff, faculty, and fellows for their feedback and suggestions.

I wish to thank the staff and archivists at the following libraries: the State Library of Victoria, the Bibliothèque nationale de France, the National Archives at Delhi, the Nehru Memorial Library and Museum, the Sri Aurobindo Ashram Archives, the Sabarmati Ashram Archives, Sri Ramanasramam, Regenstein Library at the University of Chicago, the Bodleian Library at the University of Oxford, the British Library, and the Houghton Library at Harvard University.

In other matters of detail, Timothy Campbell and Daniel Purdy were helpful on the question of Kant's clothing; James

Hevia shared resources from his ongoing research into colonial military history; and William Mazzarella shared his notes concerning the ban on cultural productions of the Royal Indian Navy Mutiny. Darrel Kwong Yung Chia has been a wonderful research assistant, always supportive and resourceful. Sarah McKeever and Matthew Sims also helped to negotiate and organize dispersed sources and materials during the writing of this book. Randolph Petilos at the University of Chicago Press shepherded the manuscript through its final stages, and Nicholas Murray has been an extremely attentive and helpful copyeditor.

I received valuable feedback on this project as it evolved from Bill Brown, Deborah Nelson, Seth Koven, Thomas Laqueur, David Levine, Dilip Gaonkar, Amy Villarejo, Michael Steinberg, Geoff Eley, Susan Bernstein, Simon During, Suzanne Stewart Steinberg, Asma Abbas, Mena Mitrano, Ania Loomba, Giovanna Covi, David Thomas, Suvir Kaul, Ruth Vanita, Ritu Birla, Vinay Lal, Paula Giocomoni, Pauline Nestor, Asimina Karavanta, R. Radhakrishnan, and Ferdinando Fasce. The two anonymous readers who kept company with the evolving manuscript have shaped this book. I cannot thank them enough.

I have been fortunate in the company of my colleagues at the University of Chicago. I learned much from them, and from the inspiring projects and conversations of my graduate students: Darrel Chia, Ian Duncan, Tristan Schweiger, Daniel Harris, Chandani Patel, Daniel Elam, Siddhartha Sathpathy, and Brady Smith. Besides the formative influence on this book of the 2009 SCT seminar, "On Anticolonial Metaphysics," I would like to acknowledge the exchanges and camaraderie of a spring 2013 University of Chicago seminar entitled "Radical Ethics." For their collegiality, kindness, and friendship, variously, in Chicago, I am especially grateful to Rita Balzotti, Lauren Berlant, Sheila Bhagawan, Bill Brown, Dipesh Chakrabarty, Becky Chandler, Jim Chandler, Kyong-Hee Choi, Bradin Cormack, Maud Ellmann, Judith Farquhar, Frances Ferguson, Michael Geyer, Miriam Hansen, James Hevia, Wu Hung, Adrienne Hiegel, Ian Horswill, Carl Kutsmode, Agnes Lugo-Ortiz, Drew McLeod, Rochona Majumdar, William Mazzarella, Diane Milliotes, Janice Misurrel-Mitchell, Gabriel Mitchell, Tom Mitchell, Santiago Moreno, Debbie Nelson, Naomi Patschke, Michelle Sanford, Anwen Tormey, Lisa Wedeen, John Wilkinson, Lida Wu, Diana Young, Fraser Young, Judith Zeitlin, and Linda Zerilli.

Through the composition of this book, I thought a great deal about my father, Ramchandra Gandhi: an ordinary language philosopher whose quest for the extraordinary in the ordinary made the simplest things both epic and magical. In recent years I have relied more than ever upon the love and backing of Indu Gandhi, Veenapani Chawla, and Bronte Adams.

The Adishakti community, Mona Bachmann, Kate Cook, Michael Dutton, Caroline Lewis, the Hindu College community, Sunam Mukherjee, Claire Murray, Raj Pandey, Mahesh Rangarajan, Sanjay Seth, Heidi Tinsman, and Ruth Vanita have also been true allies.

My indebtedness to Tamara Chin is simply incalculable. I have been the beneficiary throughout of her brilliance, idealism and erudition. Her rare example, loving support, and companionship are the conditions of possibility for almost everything, including this book.

———

Early versions of the chapters 1 and 3 appeared as "After Virtue: Notes on Early-Twentieth-Century Socialist Antimaterialism" in *English Literary History* 77, no. 2 (2010): 413–46, and as "Postcolonial Theory and the Crisis of European Man" in *Postcolonial Studies* 10, no. 1 (2007): 93–110. I am grateful to Frances Ferguson and Ian Hunter, respectively, for their responses as I worked through and revised ideas first presented in the pages of those journals.

Common cause:

1. lack of significance in individual high or low values, and
2. an objective shared with another person or a group.

Moral Imperfection: An Ethics for Democracy

A miscellany of opinions from the vanguard of Euro-American life has surreptitiously fostered the view that democracy is a uniquely Western property and inheritance. Dominant Western players in the new world order regularly condone violent territorial interventions in its name. Less predictably, a left-leaning theoretical dispensation emerging in the wake of poststructuralism has declared postcolonial perspectives harmful or at best irrelevant to democratic thought.[1] This book asserts a global provenance for democracy. The modern world has seen numerous non-Western experiments in democratic politics, many of which have been autochthonous.[2] Anticolonial movements the world over have included democracy in their revolutionary agendas by combining demands for universal enfranchisement with those for independence.[3] Important though such histories are to the case at hand, my claim has a different accent and concerns the inner life of democracy.

I argue that the global disposition of democracy, as an affect or attitude of infinite inclusivity or as predicating the interconnection of self and world, was intensified by an ethical turn in the transnational scene of early twentieth-century political thought, itself born of colonial encounter. In this milieu the concept of ethics had obtained a ubiquitous (and not always salubrious) application. No longer the denominator for right and wrong or for good and bad behaviors merely, it came to designate all projects of disciplined self-work, or *askesis*, wherein the arts of living achieved a collective reso-

nance.[4] Extremists, moderates, and radicals alike held subjective properties to be universalizable and projected self-cultivation as an occult work
not just upon the self but also upon others. Amid this stylistic ethical
variety, sympathizers and advocates of antidemocratic programs, especially, extolled an orthodox *askesis* of self-consolidation and perfectionism, distinguishing rare individuals from the common lot. By contrast, in
diverse anticolonial and antifascist quarters, many of them non-Western,
democracy was itself refashioned as a counter-*askesis*, or spiritual regimen
of imperfectionism. This comprised aberrant practices of self-ruination,
or an anti-care of the self, aimed at making common cause both with the
victims and abettors of unjust sociality (by defending the former and re-
forming the latter). *The Common Cause* deprovincializes the history of democracy by exhuming and elaborating some of these assorted genealogies
for moral imperfectionism in the first half of the twentieth century in the
context of the Indo-British colonial encounter.

Dramatis Personae

This study is by no means saturated by a single historical context, and the
arguments of individual chapters are informed by disparate material circumstances. Subsequent investigations, nonetheless, share a point of departure in the clarification of an ethics of moral perfectionism during the
beginning years of the previous century and with regard to an inchoate
opposition between the new imperialisms and new liberalisms of this era.
Setting out this framing context and clarifying the conceptual framework
for what follows are the main aims of this introduction, and its key elements are summarized directly below.

If pan-European in scope, the conflicts of New Imperialism/Liberalism
were sharply crystallized within British politics in the Khaki election of
1900, contested between the ruling conservatives and the Liberal Party,
the latter already split and redefining its values following the retirement of
William Gladstone and the controversy over Irish Home Rule. Herein, conservative New Imperialism revealed itself as the product of a conjunction
between imperial interests and proto-fascism, quite different from its liberal
nineteenth-century predecessor. It is best explained as a splenetic reaction
against the progress of various reform movements within Europe, bringing
the specter of democracy closer to home as a nightmare of representation
from the domestic public sphere: women, the unpropertied masses, working men, the lumpenproletariat, racial others, the Semite, the crowd, the
rabble, and the undistinguished mob. New Imperialist ideologues strongly

believed that the threat of democracy was best answered through totalitarian self-development based upon the cultivation of rank, purity, excellence, strength, heroism, exceptionality, and so forth. The New Liberals opposing this formation set themselves apart from orthodox liberalism while claiming direct descent from the democratizing reformisms of the nineteenth century. Yet their own emphasis on the ethicization of the political betrayed a profoundly divided attitude to democracy that opposed the values of representative government to those of egalitarian society. This position, at the heart of *belle époque* New Liberalism, is well explained by the philosopher Jacques Ranciere as incorporating the following thesis: "Democratic government . . . is bad when it is allowed to be corrupted by democratic society, which wants for everyone to be equal and for all differences to be respected. It is good, on the other hand, when it rallies individuals enfeebled by democratic society to the vitality of war in order to defend the values of civilization, the values pertaining to the clash of civilizations. . . . There is only one good democracy, the one that represses the catastrophe of democratic civilization."[5] In a related defense of "good" over "bad" democracy, and not unlike their political antagonists, New Liberal ideologues elicited a public *askesis* of their own, albeit one also premised upon a heroic ethical style ultimately antithetical to social and political inclusivity. To put the case precisely, although New Liberalism was an important adversary to New Imperialism on home ground, it nonetheless retained key investments in totalitarian premises by presenting the democracy it was supposedly defending as a comparable, if not perfected, ethos of perfectionism.

The multiple moral imperfectionisms at the core of this book emerged in chain reaction against this formative consensus across opposing political persuasions on the positive value of an ethics contrary to the ideals of radical democracy. The diverse bearers of these cultivated imperfectionisms brought together the anticolonial and antifascist sides of Europe with similar force in the colonies, so as to distill a more hospitable universalism. Including Western and non-Western players, they struggled to embrace what was spiritually durable within colonial culture: their aim was to salvage the very best of Europe in face of Europe's descent into totalitarianism. Taking the form of a self-lowering or self-negating response to the prevailing perfectionist ethico-political culture, these endeavors were simultaneously therapeutic and pedagogic (working on or improving the given materials) and also negative-critical and positive-utopian (reversing the logic of available materials or imagining the best outcomes for them). We can think of them as a reverse civilizing mission without any of the complicating detritus of rank and priority. Thus, the *Discourse on Colonialism*, written by the Martinican poet and cofounder of the négritude movement, Aimé Césaire, typically presents the colonial demand for independence from Europe as an intervention by well-wishers into the solipsistic life cycle of an unendurable friend or relative and expresses as much concern for the cultural and moral flourishing of perpetrators as for the victims of colonial injustice.[6] In his slightly later classic *The Wretched of the Earth*, Frantz Fanon, the writer and revolutionary member of the Algerian National Liberation Front, similarly describes the history of anti-colonial liberation movements as an effort to break from Europe if only for the sake of Europe. As he writes, "If we wish to reply to the expectations of the people of Europe, it is no good sending them back a reflection, even an ideal reflection, of their society and their thought from which from time to time they feel immeasurably sickened. For Europe, for ourselves and for humanity, comrades, we must turn over a new leaf, we must work out new concepts, and try to set afoot a new man."[7]

Successive chapters itemize such labors in stages, bookended by the 1900 British Khaki election that gave a popular mandate to New Imperialism, on the one hand, and the 1955 Bandung Conference, marking the era of decolonization proper, on the other. Notwithstanding our focus on the Indo-British encounter, it is nearly impossible to circumscribe the geography of empire in this period, due to the unprecedented shift in scale of European imperialism. British interests violently collided with those of other powerful nations over territories and resources, and even the most antagonistic participants collaborated in the sly vindication of totalitarianism at home and in the colonies. The South Asian experience of empire was also imbricated with various crises in Africa and Asia in the wake of war and the mass migrations of refugee populations. The complex crossovers and collaborations of this setting belong, we will see, to odd local pockets of uncodified resistance and of improvised exchange between East and West.

Our immediate task, however, is to clarify the antagonistic co-emergence of New Imperialism and New Liberalism and the resulting ethicization of politics against democracy. We will summarily review M. K. Gandhi's *Hind Swaraj* (1910) as the blueprint for an ethics of moral imperfectionism tethered to the conditioning scene of New Imperialism and New Liberalism. A concluding section considers the counter-*askesis* of imperfection as a belated postcolonial variant of philosophical cynicism.

The Ethical Subject of New Imperialism

We tend to think that postindustrial imperialisms are centered in the long nineteenth century, even though the European fervor for overseas expansion had abated by the mid-1800s.[8] The old French empire was almost no more. Britain had lost thirteen American colonies, and Spain and Portugal had lost most of their South American holdings. A fresh scramble for overseas territories during the fin de siècle resulted in the new imperialisms of the twentieth century. Most gains went to Britain, France, and Portugal, but newcomers such as Germany, Belgium, Italy, Japan, the United States, and Russia secured significant territories and interests. By the start of the twentieth century, as we learn from the English New Liberal economist J. A. Hobson, nearly twenty-three million square miles of the earth's surface were under imperial dominion, and some five hundred and twenty-two million of the world's people had been placed under foreign rule.[9]

Hobson's expressive statistics build a contrast between good and bad as much as between old and new imperialisms, explicitly praising the former (good-old) for their disinterested duty toward the backward peoples of the globe and condemning the latter (bad-new) for commercialism, self-interest, and extreme authoritarianism. These emphases were frequently canvassed by Hobson's peers in the liberal rank and file and later elaborated by the influential political philosopher Hannah Arendt in "Imperialism, Nationalism, Chauvinism" (1945), which became a starting point for her magisterial study of twentieth-century totalitarianisms.[10] Like Hobson, whom she acknowledges directly, Arendt acclaims the unselfish—indeed, magnanimous—quality of nineteenth-century liberal imperialisms, which she credits with producing, "that type of man whom one would find scattered in all the colonial services, particularly the British, who would take a fatherly interest in the peoples they were ordered to rule and who would eagerly assume the role of the dragon slayer, thereby fulfilling in a manly fashion the gallant ideals and dreams of their boyhood."[11] By contrast, she declares the new imperialisms of the early twentieth century indissociable from fascism, and constitutive of modern totalitarianism. "It may be justifiable," Arendt observes with reference to the twentieth-century European scramble for Asia and Africa, "to consider the whole period a preparatory stage for coming catastrophes."[12]

The New Imperialism was certainly characterized by a style of violent autocratic governance, unmatched, as contemporary observers insisted, in the earlier nineteenth century. So, for instance, in 1898 Herbert Kitchner and his troops massacred some ten thousand Mahdist dervishes in order to test the new Maxim machine guns at Omdurman in present-day Sudan. For this he received countless titles and promotions, the last as Secretary of State for War in 1914. In 1906, Lord Cromer, then British governor of Egypt, ordered a series of public hangings and floggings at the village of Denshawai as reprisal for the mobbing by local bird-keeping families of four British officers on an unauthorized pigeon-shoot. The British reaction was widely deemed appropriate to the death by heat stroke of one officer during the incident. A year later, Parliament awarded Cromer £50,000 in recognition of his eminent services in the Middle East.[13] In the spirit of these public accolades, New Imperial spokesmen upheld toughness in the field as proof of evolutionary advantage and, more so, as the expression of an *askesis* of decultivation proper to rare individuals in degenerate times. An anonymous essay of 1909, published in the left-leaning journal *The New Age*, praises imperial force in these terms as testimony to "the power of the strong over the feeble, of the capable over the incapable, of the cunning over the simple, of the creative over the passive, of knowledge over ignorance, of man over tiger, of the tiger over his prey."[14] In each such sequential victory, other sympathetic writers averred, power devolves to those who have refined the capacity for gratuitous violence, in which the show of strength or the act of killing is its own end, and which manifests a heroic freedom from necessity that is entirely, if perversely, on par with the purported moral disinterest in material outcomes professed by liberalism's erstwhile civilizing missionaries.

One of the strongest arguments of this type comes from two influential essays of 1919 and 1927, written by the conservative economist Joseph Schumpeter, briefly an Austrian Minister of Finance in the interwar years. Defending the rise of New Imperialism at large, Schumpeter describes the revival of brute force within this formation as ethically exigent for Europe: a clear path of access to the obscured atavisms wherein an aristocratic will to dominate is stripped of all banalizing instrumentalities, such as the need to eat, procreate, and find shelter. In this sense, he argues, modern imperialism clarifies an, "objectless disposition . . . to unlimited forcible expansion . . . without definite utilitarian limits."[15] Thus, in every instance where expansionist aggression "has no adequate object beyond itself" or cannot be explained or satisfied by the "fulfillment of a concrete interest," the valuable members of the race evince their distinction from the common dross.[16] Nonrational, purely instinctual inclinations toward war and conquest are "mainly fostered by the ruling classes," and it is oxymoronic to posit "a peasant imperialism" or a "working-class imperialism."[17] Democracy, according to Schumpeter, is the chief hindrance to this desired revivification of European man. Not only is it the political preserve of those with object-driven lifestyles, it also upholds a regrettable ethos of Benthamite utility and the over-rationalization of needs and wants. It is always building, developing, asking for more purpose and application. In Schumpeter's words, "everything that is purely instinctual, everything insofar as it is purely instinctual, is driven into the background by this development," where democracy, "in the 'bourgeois' sense—come[s] closest to political dominion."[18] Though these attitudes are hardly surprising in the general context of imperial-fascist *apologia*, they elucidate the rudiments of a totalitarian ethical emphasis from which the so-called advocates of democracy at the scene failed to extricate themselves, as we will see, to disastrous political effect. The awkward compromises of New Liberalism are described in the next two sections.

New Liberalism and the Enigma of Democracy

The rise of New Imperialism coincided with that of a self-professed New Liberalism in Britain, distinguished by stronger alliances with socialism than had been formerly admissible under the tenets of orthodox liberalism. Adding an extra chapter to the history of the movement after J. S. Mill and his generation, New Liberalism is inextricable from the gestation of the modern welfare state and the lived experience, to this day, of social democracy.[19] Its considerable achievements notwithstanding, it is also intimately yoked to New Imperialism through a contestational yet shared grammar of understanding, and its legacy carries a trace of this shadow.

New Liberalism was born of a strenuous critique of laissez-faire individualism (and its proxy, the hands-off state) by the generation that had come of age before the First World War. They believed their task, as a sympathetic editor of the *Manchester Guardian* observed at the time, "was to find the lines on which liberals could be brought to see that the old tradition must be expanded to yield a fuller measure of social justice, a more real equality, an individual as well as political liberty."[20] Contemporary enthusiasts celebrated this new program as nothing short of "a principle which unionists called socialistic."[21] Testimony to the cumulatively stirred consciences of sensitive Oxford men who had spent far too many evenings attending lectures on social reform at one or another of London's various ethical societies, the New Liberal volte-face was also pragmatic. The second reform act had liberated a new plebian electorate and lowered the bar for the possibility of a working-class movement. There was significant competition over this constituency from fin de siècle socialists looking for parliamentary careers under the umbrella of the fledgling Labor Party. An alliance that brought the benefit of electoral experience to labor novices while delivering fresh ideological content to the New Liberals was strongly endorsed by leaders from both camps. Such a front, the liberal veteran John Morley had once reasoned, would make for a meaningful contest "between brains and numbers on the one side, and wealth, rank, vested interest, possession, in short, on the other."[22] Liberals, he most certainly implied, would contribute "a great portion of the most cultivated intellect of the nation."[23]

In 1894 a small group of influential soft socialists and so-called new liberals came together as the Rainbow Circle, thus named as much for the Rainbow tavern where they convened for liquid dinners as for their political ecumenism.[24] Their aim was to refine the tenets of New Liberalism proper and to find a precise denominator for them. Of the many compound terms canvassed—*new radicalism* and *new collectivism* included—*democracy* recurs most frequently and emerged the clear winner. Somewhat contentiously, partisan propaganda from this time adduced democracy as New Liberalism's signatory contribution to the progressive development of the enlightenment universalism to which it was heir. In his book *Democratic England* (1912), Percy Alden thus invokes liberal social policy to extol imperial Britain as the most democratic nation in the modern world.[25] Yet more extravagantly, C. F. G. Masterman, a politician and liberal MP for West Ham North, claims New Liberal democratic experimentation as a singular event in world history. In his words, "given that desire in an educated Democracy, . . . there is no limit to the improvement of the world. That empowerment has never been tried on solid earth. The Greek and Roman civilization rested on a basis of slave labor. The Greek democracy had no real claim to be called a government of universal free citizens. Today the empowerment is being attempted, for the first time, of establishing a community in which every man and woman is a citizen, and every man and woman free."[26]

Masterman's grand rhetoric aside, incipient New Liberal democracy was by no means a form of universal self-government based on universal suffrage. Writing wryly about these years in *The Rule of Democracy, 1905–1914* (1932), the French philosopher Élie Halévy provides a thick catalogue of the many persons considered unfit for the vote under New Liberal dispensation, including lunatics, prisoners, paupers, menservants, sons still residing in their master's/father's home, itinerant laborers, and, of course, women and colonial subjects.[27] Also, it was quite unclear, not least of all to the New Liberals, what was actually implied by the term *democracy*. Active members of the Rainbow Circle readily conceded that this cardinal concept was, "but imperfectly explained and understood."[28] An opportunity for ideological clarification soon presented itself over the issue of the second Boer War, believed by many New Liberals to be "the test issue for this generation," which brought them into direct conflict with New Imperialism.[29] Fought between 1889 and 1902, the war concerned a British offensive against the two independent South African Boer republics of the Transvaal and the Orange Free State, both annexed in 1910 under

British dominion status as the Union of South Africa. New Liberals declared themselves pro-Boer and, by extension, anti-imperialist from the outset, on the grounds that the New Imperialism was entirely incompatible with democracy; the two doctrines, as we hear from the authors of *Liberalism and the Empire* (1900), "differ in their morals, their manners, and their ideals."[30] As L. T. Hobhouse puts it in *Democracy and Reaction* (1904), "Imperialist and democratic sentiments must come into conflict. Between these two sides there can be no reconciliation for they represent the most fundamental cleavage of political opinion."[31] The issue came to a head in the 1900 wartime Khaki elections, which the incumbents, pro-imperial conservatives won by a landslide over the New Liberals.

The nobility of this electoral sacrifice being as it may, New Liberals were scarcely anti-imperial in their attitudes and policies. Besides their admiration for earlier "disinterested" imperialisms (demonstrable in Hobson's writings), the party regarded empire as a crucial investment in British futures, at grave risk of conservative mismanagement. The youngish Winston Churchill, then president of the Board of Trade, strongly made this case in subsequent election campaigns, persuading voters that without liberal leadership, "very soon there would be very little British Constitution and very little British Empire for anyone to enjoy."[32] Also, New Liberal, pro-Boer sympathies scarcely translated into sympathetic thinking on various "native" questions. Pamphlets advertising the triumphs of liberal governance between 1906 and 1908, for instance, prominently showcase the forcible deportation of all Chinese migrant labor on the Rand as evidence of racial solidarity with the domestic workforce. "But for the agitation in Great Britain," readers are instructed, "there would have been not one single white miner on the Witwatersrand to-day, but 200,000 Chinamen."[33] These multiple contradictions of the New Liberal position on empire are concisely captured by a member of the Rainbow Circle: "Above all we must frankly accept democratic methods; and embrace our Imperial opportunities."[34] Thus contesting a project (empire) that it did not fully oppose by means of a doctrine (democracy) that it did not fully grasp, New Liberalism reveals its fault lines. The weak antagonism or, indeed, broken dialectic of its presumed countermand to New Imperialism is manifest, especially, in its parallel ethicization of democracy through a simple yet contingent inversion of the totalitarian *askesis* encountered in the previous section and encapsulated by Joseph Schumpeter as the law of an authoritarian objectless disposition. Let me explain.

New Liberal ideologues systematically recast the instinct/utility opposition at the heart of Schumpeter's schema as one between survivalism and cultivation, claiming the second term as integral to democratic ethics and as the sign of an updated moral perfectionism apposite to the demands of contemporary life.[35] The influential authors of *Liberalism and Empire*, Francis W. Hirst, Gilbert Murray, and J. L. Hammond, especially, declared the purported self-work of imperialist survivalism to be an archaic *techne*, or "stupendous anachronism," that augured the perpetuation of the best only by means of a backward step to the tooth and claw of our distant evolutionary past.[36] How absurd, they reasoned, that the conservative constituencies that once, "would not accept a monkey as a type of undeveloped man are tumbling over each other to acclaim the tiger or the wild cat as an image of his maturity."[37] Though democracy was no less concerned with the perpetuation of the fittest and the "irregular elimination of bad stock"—they added in a crucial, if confusing, footnote to their argument—it begins its work well after the matter of crude survival has been settled.[38] Hobson strongly concurred with these postulates in his *Imperialism*. With the onset of New Liberal times, he asserts, "the struggle for individual life is not abated, it is merely shifted onto higher planes than that of bare animal existence."[39] Indeed, guilty as charged, democracy implies self-extrication from animality, "a triumph of the laws of mind over the laws of matter," and of "rational policy" over "natural selection."[40] In other words, it replaces "outer struggle" with "inner struggle," or "lower struggle" with "higher."[41] It is the art, more succinctly, of "the cultivation of the species."[42] By its intervention, Hobson concludes, "individuals now struggle with all extra energy . . . for comfort and wealth, for place and personal honor, for skill, knowledge, character, and even higher forms of self-expression."[43]

This polemic, germane to the democratic agonism of the period, can be summarized as follows: the presumed ethical subject of New Imperialism who has recourse to the perfectionism of the jungle actually belongs to an outmoded natural history. In contrast, the subject of New Liberalism who has recourse to a perfectionism located in self-care and self-rule is the true, avant-garde bearer of an evolutionary ethics. But how does this inverted ethics serve the cause of egalitarianism? Its disciplinary critique of brute force, notwithstanding, in what way is the new premium on affluence, rank, cultivation, honor, and height (in character and self-expression) advantageous to inclusivity? Whither democracy? Let us assess New Liberal ethics on its own terms.

The Problem of Reformist Moral Perfectionism

Winston Churchill once declared New Liberalism, "the cause of the left-out millions."[44] This was a standard refrain in party literature and the crux of Ebenezer Elliott's stirring compositions for the *Liberal Song Sheet*, most notably, his chart-topping "God Save the People": "When wilt Thou save the people? / O God of Mercy, when? / The people, Lord, the people. / Not thrones and crowns, but men!"[45] Short of divine intervention, New Liberalism delivered worldly salvation to the impoverished public largely through the medium of welfare; or, as Churchill preferred to put it, "by the raising of the welfare of the people."[46] But a few years after achieving office, New Liberal economists had drafted and implemented advanced ameliorative and interventionist legislation concerning labor exchanges, insurance for unemployment and infirmity, and compulsory education for minors. Bodies were also protected from contingency by far-reaching factory and workplace safety acts, as well as by incidental laws such as the Dogs Act of 1906, which provided indemnity against vicious canines, and the Butter Act of 1907, which protected consumers from bogus butter.[47]

While unprecedented, the deafening promotion of like measures in pamphlets, jingles, posters, and related media, sometimes gave the impression of New Liberalism as a movement perhaps too preoccupied with the raw materiality of the excluded majority. The oft-repeated claim that New Liberalism had liberated "the People's Food" from the clutches of Tory tariff reform, is a case in point, blaming the conservatives solely for an antidemocratic budget to the detriment of supper: "A Dear Loaf and a Dear Knife to cut it with. Dear Meat and a Dearer Oven to cook it in. Dear Butter and a Dearer Dish to eat it off."[48] Turning the tables on this charge, conservative propagandists regularly lampooned the liberals as no more than a bread and meat operation—a soup kitchen, at best.

As it happens, the liberal intelligentsia were wary of predicating social transformation upon social economics alone. A nagging neo-Hegelianism, among the leadership, contributed to anxieties that welfarism had inverted the natural order of things, in which the perfect state should be the apotheosis rather than goad of perfect citizenry: the universalization, in other words, of previously enlightened subjectivities. An adjacent neo-Kantianism led to pessimism about a public spirit enforced by obedience to external law alone without the corroborating claims of conscience. Those more sympathetic to the spirit of liberal individualism past, such as Hilaire Belloc, argued that a too-zealous state would release men from the character-building "burden of private rectitude."[49] More sentimental, humanitarian thinkers maintained that welfarism was the slippery slope of Benthamite quantification, distracting from the exigencies of qualitative change among the people—namely, the production of impalpable moral values rather than the mere maximization of utilities. Reviewing these concerns, the autodidactic pamphlet *We Couldn't Care More* (n.d.) urged

New Liberals to demonstrate that "Britain stands for principle over expediency" and, above all, for "the hearts and minds of the British people"[50]—not just for their laboring bodies. In other words, most architects of welfarism concurred that social policy needed to be supplemented by a shared, felt experience of reciprocal recognition and intersubjectivity in the body politic. C. F. G. Masterman describes the ideal as vested in "a community where the interest of each is identical with the interests of all."[51]

This diacritical shift from closing the gap between rich and poor to closing the gap between self and other quite alters the sequence of democracy's life cycle. Welfare, we hear very often from thinkers of the new dispensation, is not democracy itself so much as its sine qua non: "a certain minimum standard," or "shared minimum" or "minimum of opportunity" that but facilitates the real business of democracy as a personal discipline or ethics of "the common good."[52] "Our social system must have an ethical basis," we learn from Percy Alden.[53] Herbert Samuel concurs in his *Liberalism* (1902), insisting that "the trunk of the tree of liberalism is rooted in the soil of ethics."[54] And, speaking for his colleagues at large, D. G. Ritchie confesses the following: "We have to come to recognize, with Aristotle, the moral function of the State."[55]

The New Liberals could have looked closer to home than Aristotelian antiquity for due precedent. The ethicization of democracy was a well-established trope within the fin de siècle socialist subcultures to which New Liberals had direct access through key interlocutors in the Labor Party. Edward Carpenter, a surviving radical from that era, had strongly emphasized the personal and intangible dimensions of democratic revolution over its practical merits in his best-selling *Toward Democracy* (1883). In a later volume commemorating this socialist sage, liberal MP, Gilbert Beith recalled these sentiments in the context of the success of reformist legislation in Britain. In his words, "To Carpenter the word 'democracy' meant a thing of the heart rather than a political creed, whereas the democracy that has established itself is an organized one and too much intent on organization. Unless it manages to make itself loveable it will dry up from within and fail. No one realized this more than Carpenter himself. . . . He never had much use for organizations or for committees or for dialectic."[56] Despite obvious continuities, there are significant differences between this vision and the New Liberal ethical project.

Carpenterian ethics (the realm of lovability, the heart, inner qualities and subjective effort) actively protests the political (the realm of creeds, organizations, and exsiccative laws), charging it with the premature foreclosure of ideal possibilities for the sake of concrete and compromised results and with interference in the psychic transformations born of direct, unmediated relationality between sympathetic, if slow-moving, entities. More specifically, Carpenter's ethics of shared or common life improves on democratic politics through the lived practices on the part of individuals of becoming common—of achieving voluntary identity with those who have been stripped of civilizational and, especially, institutional value. As Carpenter clarifies in *Civilization: Its Cause and Cure* (1889), true democracy consists in the spiritual realization of "the Mass-man, or Demos, in each unit-man."[57] An underlying philosophical naturalism helps this premise along by supplying a general disdain of so-called higher faculties and upper echelons.[58] In contrast, New Liberalism does not seek to displace the political, which it takes as incumbent in social life. Rather, its ethical project consists in raising the general masses to the already exalted level of the political—that is in the cultivation of an improved citizenry. Herein, democratic coexistence implies shared responsibility for evicting demotic elements—in the sense of all that is unexceptional, ordinary, unremarkable, unworthy of note—from civic life, so as to secure a culture of maximal communal achievement. This modality, whereby individual citizens commit to work upon themselves in order to catch up with and live up to progressive political structures, forms the nucleus of New Liberal moral perfectionism.

New Liberal policymakers found the philosophical ratification they needed for their preferred ethicization of democracy in the parallel milieu of British idealism, a leading school of Western ethical thought in the early twentieth century, to which many New Liberals were exposed under the tutelage of the Oxford philosopher T. H. Green.[59] Green's pertinent thinking is epitomized in his catechisms on the "common good," which he asserts as democracy's categorical imperative in an influential series of lectures posthumously collated as *Prolegomena to Ethics* (1883). The common good, he argues, is that irresistible and universalizable "ought" that supplements both law and authoritative custom.[60] However, it is also the basis for a bracing evolutionary ethics that requires us to do our best for our *genus* (community/nation/family) by being committed to personal excellence. This program is communicated by way of the following explicandum. First, to say we are common means that each personality is but the trustee or custodian for the wider community of certain traits and circumstances. By this route, Green avers, "the individual comes at once practically to conceive his personality—his nature as object to himself—as belonging to others."[61] Second, living an ethical life does not mean being good so much as becoming perfect through the realization of our highest capabilities. This involves "that effort after the Better which, at least as a conscious effort, implies the conviction of there being a Best."[62] Third, the common good (or ethics of commonality) is therefore a project of collective perfection that is founded on exemplary individuals who maintain strict fidelity to what Green calls "a system of social requirement and expectations."[63]

This is hardly asking too much—who doesn't want personal investments in a self-reforming community?—but Green's formula divides internally into a discomfiting split in the way it applies to the haves and the have-nots, generally considered. Moral perfectionism for the haves is a matter of anodyne altruism based on the transcendence of pleasures or of conformity to mere self-interest within the provincial circle of their "loves or likes."[64] Perfectionism for the have-nots, however, is a more strenuous affair that entails the transcendence of the pain resulting from the state of helpless confinement to the handicaps and burdens of their given circumstances. Addressed to the unfortunate citizenry (the subjects of pain rather than of pleasure), have-not perfectionism inveigles the common laborer to rise above his abjection and develop capacities beyond the "conditions of the animal soul, 'servile to every skiey influence.'"[65] He must endeavor relentlessly, Green writes, to lift himself above "present imperfections" in order "to have more intellectual excellence; to be more brave, . . . more perfect."[66]

Green's influence imbued New Liberal democratic ethics; his lessons for the have-nots especially furnished a compendious pedagogy for the oppressed, or civics for new citizens. Books with titles like John Maccum's *Ethics of Citizenship* (1921), Sir Henry Jones's *The Principles of Citizenship* (1919), and Masterman's *How England Is Governed* (1921) struggled, in Greenian spirit, to show those "breaking through the former disability of poverty and discomfort" how to attain sovereignty by participating in the "moral structure of the State."[67] Welfarism, they argued repeatedly, did not really address those who were still trying to keep body and soul together. It was not, thus, a safeguard against destitution so much as a prompt to self-improvement—that is, "to brains," and to the self-selection of "the best and most gifted beings in every generation, . . . the wisest, the bravest, the most generous, the most skillful, the most beautiful, the strongest, and the most virtuous."[68] Accordingly, the true identity of ruler and ruled ratified by democracy, or the principle of "the State it is me" (to borrow a phrase from the New Liberal economist L. T. Hobhouse), consisted in cultivating the *"noblisse oblige* . . . all men feel" and competing aggressively for a rank in "nature's aristocracy."[69]

The social theorists Antonio Negri and Michael Hardt have recently described democracy in similar terms as an art for the multitude of "Becoming-Prince," which entails "inventing lasting democratic forms of social organization."[70] In its proximate New Liberal origins, however, becoming-prince, or the concept of self-rule, was scarcely about inventing rights so much as the imperative to qualify for the political by first pulling up one's socks and then oneself by the bootstraps. The man stuck in a mine shaft (or the woman in a jam factory) could achieve this by imitating social betters, though without presuming parity with them.[71] In the main, however, the self-work of have-not perfectionism meant conceding the inadmissibility of non-excellence in democracy through a practiced zero tolerance toward the personae and hinterlands of one's own destitution. The poorest person achieves the common good, we learn from an influential liberal idealist, through the discovery of shame: the sense that she can no longer live on her disreputable street; or subsist on a cheap soup of water, barley, and four ground red herrings; or resort to low tricks and hand in disgraceful work; or permit her filthy offspring to roam untended through the neighborhood.[72] Writing in this vein on poor relief and charity organization, the redoubtable Bernard Bosanquet (a thinker admittedly at the conservative end of New Liberalism), declared pauperism to be an ethical lapse rather than economic contingency. In his words, "The spirit of pauperism may be found in all social classes, and means a weakness of the citizen mind which prevents it from being equal to the situation. In other words, it is a defective participation in the social mind, on which the adjustment of life to social standards depends. . . . Pauperism, then, as an external fact, is . . . a failure of the citizen mind."[73] Thus conceived, the New Liberal common good is as much a process of "un-becoming pauper" as of "becoming-prince." And, thus conceived, moral perfectionism turns against democracy through the very gestures with which it turns toward it.

The doubleness of this ethics reappears and is clarified in the richly textured writings of the American philosopher Stanley Cavell. Moral perfectionism, Cavell avers in New Liberal register, is a project of "declining-decline" that elevates the body politic above the coarsening and leveling effects of false democracy. In doing so, it conveys the message that "the alienation of the relatively advantaged is as great a threat to the life of a democracy as is the alienation of the relatively disadvantaged."[74] To the latter, it bequeaths, as we have seen, the complicated moral gifts of disappointment and desire, self-loathing and envy, through which to enter the history of sovereignty. In the period we have been reviewing, such conclusions brought democracy into intolerable proximity to the cultures of totalitarianism. This is the point I've been making. Consider, at one extreme, the philosophy of Carl Schmitt (1888–1985), the influential German jurist whose writings from the early twentieth century make the case that a substantive democracy of equals is built upon a necessary correlative of inequality: either through the social subjection of some categories of person, or by the *asketic* exclusion of some states of being and forms of life. A democratic spirit of this type, he insists, is entirely compatible with dictatorship. "In the history of democracy," Schmitt writes, "there have been many dictatorships." He adds elsewhere that "dictatorship is not antithetical to democracy" and that "dictatorship is just as little the definitive antithesis of democracy as democracy is of dictatorship."[75]

New Liberalism was a dangerously inadequate critique of New Imperialism. Its tremendous contributions to the history of social welfare notwithstanding, its ethical innovations all but banished the properties that lie on the other side of perfection, of which the vast terrain of social and, indeed, human life is composed: failures of nerve, incapacities of mind, improprieties of love, lapses of the body, the end of life. How very self-indulgent it would be to cleave to such properties, given the promise of amelioration. And how utterly wasteful to deny them the truth of their being.

Moral Imperfectionism; or, Gandhi in London (Midlife Remix)

It is entirely possible to conceive of democracy without ethical supplement as something that falls solely under the remit of distributive justice rather than the good, abstractly considered. The moral and political philosopher John Rawls famously argues that ethics, especially when it takes the form of moral perfectionism, may be impertinent if not downright baneful for the enterprise of just society.[76] Though we have seen this verdict amply corroborated in the preceding discussion, a stringent dissociation of politics and ethics would not have been beneficial for the agents of radical democracy who are at the core of this study. Many of them, such as the subject peoples of empire, had no substantive recourse to the domain of politics proper in which to air their grievances. The newly politicized terrain of the ethical, however, to which everybody notionally had free access, was readily available for appropriation. Also, we have been arguing, the distortions of early twentieth-century politics had distinct ethical causes that many believed were best assuaged through an opposing ethical idiom.

In the following chapters we encounter varied experiments in this opposing ethical idiom, all defying global mutations of perfectionism in the first half of the previous century. M. K. Gandhi, a presiding genius for such experimentation, makes guest appearances in several succeeding discussions. Yet nowhere are his contributions to our themes better exemplified than in *Hind Swaraj* (1910), Gandhi's early manifesto for radical democracy, which serves as a starting point for the explorations to follow and is intimately linked to the inaugural contexts sketched above in this introduction.[77] The 2010 centennial anniversary of *Hind Swaraj* has provoked a rich and substantial interpretive literature about its multiple contexts, rhetoricity, and political trajectory. The text was once commonly regarded as but a vindication of the claims of Indian or non-Western civilization with respect to an abstract imperial *mission civilisatrice*. We now know to read this manifesto as a moveable feast, as much situated in the lexical peculiarities of the Gujarati language as shaped by the changing cultures of the Indian Ocean—both mainstream and subaltern.[78] Moreover, though the book is rife with the oratory of colonial contestation and frequently touts the questionable belief "that Indian civilisation is the best," its polemic was nourished by numerous Western critiques of Western civilization.[79] We are directed to these self-critical, subcultural traditions and to the collaborative aspects of *Hind Swaraj*'s anti-imperial polemic in its eclectic bibliography. Included here in a dense intertextual nexus are works such Edward Carpenter's *Civilization: Its Cause and Cure* (1889), describing democracy as the ethical realization of the Demos in each individual life; Thomas Taylor's *The Fallacy of Speed* (1909), condemning New Imperial culture for the instrumentalization of time and space; Thoreau's famous pamphlet "On the Duty of Civil Disobedience" (1849), teasing at the agonism of inner and outer in political affect; and Tolstoy's *Letter to a Hindoo* (1909), inviting anticolonial subjects to spiritualize political and civic life for everybody. Even as these dense circuits and paths of transmission come more clearly into view, however, it is little acknowledged that Gandhi's foundational work was directly provoked by his encounter with New Liberalism in the mix of the latter's challenge to the rise of totalitarianism in Europe. Let me recall the familiar story of the book's composition before elucidating these lesser-known conditions by which it was in fact catalyzed.

Between November 13 and 22, 1909, on a return voyage from England to South Africa on the ship *Kildonan Castle*, the forty-year-old, Indian born, London educated, Natal based lawyer-activist Mohandas Karamchand Gandhi composed the Gujarati manuscript first published as *Indian Home Rule, or Hind Swaraj* in 1910. Legend has it that Gandhi worked on the book without pause for some ten days, using the ship's stationary and writing with his left hand when the right was tired (commentators have calculated that at least 40 of the 275 pages of the manuscript may be attributed to the right-handed author's left hand). This first occurrence of ambidexterity in Gandhi's writerly practice is often invoked, poetically, as confirmation of his place in the mythic genealogy of the *savyasachi*: a type perfected in the figure of Arjuna, epic hero of the *Mahabharata*, who can wield a bow and shoot fatal arrows equally well with either hand. Yet, if anything, it is hardly a fluency in violence that the preparation of *Hind Swaraj* achieves or advocates so much as its opposite, namely, a fluency in the complex technologies of *ahimsa*, or nonviolence. This *ahimsaic* subject is not born of prodigious ambidextrous skill so much as from the dissonant commensurability of skill and shortcoming; the insistent partnership, that is, of a proficient right hand and its deficient double.

Fully cognizant of *Hind Swaraj* as an epochal spiritual event in his own formation as demi-yogi and partly political leader, Gandhi consistently claimed its advent as conclusive clarification of his spiritual vocation in the world of twentieth-century imperialism. "The thing," he wrote to collaborator Henry Polak, "was . . . the progressive step I have taken mentally."[80] Gandhi's unabashed enthusiasm about his own book notwithstanding, he was bitterly disappointed by its subsequent reception. On March 10, 1910, copies of the newly minted Gujarati edition were intercepted at Bombay upon order of the Madras High Court and fourteen days later, subsequent to a hostile state-interpreter's report, the book was banned in India by the Home Department on grounds of sedition. This ban on the Gujarati text, which remained in place until December 1938, fuelled among the general English reading public the rumor that M. K. Gandhi had penned a poisonous invective against the English race, thus eschewing all former loyalties to the numerous individuals and organizations that had offered him generous hospitality from the time of his first arrival in London, in 1888, as a somewhat gormless law student. Gandhi was clearly piqued by the proscription and negative press. In the preface to the English translation of the work, he takes pains to distinguish his condemnation of English civilization from his regard for English people: the latter merely misguided, he insists, by the pernicious values of the former. Here Gandhi projects his book as an act of love or a reverse civilizing mission aimed to help Westerners liberate themselves from the backward condition and bad habits of colonialism. It is through this stance, actively on display throughout the work, that *Hind Swaraj* presents a pointed rejoinder to *belle époque* moral perfectionism and a vital historical conjuncture for our discussion.

Nearly a decade and a half after his first departure from fin de siècle London as a radicalized, late-Victorian barrister, Gandhi returned to Britain twice in a short spell, first in 1906 and again in 1909. His purpose on both occasions was to represent the languishing claims of colored migrants in South Africa following the second Boer war. The conditions for resident and nonresident "native" populations had worsened considerably under British jurisdiction. A liberal-led proposal for a Union of South Africa further threatened the creation of a multinational, monoracial dominion with no indemnity for multiracial workers and their dependents. These battle lines notwithstanding, the early years of the twentieth century found Gandhi immersed in the prevailing New Liberal ethos and entirely susceptible to liberalism's heady condemnation of empire in the name of democracy.[81] Once back in London, on November 7, 1906, Gandhi successfully addressed a gathering of more than a hundred members of Parliament, the majority of them liberal, in the Grand Committee Room of Westminster Palace. Through these contacts he also came under the influence of the New Liberal Ethical Societies movement, which he praised enthusiastically for its ecumenical emphasis on inner life in public matters.[82] But two years later, by the end of 1909, he declared the New Liberal government incapable of "elementary equality," and announced a comprehensive renunciation of its testament, albeit in the name of ethics.[83] Speaking before the Union of Ethical Societies in London, on October 8, he named this enterprise "The Ethics of Passive Resistance": a practice of becoming-common, *a la* Edward Carpenter, crystallized around the traits of "self-restraint, unselfishness, patience, gentleness, . . . flowers which spring beneath the feet of those who accept, but refuse to impose, suffering."[84] This is the germane motto at the heart of *Hind Swaraj*.

Written in a mood of indignation, *Hind Swaraj* unambiguously rejects the culture of New Liberal democracy, attacking it at the cardinal point of its ethical credo. This democracy, Gandhi avers, is no more than a parliamentary ruse that runs on legislative bribes to the people: all institutional machinery and no "living conscience."[85] The model is clearly unworthy of imitation: "The Government of England is not desirable and not worth copying by us."[86] Its renunciation, he adds, will be simultaneously political and ethical for all those as yet without franchise. Gandhi's preferred term for Indian home rule, *swaraj*, strictly translates as "self-rule," "self-mastery," "control of the mind," "good conduct," and "a good way of life."[87] At this early stage of the national movement, Gandhi favors the latter meanings when engaging the question of true independence for the colonial world. As he puts it, "If we become free, India is free. And in this thought you have a definition of *Swaraj*. It is *Swaraj* when we learn to rule ourselves; . . . such *Swaraj* is to be experienced by each one for himself."[88] The self-work that is *swaraj*, nonetheless, always involves the common cause or collective dimension, although, in this variant, participants pursue less rather than more and practice the arts of handicap not advantage. "Our ancestors . . . set a limit to our indulgences," Gandhi declares, before itemizing an intricate taxonomy of constraint.[89] "No system of life-corroding competition," he writes in grand Ruskinian pitch; "we should only do what we could with our hands and feet"; "be prepared to lose every penny."[90] The soul of this grim asceticism (the author, by the way, put out an incredible two pounds to secure a bottle of patent hair restorer in the midst of his hectic London negotiations) is a "sacrifice of self."[91] By this route, the subject of *swaraj* makes strong alliance with her own existential precariousness and thus acquires the paired gifts of immunity to the figures of superiority and susceptibility to the figures of destitution. The former is experienced as reduced awe for commanders and "sovereigns of the earth."[92] In Gandhi's words, "kings and their swords [are] inferior to the sword of ethics."[93] The latter, more dimly articulated, registers as increased consideration for those consummately uncommanding of attention.

Hind Swaraj was profoundly influential in the anticolonial world. Gandhi's controversial modifications in that work of the ideal of the common good were also registered in Europe during the long aftermath of the New Imperial/New Liberal polemic. In 1938, a theosophical journal called *The Aryan Path* staged, in its pages, a belated roundtable among eminent Britishers on the relevance of *Hind Swaraj*.[94] Contributors to this special issue included many former members of the Ethical Societies movement, among them some liberals and parliamentary socialists who had augmented the contentious welfarism of the era. All agreed that Gandhi's manifesto was a salve to the crisis of war-torn, imperial-fascist Europe. Through its idealistic commendation, in every circumstance, of selflessness over self-interest, it clarified a congruent sequence of discursive oppositions for the times, privileging obligations over rights, service over consumption, principles over expediency, altruism over acquisition, and so forth. Participants also noted that the most therapeutic, albeit most demanding, antinomies within this series further privileged self-suffering over violence, injurability over injuriousness, and failure over conquest. In a word: imperfection.

A Postcolonial Cynicism

The characters and groups presented in the ensuing pages participate in the genealogies we have been canvassing though their efforts concatenate around discrete histories, and their variations on our leading themes are as diverse as the contexts by which they were occasioned. Yet there are shared elements across the field that we may provisionally characterize as a form of modern, postcolonial cynicism. It is exemplified in Gandhi and indirectly revealed by Michel Foucault's final lectures and writings on the life and thought of the Cynic philosopher Diogenes of Sinope.[95]

Foucault describes Greek Cynicism as a revolutionary ethics that communicates itself through the modality of *parrhesia*: free speech or truth telling. Attending characteristics evoke the domain of discussion, upheld by modern thinkers such as Jürgen Habermas as integral to democratic procedure, whereby members of the public sphere exercise the right to inform prevailing opinion and sometimes the law itself. Though Cynic *parrhesia* certainly addresses power/government, it does so to contradict all normative opinion that participates in law and custom and concerns established prohibitions and observances deemed sufficient to the achievement of a meaningful life. Historically the preserve of fallen figures, *parrhesia* comes from below and is directed above; and its cynical bearer, Foucault writes, "is the man with the staff, the beggar's pouch, the cloak, the man in sandals or bare feet, the man with the long beard, the dirty man. He is also the man who roams, who is not integrated into society, has no household, family, hearth or country, . . . and he is also a beggar."[96] From this debased vantage, Cynicism is directed against the social requirement. It is in every way, as Foucault notes, the "opposite of what was traditionally recognized as the true life."[97] This topos of reversal is tethered to the founding story, within the school (if we can call it that), of the sentencing of Diogenes on charges of falsifying state currency—a lived metaphor that we learn from Diogenes Laertius (in a short biography of his namesake), for "adulterating currency in the very truth, allowing convention no . . . authority."[98] Three features of Cynic reversal are germane to the case studies in subsequent chapters: respectively, the history of nonsovereignty, the currency of non-value, and the art of the un-manifest. They are sketched below and are elaborated as we go along.

The History of Non-Sovereignty. The slim sources for Greek Cynicism all emphasize Diogenes's scorn for kings, rulers, and powerful citizens. In the most famous story of this type, recounted in the *Lives of Eminent Philosophers*, Alexander comes and stands over Diogenes, who is sunbathing. The emperor says, "Ask of me any boon you like." Diogenes replies, "Stand out of my light."[99] Contempt for sovereigns is matched by the Cynic's disregard for his own sovereignty or excellence and so also for the self-care and cultivation appropriate to orthodox ethics. By this contrarian demeanor the Cynic swerves away from the self toward the care of others, or what Foucault calls an other life, *une vie autre.*[100] In concrete practice, the agent of Cynicism's ethics-for-other-lives concentrates on transforming herself into a figure of destitution for the privileged to practice upon so that they may better learn to conduct themselves when they encounter real destitution. When playing the beggar, Diogenes was said to have used the following form of address: "If you have already given to anyone else, give to me also; if not, begin with me."[101]

The Currency of Non-Value. In impersonating occluded figures from the history of non-sovereignty (e.g., beggars, paupers, insects, frogs, dogs, lunatics, and slaves), the Cynic defiantly acts out the scandal of misfortune and thereby brings it out from under the cover of epistemic darkness into the light of philosophy: a truth that can be told to everyone and is drawn from the template of allegedly worthless lives. She also announces the uninjurability of debased existence in her own person by showing herself indifferent to humiliating circumstances in a bold rhetoric of survival. This is how Dio Chrysostom, the Greek orator and sophist, portrays the true Cynic in his discourse "Diogenes; or, On Tyranny":

I am not afraid to go even through an army if needs be, without the herald's staff, yea, and amid brigands. . . . If all the gold, all the silver, and all the copper should give out, that would not injure me in the least. And if an earthquake lays all the houses low, . . . and all the sheep are killed so that not a single man has wherewithal to clothe himself, . . . I shall fare none the worse nor be the more destitute. For how much more naked shall I be than I am now, how much more homeless?[102]

This attitude was later claimed as a stoic commonplace recommending the existential courage wrought by self-armoring practices of detachment from people and things. Secreted herein, however, is another more exacting emphasis on non-evaluative nondiscrimination, gleaning a democratic disposition from the premise that everything matters; in other words, even the most abject states of being can be transformed into a living currency or resource. "All elements," as Diogenes is credited with urging elsewhere, "are contained in all things and pervade everything."[103]

The Art of the Un-manifest. Breaking sharply from what is established (thus stripping the world bare of received value), Cynicism also eschews *telos* and perfectionism through a rigorous anti-idealism. We learn this from accounts of the many alleged verbal skirmishes between Diogenes and Plato. In one of these, Diogenes berates Plato (as perhaps a Wittgenstein might a Heidegger) for his fascination with perfect forms and immutable essences: "As Plato was conversing about Ideas and using the nouns 'tablehood' and 'cuphood,' he said, 'Table and cup I see; but your tablehood and cuphood, Plato, I can nowise see.'"[104] Yet Cynicism does not designate alternative content in lieu of the teleologies and, concomitantly, the goals and objectives that it abolishes. It is not another system or dogma so much as a technique of unsystematicity that equips beneficiaries to listen otherwise—to disarticulated themes and lives. Foucault depicts cynical style, accordingly, as a lifelong preparedness for the "irruption of what is underneath, below, of what in a culture has no right, or at least no possibility of expression."[105] So we learn from Diogenes Laertius that the Cynic Diogenes would always praise people not for the things they had accomplished but for those they had failed or refused to accomplish—that is, for an *askesis* of de-realization. "He would praise those who were about to marry and refrained, those who intending to go on a voyage never set sail, those who thinking to engage in politics do no such thing, those also who proposing to rear a family do not do so, and those who make ready to live with potentates, yet never come near them at all."[106] In these ways, swerving from all the paths leading to predictable, known, or sanctioned outcomes, the Cynic is alert to the unimaginable. A student of Diogenes is reputed to have requested that he be buried on his face because, said he, "after a little time down will be converted into up."[107] Thus, we could say, Cynicism combines what might otherwise seem like an unforgiving contempt for the world with an ethics of world-making, albeit from the remains—that is, from wasted elements customarily beyond regard and repair. In this way it is a scavenger's art or the pauper's gift.

The figures who populate this book are not always non-Western, though all approach the redemption of Europe from a position of intimate exteriority. As such, the postcolonial variation on Cynic ethics gains traction from the fable that Greek Cynicism was inflected with influences from the East in the wake of the globalizing Macedonian empire.[108] In his *Life of Alexander*, the Greek historian and biographer Plutarch speaks of transactions between Cynic thought and Indian "gymnosophists" or "naked philosophers"—the latter held responsible by the emperor for provoking native revolt against invading Macedonian forces. Ten such rabble-rousing thinkers are captured by Alexander and tested (upon pain of death) through questions that they answer in riddles and inversions, emphasizing that the greatest power is invested in those who inspire the least fear. Intrigued by the Indian philosophers, Alexander sends Onescritus, "one of Diogenes the Cynic's disciples," to further investigate their thought.[109] In subsequent deliberations the gymnosophists learn of Cynic principles, which they claim to find estimable albeit insufficiently cosmopolitan: "Dandamis received him with more civility, and hearing him discourse of Socrates, Pythagoras, and Diogenes, told him he thought them men of great parts and to have erred in nothing so much as in having too much respect for the laws and customs of their country."[110] In his *Lives of Eminent Philosophers*, Diogenes Laertius also refers to these philosophers and reports that the skeptic Pyrro of Elis (a likely contemporary of the Cynic Onescritus) traveled afar and "foregathered with the Indian Gymnosophists," in whose company he refined a trenchant critique of power and sovereignty: "He would withdraw from the world and live in solitude, rarely showing himself to his relatives; this he did because he had heard an Indian reproach Anaxarchus, telling him that he would never be able to teach others what is good while he himself danced attendance on kings in their courts. He would maintain the same composure at all times, so that, even if you left him in the middle of a speech, he would finish what he had to say with no audience but himself."[111]

The emblematic potential of these cross-cultural encounters is sufficient for our purposes. Yet it is intriguing to follow conjectures about who the heavily mediated gymnosophists might have been. A standard account privileges the Jains, followers of Mahavira, and the Buddhists; both groups are notable for their antinomian rejection of scriptural authority and democratic outlook.[112] It is also possible that the sects referenced in Greek sources are two influential earlier factions: the Ajivikas, (anti-soul) followers of the teacher Makkali Gosala, named (according to legend) for the cowshed in which he was born in poverty; or the Charvaka/Lokayata (popular-democratic) followers of the heretic Ajita Keshakamabalin, so named for his sole garment: a filthy blanket of matted hair (likely his own). Their strong internal differences notwithstanding, all of these groups—Ajivikas, Lokayatas, Jains, and Buddhists—can be placed in context of the broad-based, materialist-ascetic Sramana tradition of Indian philosophy, itself of interest to our discussion. In stiff religious competition with the orthodox and elite Brahmana tradition, the Sramanas, meaning those who toil or labor, rejected the metaphysical hierarchies vested in the notion of a supreme deity as well as all contingent worldly hierarchies—especially those ratified in the social system of hereditary castes and ranks.[113] The more extreme Sramana groups professed an equalizing vision born of radical nihilism, wherein the felt absence of an afterlife or of karmic consequence (otherwise, strict moral causality and calculability) implied the pointlessness of self-importance and overlordship over others.[114]

Such details scarcely come into view in the sources cited above. Yet the Greek geographer Strabo credits the early ethnographer Megasthenes with making "another division in his discussion of the philosophers, asserting that there are two kinds of them, one kind called Brachmanes and the other Garmanes."[115] In his account the "Brachmanes" are in agreement with dogma and, "engage in affairs of state and attend the kings as counselors."[116] In contrast, he describes the "Garmanes" as "humanitarian philosophers" who follow nature merely and include ascetics, beggars, and healers.[117] These philosophers (who include both male and female ascetics) willingly teach anybody, and their instruction bears resemblance, or so Strabo avers, to the doctrines of "Pythagoras . . . Socrates and Diogenes."[118] He further suggests, albeit inconclusively, that the ascetics encountered by the Cynic Onescritus on behalf of Alexander may have been among the latter camp.[119] As a footnote to this elusive archaeology of philosophical exchange on Indian soil, we can add the surmise that Diogenes' birth city of Sinope lay on the trading routes between Greece and India.[120] Itinerant merchants in need of a moneychanger may have chanced upon the Cynic and his kind and altered (falsified) the currency of their emerging thought with stories and influences from variant, near-subject cultures. Or vice versa.

The transnational imperfectionist *askeses* at the core of this book conjure (and are summoned by) these likely imaginary transactions between prior/coeval democratic-ethical traditions, which together troubled the conscience of global antique supremacy, whether based on hereditary systems of caste, race, and rank, or on territoriality, conquest, and aggression. Our themes come to a focus in one work of late classical Greek antiquity, *The Greek Alexander Romance*, which embellishes the legendary colloquy between the world-conquering Alexander and the unconquerable (because they had nothing to lose) gymnosophists, or naked philosophers, of India, whoever they really were. The extended dialogue between the emperor and the gymnosophists, who are "entirely without clothing and living in huts and caves," parallels scenes of improvised pedagogic exchange between Alexander and Diogenes in a shared thematic of king baiting.[121] The following excerpted parley is a good place to end and an even better one to begin: "Then Alexander said to them all, 'Ask me for whatever you want and I will give it to you.' At once they all burst out, 'Give us immortality.' But Alexander replied, 'That is a power I do not have. I too am a mortal.' Then they asked him, 'Since you are a mortal, why do you make so many wars? When you have seized everything, where will you take it? Surely you will have to leave it behind for others.'"[122]

The Plan for This Book

Chapter 1 of this book is historically close to the milieu of moral perfection described in this introduction. It concerns British labor agitations between 1910 and 1913 that involved workers from disparate industrial sectors. Directly fueled by the duplicitous welfarism of the New Liberals, these strikes exemplified a complicated, nonvirtuous antimaterialism among proletarian constituencies that went against the grain of the dominant *belle époque* critique of consumption. Born of ideological continuities between the early twentieth-century liberalisms and totalitarianisms we have been tracking, the orthodox antimaterialism of the era was an ethics of *phusikaphobia*, or recoil from the physical world, that lent itself to pro-vincial anti-collectivism. In contrast, the heterodox antimaterialism of some labor agitators crystallized as *philophusikia*, or a reparative love of things, particularly the alienated objects of possession. This may be read as a resourceful will toward collectivity. The discussion draws on journalistic testimonies, syndicalist journals, and guild socialist literature, especially the writings of R. H. Tawney.

More disparate sources inform the discussion, in chapter 2, of a dis-cursive dialectic between European racial ethnology, an important source for imperial fascism, on the one hand, and antinomian, modern Indian spirituality, an important source for radical democracy, on the other. Call-ing the first a "science of ascent," and the second an "art of descent," I elaborate the *asketic* concept of descent as an egalitarian disregard of the self. The arguments concern the collective corpus of four gurus of mod-ern India (as developed in their cosmopolitan ashrams): Sri Ramakrishna Paramahamsa of Dakshineshwar; Mahatma Gandhi, of Tolstoy and Phoe-nix farms in South Africa and of Sabarmati and Sevagram in India; Sri Au-robindo of Pondicherry; and Sri Ramana Maharshi of Tiruvanamallai. The transnational elaboration of the works of these gurus by Western disciples and followers takes us farther afield across three terrains: interwar Freudian psychoanalysis; the international pacifist movement during the Second World War; and, finally, the photojournalism associated with Magnum Photos and transformed into a style of democratizing portraiture by Henri Cartier-Bresson, the French photographer who captured rare images of many modern Indian gurus during his momentous visits to postcolonial South Asia. This story has another gloss. Fin de siècle racial ethnology built its case for European Aryanism and race supremacy, as we will see, upon an invidious defense and reanimation of the rigid caste hierarchies codi-fied within Indian tradition. In this way early twentieth-century totali-tarianism, or "ascent," was partly born of a perverse genealogy connecting ancient South Asian caste tyranny to modern European imperial fascism. When brought to view, this globalizes the scandal of caste injustice in South Asia and also demands that any objection to Western perfectionisms be combined with a like attitude toward their non-Western counterparts. The transnational practitioners of "descent" were well aware of these obli-gations; the Indian figures among them were especially so as members of privileged caste groups protesting their own historical and scriptural access to rank and priority. Such projects are crucial to the "annihilation of caste," to borrow a phrase from the reformer and revolutionary, B. R. Ambed-kar.[123] Yet they must be noted as a corollary to the ethical-politics of those directly victimized by caste oppression. Salient here is an emphasis on willfully inhabiting the hard ground of enforced commonization—or refusing to ascend—evinced in the preference of Indian "untouchable" castes to go by the pejorative name *dalit*, meaning those who have been broken and ground down and whose egalitarianism is born of a bracing fidelity to ruination. The theme of modern *dalit askesis* is beyond the scope of this study, though it is germane to its abiding commitments.[124]

In chapter 3 we survey the macabre cosmopolitanism of the First World War, with its complex migration of soldiers from colonial outposts to the battlefields of Europe and back again, as a setting for an inter-civilizational ethics of intimate enmity that is devoted to rescuing the endangered spirit of Europe from the clutches of imperial fascism at the cost of immediate, anticolonial, nationalist aims. Based on nationalist war-recruitment records and letters written by Indian peasant soldiers, the chapter gleans from the rhetoric of sacrifice therein a discrepant genealogy for moral imperfectionism and tracks its development through the decolonization era. This trope of sacrifice, I argue, may well be the most elementary virtue of anticolonial, antifascist democracy as a work of self-ruination. Its clarification, and with it the clarification of the obscured story of colonial participation in the violent European wars of the previous century, answers some of the key questions that have provoked this book: Did non-Western decolonization movements ever refuse the spoils of anticolonial nationalism and of culturalist primordiality for the sake of reparative solidarity with colonial cultures? Did these movements conceive demands for independence from Europe not just as a rejection of Europe but also as a desire to salvage the very best of Europe? What does this best of Europe look like after its non-Western rehabilitation? While the heart of chapter 3 deals with cooperative native soldiers, chapter 4 concerns the outbreak of anti-imperial global mutinies in the demobilization era, with a particular focus on the Royal Indian Navy Mutiny of 1946. It draws upon trial proceedings for the perpetrators of this outbreak and analyzes its negative reception in the national and world media. My claim is that the inconsequentiality with which the naval mutineers were frequently charged was in fact a motivated ethics of non-generativity or symbolic celibacy, protesting considerations of causality in moral and political procedure. Read sympathetically, the oddly self-trivializing practices (and testimonies) of the mutineers can be shown to be rooted in the buried history of anticolonial mutinies in general, beginning with the revolt of 1857. Much like their predecessors, the rebels of 1946 refuted the perpetuation of empire within themselves (along with the protracted conversion of colonial worlds into garrison states) performatively, by falling short of military regimen and the contingent culture of perpetual war.

An epilogue to the book addresses questions of methodology arising from the problem of accurately describing and historicizing a property as diffuse as moral imperfection—that is, a cynic art of the un-manifest that consists more in dismantling existing systems than in clarifying modular alternatives. Always conjectural and provisional, as also geared toward the unimaginable, does the ethics of imperfection require an imperfectionist style of narration and of thought? The present study is framed by the styles of an *ahimsaic*, or nonviolent, historiography. Building on M. K. Gandhi's conviction that history proper is but, "a record of every interruption of the force of love or of the soul," I have long sought out subjugated narratives of accord and collaboration among oppressors and oppressed (at the scenes of colonial encounter, especially), concerned with visionary commitment to the end of institutional suffering.[125] Such a method or historical apperception demands fidelity to small things, barely visible subcultures, occluded political forms, affective *micrologoi*—in other words, to the unobserved and uneventful reconciliation, as Gandhi has it, of quarrelsome siblings.[126] That said, I wish to invest these most minor and apparently inconsequential events with seemingly unmerited global significance or world-transforming propensity. Sometimes this entails creating narrative and theoretical conditions of possibility for imagining such significance by substituting the "what happened" of history proper with the "what might have happened" or "what could happen if" of *ahimsaic* historiography. To this end, the hesitant and muted documentary of accord has to be compelled into conversation with grander, more canonical, and, oftentimes, hermetically sealed annals. It also must be yoked into oxymoronic alliance with other minor, generically and geopolitically unexpected or unlikely scenes of rapprochement. These multiple scenes of archival engagement are sometimes coeval with each other. At other times they concern mutually irrelevant or remote periods and genres. The simultaneous and polyphonic opening up to each other of incommensurable records, intended to stage the global import of small stories of accord, is key to my endeavor in *The Common Cause*.

ONE

After Virtue: The Strange Case of *Belle Époque* Socialist Antimaterialism

Subsequent chapters pursue the development of moral imperfectionism farther afield than Europe and later in the twentieth century. The characters and events examined in the present chapter, however, belonged to the same moment as New Imperialism and New Liberalism and protested their part in it. What follows is an inquiry into shifts in imperial and capitalist style and then in anti-imperial and socialist style that occurred during the *belle époque*—that beautiful era of European history commencing sometime toward the end of the nineteenth century and ending in the midst of the First World War. As we saw in the introduction, critics of diverse political persuasions alleged that these early years of the twentieth century saw the emergence of new kind of imperial-capitalist culture, driven by economic rather than civilizational motivations. Such objections were so cogent that even the strongest champions of New Imperialism attended to them, defensively emphasizing the totalitarianism, or brute force, rather than the commercialism, of new ventures in Asia and Africa as evidence of the objectless disposition of New Imperialists and, accordingly, of a shadow form of moral disinterestedness in mere material outcomes. This pervasive critique had direct consequences for the domestic countercultures of anti-imperial socialism as well, in Britain mainly, but also in Europe.

When profit, commercialism, mercantilism, materialism, expediency, and practicality were postulated as the leading, and most regrettable, tropes of contemporary dominion, contemporary socialists reacted strongly with an ideology of antimaterialism, characterized by abstract thinking, theory, unprofitable speculation, and amateur metaphysics. This discourse was internally divided by a schism between a type of *phusikaphobia*, or recoil from the physical world, on the one hand, and a type of *philophusikia*, or love for things, specifically for the alienated objects of possession, on the other. The former, which sought to quarantine the human subject from the threatening contagion of matter, fashioned a neo-idealist invective against the objects and practices of consumption allegedly typical of the world of capitalist imperialism. The latter tried to bring the human into reparative fellowship with things by laying claim—often through the popularized philosophy of Henri Bergson—to an updated metaphysical empiricism. It formulated a self-reflexive critique directed not only against objects of possession but also more strenuously against the virtuous subject of nonpossession—in this case the ethically self-righteous, anticapitalist antimaterialist. I argue that, notwithstanding its greater ideological clarity, the *phusikaphobic* ban against cohabitation with the nonhuman and inanimate lends itself, historically speaking, to a provincial anticollectivism. In contrast, *philophusikia* manifests a resourceful will toward radical democracy and collectivity. Its provisional suspension of left-revolutionary aims subtly countermands a tendency toward totalitarianism secreted within several past and current manifestos of anthropogenic antimaterialism. To make this case, we will need to consider questions such as these: Did the *phusikaphilic* critique of nonpossessive virtue, conducted in the name of antimaterialism, supply the rudiments of a recuperable anti-totalitarian politics? Or was this politics but a relapse into the comfort zone of European affluence—a furtive concession to the considerable material advantages of capitalist expansionism? Finally, who or what appears upon the stage of socialist antimaterialism, as it were, after virtue? Directly below is a précis of some pertinent historical and theoretical markers for the ensuing discussion.

Context 1: The Field of Nonpossession

During the late years of the *belle époque*, partly in reaction against the scramble for empire between competing national economies, antimaterialism emerged as the governing idiolect of insurgency, whether radical or conservative, Western or non-Western. As historian Zeev Sternhell writes, "'Anti-materialism' was the dominant trait and the common denominator of all the movements of revolt before the world war and between the two world wars. . . . It was in the name of 'anti-materialism' that men who had issued from different political streams condemned Marxism *and* liberalism. . . . All of them shared a common hatred of money, speculation and bourgeois values."[1] Broadly speaking, there were two cultural sources for the socialist chapter of this revolt. European antimaterialism grew out of French syndicalism, while its British counterpart was rooted in guild socialism.

French syndicalism was a movement of direct proletarian action, launched through a series of spectacular strikes by the Confédération Générale du Travail (CGT). Its compelling theoretical gloss came from the fiery writings of the irascible autodidact George Sorel (1847–1922), especially his *Reflections on Violence,* first published as a series of articles between 1905 and 1906, and translated into English in 1914.[2] A response to the revisionist crisis provoked by Second International Marxism, Sorel's syndicalist antimaterialism began as an attempt to eliminate economicism as the only basis for class unity. It developed, by degrees, into an apoplectic denunciation of affluence in all its historical and civilizational mutations.[3] Thus, in a somewhat idiosyncratic history of ancient philosophy, Sorel credits the decline of the West to "optimistic" Greek thinkers (it is never clear whom he means) from "rich and commercial urban populations who were able to regard the universe as an immense shop full of excellent things with which they could satisfy their greed."[4] In contrast, he valorizes equally obscure mountain-dwelling and warlike Greek "pessimists," "whose material conditions were correspondingly poor," and who are (or ought to be) the direct ideological forbears of the modern worker-producer.[5]

An English chapter in anti-economicism emerged out of guild socialism. The latter was an eclectic movement spreading outward from the amateur Leeds Arts Club of 1902, through the dissident Fabian Arts Group of 1907, and finding its first true platform in the pages of *The New Age,* a defunct Christian socialist journal purchased and revived by A. R. Orage and Holbrook Jackson upon the donation of £500 by Bernard Shaw and a little extra help from theosophist banker Lewis Alexander Wallace. Launched in 1907 as "An Independent Socialist Review of Politics, Literature and Art," *The New Age* quickly formalized a manifesto in which wage reform was superseded by demands for the right to perfection of work or labor on the grounds that the aesthetic and creative well-being of the worker was far more important to the socialist refabrication of the world than her material well-being. The theme is clarified in an editorial of October 3, 1907:

We have suggested more than once that the Trade Unions, if they are to command moral as well as political respect, will have to organise themselves for the sake of their work as well as for the sake of themselves. A plasterer's union, for example, that went on strike, not simply for higher wages, but because their employers were demanding of them shoddy work, and thereby defrauding the public, would command the support not merely of the fighting political sections of the community, but of all the best elements in society. So too, any Union whatever that is formed to maintain a standard of workmanship as well as a standard of pay becomes . . . intellectual or moral.[6]

While trying to engage the attention of the unions, writers for *The New Age* also proclaimed the incompatibility of parliamentary laborism with the aims of socialist renunciation. This led to closer ideological association with the anti-statist syndicalism already well underway across the channel. By 1909, the journal had explicitly claimed syndicalism as a crucial interlocutor and collaborator in the guild's project, and in 1910, with the publication of union leader Tom Mann's monthly, *The Industrial Syndicalist*, the alliance appears to have been sealed. It found its proper course and expression in the labor revolution of this period, a movement of direct proletarian action, disdainful, in its rhetoric, of New Liberal welfarism: the "sops," the "bread and circuses," the bribes of "profit-sharing and Old Age Pensions," regularly "thrown" by the master class to "the snarling Demos."[7]

Even as we start to become aware of *belle époque* socialist antimaterialism as an amalgam (at least within some quarters) of English guild socialism and continental syndicalism, however, we can also dimly perceive the lines of two incongruous, antipathetic figures derived from each of the traditions under review. The first, sharper and better known, is the frugal, aristocratic, heroic, sovereign champion of Sorel and the Sorelians, whose ideological itinerary includes a prolonged stopover in the dark places of early twentieth-century European fascism. To cite Sternhell again, he is amenable to "a fascist revolution directed against materialism."[8] Let us call him (advisedly) "the man of exemplary properties" and the bearer of *phusikaphobia*. The other figure is more shy and elusive—much like the Nowhere Man of the 1965 Beatles hit single, who is largely without itinerary or aim. We can call him "the man [once again, advisedly] without properties of self," and the bearer of the practices of *philophusikia*.[9] Though arising in Britain, this latter entity is cosmopolitan in disposition and generically diffuse. He sometimes appears as a historical figure and at other times as a fictional character or indistinct trope. He is firmly embedded in the scene of contemporary socialism with its will-to-democracy: an everyman with strong anti-imperial credentials (and ancestors) whose challenge to materialism, nonetheless, falters unnervingly in the course of several uncoordinated skirmishes with the heroic renunciate of extremist revolutionary syndicalism. The discursive encounters between these two types of variously traumatized subjectivity (the one seeking reconstitution; the other, decomposition) result in a profound modification of the very field of nonpossession.

Taking the scene of the 1910–1913 labor unrest in Britain as our principle historical setting, I elaborate these competing paths within *belle époque* socialist antimaterialism in their ethical, metaphysical, and political dimensions, each one linked to and informing the others. As an ethics, *phusikaphobia* argues that the eschewal of material possessions results in rich accrual of compensatory moral assets. The discourse of *philophusikia*, in contrast, claims that true nonpossession demands the relinquishment not only of material but, more significantly, of associated moral goods. In the metaphysical iteration of this debate, *phusikaphobia* manifests as a form of neo-idealism that requires the human subject to close itself off from the realm of onticity, namely, physical, real, or factual existence. Here, *philophusikia* manifests as a neo-empiricism, inviting the human subject to risk cohabitation with muddy, ontic existences. Finally, *phusikaphobic* politics expresses itself as the theme of sovereignty organized around a figure who is "better than the rest," while *philophusikia* assumes a counterpoint that resembles but is not quite the theme of equality, and is organized around a figure chronically "lesser than the rest." In what follows, while delineating these contrasts, my elaborations implicitly favor the inchoate content of *philophusikia*. To clarify my investment in the contrarian forms of antimaterialist ethics, metaphysics, and politics outlined above, I present below three disparate sightings of the *phusikaphilic* "man without properties"— the antiheroic hero of the present discussion.

Becoming Zero: Phoenix Ashram and After, 1908. In the intense phase of his very first South African experiments in *aparigraha* (nonpossession), M. K. Gandhi reintroduced into the multifaith prayers regularly convened at Phoenix Ashram, Natal, a *bhajan* (hymn) composed by Narsinh Mehta, a fifteenth-century poet-saint of Gujarat. Written in praise of the true renunciate, the song *"Vaishnava Jana"* may be paraphrased as follows: "He alone can be called a *vaishnava* [person marked by God], who knows the other's pain and praises the entire world. So complete is his abstention, he forgets/does not possess/has renounced, his own virtue, and is most distinguished by his eschewal of distinction."[10] In the ensuing years, notable for Gandhi's progressive valorization of *aparigraha* as the foundation for *abhaya* (fearlessness) and *ahimsa* (nonviolence), he also refined Narsinh Mehta's ethical sequence into one of his characteristic semantic distillates whereby nonpossession emerged as shorthand for the radical encipherment of personality. In a 1927 address to the Young Men's Christian Association (YMCA) in Cuddalore, South India, for instance, Gandhi's particular take on the vow of nonhoarding translates as the assertion that the greatest challenge to a life of renunciation is not the temptation of worldly comfort so much as the invidious "build[ing] up of self," or accumulation of personality, that follows in its wake.[11] Thus, it is spiritually expedient, as a letter of October 7, 1930, advises Narandas Gandhi, that the proprietor of ascetic humility remain scrupulously "unaware of its existence." In other words, as another interlocutor is instructed, the chief burden of renunciatory *praxis* consists in an art of cultivated blindness toward those "incidents in one's life which show one's virtues," for the reason that "our virtues are for others to see."[12] In the labor of imagining no possessions, then, the accomplished *aparigrahi* must first give up attachment to the "goods" of pious subjectivity: "One has to forget the sense of 'I' and become a mere cipher."[13] The path of "poverty and non-possession," as Gandhi reiterates during a lecture of 1931 to conscientious objectors in Lausanne, is quite simply the path of self-expropriation: "You must reduce yourself to zero."[14]

The Uses of Pleasure: Manchester, 1912–1914. Just before the outbreak of the war in which he would enlist as a private and suffer serious injury at the battle of the Somme, R. H. Tawney, the Christian and Guild socialist, spent two formative years in Manchester as a tutor for the Workers' Educational Association (WEA).[15] In this period, while clarifying ideas on socialist equality and antimaterialism that would eventually find expression in books such as *The Acquisitive Society* (1921), *Religion and the Rise of Capitalism* (1926), and *Equality* (1931), Tawney privately recorded a series of spiritual exercises for the twentieth-century socialist renunciate. Teasing out the uncongeniality of satisfaction to enjoyment (in somewhat unbefitting notes on the proper uses of pleasure), he recommends the calculated decrease of inessential objective and subjective property: "Never be afraid of throwing away what you have," he insists.[16] "If you *can* throw it away, it is not really yours. If it is really yours, you cannot throw it away. And you may be certain that if you throw it [a]way, whatever in you is greater than you will produce something in its place."[17] Tawney's subtle projection of impersonality into the theme of non-possession gathers force in aphorisms such as these: "The secret of growth is self-surrender. . . . A man . . . must become impersonal, suppress his own fancies and predilections"; "the elevation of man out of himself . . . is the supreme good," and so forth.[18] In each case, however, Tawney's emphasis on the exfoliation of personality in the work of nonpossession opens an enchanted corridor to surreptitious and compensatory enrichment, enhancement, and amplification that is quite distinct from the rhetoric of frugality otherwise in vogue for antimaterialist catechism. As he observes, the relinquishment of properties of self opens a path to "whatever in you is *greater* than you"; "self-surrender" leads to "channels of *expansion*"; suppression of personal predilection posits an "*elevation*."[19]

Potentiality: Vienna, 1913–1914. Shortly after the First World War, the Austrian writer Robert Musil began work on his epic novel *The Man without Qualities*, which remained unfinished upon his death in 1942. In this *magnum opus* the author returns to the scene of prewar, Austro-Hungarian imperialism and its production of social cohesion through various projects of identity: nationalist, racist, fascist, and otherwise. As recent critics have clarified, Musil draws up a riposte to this scenario in his antihero, Ulrich, a new post-expressivist human being unavailable to appropriation by essence-seeking fundamentalisms.[20] Susceptible to a rare personality disorder, Ulrich does not know the "possession of qualities."[21] A renunciate par excellence, he experiences subjectivity as an inclination toward a void or vacuum that reopens the cloistered self to the world and renders it cosmological: "Here inside, at the world's personal end, a certain lack of inner substance makes itself felt, in the form of a big, vacuous, round O. The condition is the classic condition of making contact with all that is eternal and great, like dwelling on the peaks of humanity and nature."[22] Thus cognizant of an affective continuum between unfinished and empathetic selves, in the years when he was composing *The Man without Qualities*, Musil was also planning a collection of essays with the title "An Attempt to Find Another Human-Being." In this combined oeuvre Musil describes the psychic viaduct between the twin projects of lacking qualities and gaining (or finding) others as a state of pure potentiality or radical possibility: "Whoever has it does not say, for instance: Here this or that has happened, will happen, must happen; but he invents: Here this or that might, could, or ought to happen. If he is told that something is the way it is, he will think: Well, it could probably just as well be otherwise. So the sense of possibility could be defined outright as the ability to conceive of everything that might be just as well. And to attach no more importance to what is than what is not."[23]

Keeping in mind the symptoms "becoming zero," "the uses of pleasure," and "potentiality" as typical, in some ways and under some conditions, of the man without properties, we can proceed with our inquiry into the wider scene of *belle époque* socialist antimaterialism as a setting for the dramatization of an ethical, metaphysical, and political conflict between the imperatives of *phusikaphobia* and *philophusikia*, respectively.

Context 2: The Scene of *Belle Époque* Socialist Antimaterialism

Commentators such as the American sociologist Thorstein Veblen (1857–1929) attributed the ethical irresistibility of antimaterialism to *belle époque* radicalism to a staggering shift in the quality and quantity of private wealth in the era. "Those thoughtful men in the eighteenth-century," Veblen reasons, "who made so much . . . of the modern point of view did not contemplate anything like the system of large wealth, large-scale industry, and large-scale commerce and credit which prevails today. . . . It is a division, not between those who have something and those who have nothing, . . . but between those who own wealth enough to make it count, and those who do not. . . . It is a division between vested interests and the common man. . . . A vested interest is a legitimate right to get something for nothing."[24] Catalyzed by the decisive transition within capitalism proper from private enterprise to oligopoly and *grossindustrie*, these changes oversaw the rise, at home, of a vulgar new financier: the plutocrat. Overseas, New Imperialism yielded figures like the unscrupulous South African Randlord.[25]

Writing about the contemptible new rich of the times, the English economist and novelist, W. H. Mallock (1849–1923), holds that while there were fewer than five hundred people outside of the landed gentry with incomes greater than £5,000 a year at the time of the Battle of Waterloo, at least thirty men were worth £2 million upon their demise between 1895 and 1914. To cite Veblen again, this was money available for "an indefinitely extensible consumption of superfluities."[26] Some of these arrivistes built their stuccoed palaces with marbled bathrooms and gold taps in Piccadilly and Park Lane. Others opted for orgiastic shooting parties at rural retreats where thousands of birds were felled for pleasure prior to evenings where the champagne flowed like a veritable river. Champagne itself achieved unprecedented popularity as the first decade of the century progressed, with sales from the Marne alone averaging a total of 39, 294, 526 bottles between 1909 and 1910. Sales for this beverage among new millionaires in the United States quadrupled between 1900 and 1909, notwithstanding exorbitant duties. In a tableau exemplifying the crude excesses of the era, it was with his hand resting theatrically upon an empty magnum of champagne that the great tenor Caruso sang an aria from *Carmen*, in 1906, at the Pacific Coast residence of the absurdly wealthy James Ben Ali Haggin, only two hours before San Francisco was hit by the devastating earthquake of that year.[27]

Responding to such scenes with due moral outrage, pious observers tediously elaborated the grim symbiosis between material excess and ethical impoverishment to which the rich were so susceptible. The most coherent of these sermons included Veblen's theses on "conspicuous consumption," condemning the wealthy for their reduction of human worth to "unremitting demonstration of the ability to pay."[28] Socialism, no less than other radical credos, readily joined the prevailing chorus of lamentation for the endangered souls of *belle époque* billionaires. It took its cue, internationally, from George Sorel's bristling syndicalist polemic against the imperial-capitalist transformation of the world into a monstrous shop replete with decadent luxuries. In Britain, R. H. Tawney, among others, began his painstaking diagnosis of capitalism's intense "appeal to the acquisitive appetites and the skill with which it plays on them."[29] In a more populist pitch, the *Irish Times,* also an acknowledged mouthpiece for the Dublin labor unrest of the moment, lampooned the Midas touch of plutocracy. A typical example is this doggerel from the print campaign directed against the voracity of the local plutocrat William Martin Murphy, a man grown rich on tramway construction and railway enterprise: "I went to heaven. The Jasper walls / Towered high and wide, and the golden halls / Shone bright. But a strange new mark / Was over the gate, viz., 'Private Park.' / 'What is the meaning of this?' I cried. / And a saint with a livery on replied: / 'It's Murphy's.'"[30]

Though such denunciations suggest untroubled consensus at the scene of *belle époque* socialist antimaterialism, a countervailing subcurrent appears whenever antimaterialism manifests as a moral nausea directed not against the consuming rich but against the consuming poor. A case in point is Veblen's claim that the proper peril of "conspicuous consumption" is that it sets off a materialist contagion (or sets down a canonicity of consumption) to which the laboring classes conform through self-corrupting forms of "pecuniary emulation."[31] This last, Veblen adds, is "an ideal of consumption that lies beyond our reach, or to reach which requires some strain. The motive is emulation—the stimulus of an invidious comparison, which prompts us to outdo those with whom we are in the habit of classing ourselves."[32] It was in Britain, especially, that the charge against "pecuniary emulation" found potent fuel in current political developments.

From about the late 1880s onward, British "new unionism," as it was called, had put itself firmly on the course of political respectability for labor leaders and material well-being for the common man and woman. These efforts were finally poised for success with the resounding Liberal majority returned in the elections of 1906. The New Liberals who had promised to secure access for "working men to . . . manage Parliamentary affairs," carried twenty-nine labor candidates into Parliament, and prepared the way to the historic founding of the British Labor Party.[33] Subsequent efforts by the new Lib-Lab alliance to redistribute the ill-gotten gains of empire more equitably resulted, as we have seen, in the historic inauguration of welfarism, with the new government's "People's Budget" of 1909 controversially proposing to tax the rich to repay the poor. The years between 1906 and 1911 were especially devoted to the economic propitiation of the worker. They were bookended to this effect, on the one side, by the Trades Disputes Act, granting unions indemnity against damages incurred during a strike and, on the other, by the Health Insurance Act—a brainchild of Lloyd George, the chancellor for the Exchequer—granting every worker medical, maternity, disability, and sanatorium benefits upon the payment of a mere four pence a week.[34] In the same period, a subsidiary Liberal program of wage reform, buttressed by input from libertarian economists such as J. A. Hobson and formalized by a Living Wage Commission, also worked at policies to expand working-class purchasing power, on the view that thrift, especially amongst the poor majority, would ultimately jeopardize the extension of public ownership.[35] Enthusiastically supporting the projected shift in spending from Bond Street and Monte Carlo to the East End, some voices on the Left were quick to endorse the rearrangement of imperial spoils. In an essay for *The New Age*, Frank Holmes, a rags-to-riches oil-concession hunter, demands compensatory pecuniary benefits for the imperialist worker on the grounds that "if our Empire is worth having at all, it is worth paying for."[36] The argument is iterated by another union leader, who augments the prevailing clamor for wage increase with the slogan, "Don't think of an Empire on which the sun never sets; think of the wage that never rises."[37]

It was precisely demands for equity in consumption that provoked a virulent bourgeois reaction against working-class greed. Protesting the "illimitable feast of health" promised by Lloyd George's health reforms, physician Dr. Henry Roberts pours scorn in a piece for *The Nation & Athenaeum* upon the eager commoditization of medicine by the uncomprehending working poor in London's slums and tenements:

Mr. Lloyd George's new Act . . . was to do wonderful things. Every poor man was henceforth to have at his disposal all the medical and surgical science and skill that had hitherto been at the service only of the rich. There was to be a bottle of "real medicine" on every tenement mantelpiece, . . . and today there can hardly be a working-class home in the land without a partly consumed eight or ten ounce bottle of bitter or sweet brown or pinkish, mixture, composed of ingredients in the efficacy of which not one doctor in fifty has the slightest faith.[38]

In a private letter of March 1912 to the labor leader Robert Smillie, the Liberal prime minister's wife, Margot Asquith, makes another sort of case against the moral bankruptcy of welfarism, which she faults (in a familiar argument) for the enervating assumption that wealth alone will redeem the poor. As she puts it, in rising crescendo, "Do you think quality of brain could be made equal if we had equal prosperity? Do you think in trying or even succeeding in making Human Nature equal in their bankbooks, they would also be equal in the sight of God and Man? Equal in motive, in unselfishness, in grandeur of character?"[39]

To get to the heart of the matter at hand, how did the British labor and socialist movement respond to this new invective against the consuming poor? With, I submit, consummate creative inconsistency. On the one hand, it reacted to the scandal of its alleged avarice in recoil from worldly gain. On the other hand, it distanced itself, simultaneously and symbolically, from the fetishization of the virtue of nonacquisition. This story, such as it is, can only be told in two versions of the same events, each of which possesses its own veracity and unique conclusion. The friction between these two accounts clarifies the ethical conflict between the men of exemplary properties and those without properties. It also points the way forward to the metaphysical and political ramifications of this disagreement at the scene of socialist antimaterialism.

Ethics: Asceticism and Eudaimonism

Version A: The Worker as Ascetic

By the 1910s the ongoing bourgeois polemic against welfarism as a perilous stimuli to working-class covetousness had provoked a self-defensive reaction against the material advantages of parliamentary laborism within socialist ranks as well. In 1907 *The New Age* was plangent with endorsements of the Lib-Lab electoral victory for securing representation for a constituency hitherto remote from the corridors of power. It had quite changed its tune by 1909, now giving unexpected support to the controversial Osborne Judgment of this year, which denied unions—much to detriment of the fledgling Labor Party—any direct allocation of their funds for political purposes. Notably, it was in the name of socialist temperance and working-class abstinence that an editorial of September 1910 hailed the judgment as welcome liberation from the multiple corruptions of representative democracy:

It is all very well to argue that working-men are entitled to representation, that trade unions are compelled by economic pressure to enter politics, that they can point already to advantages won for their class, . . . [but] the fact remains that delegacy of any kind is contrary to representation. . . . The ideal member is undoubtedly the man who employs his talents under the guidance of his constituents. . . . In so far as he is merely the incarnate greed of any single constituency striving to win some local advantage at the expense of the general good, he is politically corrupt. And he is not at all less corrupt for being the mouthpiece of the selfishness of a whole class.[40]

Distinctly syndicalist in tenor, this antipathy against the institutionalization of self-advantage ranks high among the factors that caused British socialism to swerve dramatically, albeit briefly, from the comfortable path of representative democracy into an oftentimes incoherent carnival of direct labor agitation that began in January 1910 and lasted almost to the end of 1913. What happened? Arising, it could be argued, from the very political unconscious of the procedural politics ratified by parliamentarism, the great prewar labor strikes spread upon a logic of pure conjuncturality, spontaneously, sympathetically, and without cogent purpose among workers in disparate industrial sectors. In the aftermath of the protests, Ramsay MacDonald, then chairman of the Parliamentary Labor Party, offered baffled testimony to the manifest atavism of the strike tendency in grown men and women: "The labor world responded to the call to strike in the same eager, spontaneous way as nature responds to the call of the springtime. One felt as though some magical allurement had seized upon the people."[41]

So, on January 1, 1910, in protest against the replacement of the two-shift system by a three-shift system that would prevent male members of a household from reliable participation in domestic chores (such as feeding babies, cleaning homes, and shopping for groceries) to which they were so clearly committed, more than a third of the miners from the Northumberland and Durham districts stopped work apparently in the cause of spousal harmony. In early July, once again for diffuse causes, more than ten thousand fairly well paid employees of the North-Eastern Railway held up all traffic for some three days and then unaccountably returned to work. September 1910 witnessed such riots in the coalfields of South Wales that the infantry and cavalry were sent in—not for the first time in the course of these upheavals. More than a year later, in February 1912, the settled direction of the miners' strike in Manchester suffered arbitrary but welcome disruption when activist leader Tom Mann courted arrest for incitement to mutiny by publicly reading the following letter from railwayman Fred Crowsley, urging the British armed forces to join in solidarity with all striking workers:

Men! Comrades! Brothers! You are in the army. So are we. You in the army of Destruction. We in the Industrial, or army of Construction. . . . When we go to strike to better Our lot which is also the lot of Your Fathers, Mothers, Brothers, and Sisters, YOU are called upon by your Officers to MURDER US! Don't do it. . . . Immediately you are ordered to murder Us, as You did in Mitcheltown, at Featherstone, at Belfast. . . . Boys, Don't do it. "Thou shalt not Kill," says the Book. Don't forget that! It does not say, "unless you have a uniform on."[42]

By 1913, with the inauguration of an Irish chapter in the history of the unrest, the city of Dublin erupted in a year-long revolt that would include every conceivable branch of the skilled, semiskilled and unskilled trades, each paralyzing the motions of industry in an effort, it sometimes appeared, simply to impose a remedial regimen of hunger upon the culture of consumption itself.

In this spirit, in each passing year scores of productive workdays were wasted (calculated on the basis of one day per head; thus, 10,319,591 days in 1911), and scores of laborers extracted themselves from the life cycle of work—that biorhythm perfected by modern power that makes us, in the words of R. H. Tawney, "go to work to earn the cash to buy the bread to get the strength to go to work and earn the cash."[43] Those accustomed to the greater luxuries of industrial capitalism in the Thames Valley were, likewise, brought to the brink of famine in 1911 when a relentless, combined action of stevedores, tugboatmen, crane porters, coal bunkerers, and sailing bargeman, among others, brought the services of coal, water, gas, electricity, river, road, and railway transport to a complete halt. "Vegetables and flour grew scarcer and scarcer," George Dangerfield observes. "Great piles of fruit lay perishing in the docks, . . . the Danish butter . . . was growing rancid in the mounting heat. The frozen meat from Argentina, the United States and New Zealand—on which the city largely depended—was going bad, . . . and the refrigerating ships themselves lay useless in the river without coal."[44]

The prewar labor agitations were largely disjointed and unintelligible. Yet, the divergent scenes of waste, self-sabotage, hunger, and the enforcement of austerity canvassed above, and common to all the protests during this period, disclose something like a shared moral contraction in the face of privilege and property per se. Contemporary spectators of the unrest also underscore a contingent elision of the wage issue in most strike actions. The Scottish philosopher John W. Scott (who was in empathetic correspondence with the perfectionist New Liberals and Oxford idealists encountered in the introduction) insists that the industrial unrest reached continually toward "something vaguer and vaster" than mere "wage increase."[45] Philip Mairet, from the *New Age* circle, maintains that the protests aimed "to organise and to strike, not for wages" but for the sake of the strike itself.[46] Speaking specifically of the Dublin disturbances, eyewitness Arnold Wright reports that "it was in essence a revolutionary rising, one in which the ultimate aim of its promoters involved the destruction of Society quite as much as the betterment of the wage conditions of the workers."[47] Giving credence to such readings, James Larkin, the unruly leader of the Irish unrest, proclaimed his "divine mission" to be not the securing of comfort for the working poor so much as the effort conscientiously "to make men and women discontented."[48] To these performances of socialist renunciation on the docks, streets, and tenements of London, Dublin, Liverpool, and Manchester, we can add the gloss of various augmenting moral pietisms from intellectual interlocutors of the movement: "A Socialist State as a happy hunting ground of friends is . . . a far finer idea than a Socialist State as the fair divider of the spoils of labor"; "we believe what is morally right is economically right"; the members of a functional society must "renounce the opportunity of gains," and so on, ad nauseam.[49]

Version B: The Laborer's Eudaimonia

Morning arrives on August 14, 1911, after a sweltering night in Bermondsey, an epicenter in the black patch of working London. The tenement dwellers, each family crowded into a single room, have felt this summer acutely. It is the hottest, some have been saying, on record and certainly among the most onerous in memory, what with the men fractious and unoccupied following the bitter transport strikes of the season at the very height of the ambient unrest. The women leave for work as they have been doing all summer, in a mess of babies and unfinished chores, to resume positions within the numerous confectionery factories where they are employed: "jam, biscuit and food preparation factories; . . . workshops where girls . . . [make] sweetstuff, glue or tin boxes, . . . teapacking and perambulator works."[50] Upon the conclusion of this day, whereon the grim regularity of factory time and the routine motions of labor and domesticity, no less, will be quite undone, the women will talk unreliably about the appearance as though out of thin air of a very fat woman, threatening employers and asking the girls to leave, for no apparent cause than the pleasure of pouring out upon the dismal streets. No one has really seen her, but everybody believes in her. Once upon the streets though, the workers will discover that they too are on strike (much like their men and the comrades of their men), marching, in this instance, for a wage increase over the seven to nine shillings that the women get each week, and the three shillings reserved for the girls. Somewhere between the inchoate flaring of the strike impulse and the clarification of political objectives—that is, between the visitation of the fat lady and the mathematics of a wage increase—however, many of the women find time and the means to don their finery.

Let us rewind this frame for a moment, briefly to interpolate some content from version A of our unfolding narrative for the sake of this description: even as the workers, activists and thinkers of *belle époque* socialist antimaterialism clarified their renunciatory catechism, the women workers of Bermondsey materialized on the streets, the *Daily Chronicle* of August 15, 1911, tells us, "in the highest spirits. They went laughing and singing through Bermondsey shouting 'Are we downhearted?' and answering the question by a shrill chorus of 'No!' It was noticeable that many of them had put on their 'Sunday best.' In spite of the great heat, hundreds of them wore fur boas and tippets." Turning the austere arena of the unrest into a catwalk, the women filled the air also with the smell of revolutionary confectionery. "In the heat," another account tells us, " the air [was] fetid with the mingled smell of jam, . . . biscuits and pickles, the sickly odour of jam predominating, the streets packed with people."[51]

Here, in unmediated form, we can observe the rudiments of a political performance in which an unmistakable aura of consumption mingles with the regimen of starvation proper to the emerging manifesto of socialist asceticism. The adulteration of ethical intent in this scene, furthermore, proves emblematic in the setting, which is noteworthy for its disruptive iteration across the wider theater of the unrest in countless similar examples of willful impropriety and excess. We learn, variously, that the sweat-workers of Lancashire find the sermons of union leaders rather more recreational than moralizing, "better," one worker puts it, than a trip to "t'sea-side"; that Jim Larkin, the putative prophet of working-class discontentment, inaugurates the great riots of August 31, 1913, on O'Connell Street in Dublin by dropping a bottle of something from the first floor of the Imperial Hotel into the crowd below, while smoking a cigar and clad in unimpeachable silk hat and frock-coat; and that the motley, semiskilled transport workers of Liverpool were, likewise, always beautifully dressed when in contravention of the law.[52] In this period, in a perverse twist upon the otherwise puritanical antiwelfarism of the movement, the *Irish Worker* also recommends sedulous conversion of Lloyd George's health insurance benefits into a free drinking allowance: "Homeward those sick ones went, / With money to pay the rent, / Which Lloyd George had kindly lent—/ Happy Sick Hundred! / And tho' they're badly crushed / Into the pub they rushed. / Later with faces flushed, / Homeward they went."[53]

We could say of these vignettes that they point to a stylistic modification of socialist antimaterialism wherein renunciation displays itself anew as a type of inspired hedonism. The theme is crystallized in the writings of R. H. Tawney, which represent the eschewal of material possessions as a careless profligacy of spirit. Here, self-denial consists in an extravagant "throwing away [of] what you have"; drawing its model from "commercial ethics" where one must "trust the future and take risks." In moral as in economic affairs, the rash man is "he who does not speculate."[54] This recasting of the antimaterialist as ethical spendthrift and bon vivant is supplemented by direct inducements to working-class desire in Tawney's scattered aphorisms, contradicting his more formal lessons against acquisitiveness and increase: "It is the ineradicable assumption of the upper classes that a workman should . . . want . . . not to live but to work. The slightest extravagance in him is condemned by the very people who . . . never dream of denying themselves . . . pleasures and luxuries." "There is no reason why the community, by provision, should not make the life of the ordinary workman as rich and interesting as that of the fellow of an Oxford College." "The purpose of Industry [should be] . . . to supply men with the material means for a good life," and so on.[55]

To summarize the discussion so far, our attempt to seek a historical modality for socialist antimaterialism at the scene of the prewar labor unrest in Britain reveals a creative confusion within this discourse at the point when it turns into an exculpation of the consuming poor. To participate in such a project and rise to renunciatory exemplarity the laborer must internalize the prevailing invective against her own petty materialism in this time of champagne and pheasant-massacre. She can only silence her bourgeois detractors through a performance of sovereignty precisely over those signatory desires for advantage by which she may otherwise claim common membership in her class and collectivity. This enterprise, seeking, in the words of one commentator, to convert the "fighting strikers" into "the monks of the working class movement," we may describe as a manifesto *for poverty and against the poor*: a program, à la version A of our narrative, of ascetic antimaterialism.[56] This program, in due course, found fulfillment within the revolutionary syndicalism of the later Sorelians — among them were Edouard Berth, George Valois, Robert Michels, Arturo Labriola, Marcel Diat, and Henrik de Man, each claiming affiliation with various fascist organizations and publications through the interwar years and each committed via a structuring anti-Marxism to the supersession of economicism by an antimaterialist ethics. It would take only a slightly increased bias toward antimaterialism for this undertaking to declare class interest altogether irrelevant to the socialist project and then to replace the proletariat with a nation in which repugnance for majority rule would translate all too readily into a catastrophic repugnance for the body of the people themselves.

Against this program, version B of our narrative delivers little that might pass muster as a manifesto among serious revolutionaries. At best a politics of gesturality or, more concretely, of the self-contradictory gesture, it performs with one hand the frugal ethics of asceticism that it forgetfully undoes with the other through a counterethics of eudaimonia. It reaches for the themes of fortune, flourishing, and plenty as essential Derridean supplements, which displace even as they substantiate the claims of virtue alone.[57] To pursue these thoughts in another way, via Hannah Arendt's idiosyncratic readings of Jesus of Nazareth, we could posit the self-contradictory gesturality of British socialism during the unrest as a type of negative goodness, the efficacy of which demands disciplined authorial ignorance of self-virtue, namely, of the properties of self. "For it is manifest," Arendt tells us, "that the moment a good work becomes known and public, it loses its specific character of goodness, of being done for nothing but goodness' sake. When goodness appears openly it is no longer goodness. . . . Goodness can exist only when it is not perceived, not even by its author; whoever sees himself as performing a good work is no longer good. . . . Therefore: 'Let not the left hand know what the right hand doeth.'"[58] Conceding in this way the ambiguation and ideological dispersal of their own ethico-political project—thus foiling its formal perfection—the actors of version B may be said to enable "the people" to repossess the space of an improper socialism. In a minor key, their interception of working-class self-loathing (in the name of antimaterialism) insinuates something like a caesura between the time of socialism and that of revolutionary antipopulism.[59] Let us call this variant a *eudaimonian* politics *against poverty and for the poor*.

How exactly do these two forms of socialist antimaterialism engage each other and to what effect? I would like to propose that ascetic socialism (for poverty and against the poor) and eudaimonian socialism (against poverty and for the poor) respectively comprise the idiolects proper to the *phusikaphobic* man of exemplary qualities and the *phusikaphilic* man without properties encountered at the outset of our inquiry. These antagonistic figures only come into their revolutionary patois, however, via the founding grammar of a new metaphysics. To put this another way, their constituting antimaterialisms signify two types of metaphysical yearning—a discrepant reterritorialization of metaphysics itself. Traversing the epistemological path of revisionist idealism, socialist asceticism declares war not only on everyday materialism but also against the perceived philosophical hedonism of contemporary Marxism. The thinker Ernest Belfort Bax (1854–1926) is representative in his view that a "crude and dogmatic materialism" is enshrined within the Marxist doctrine of class interest and given new vigor in Engels's *Anti-Dühring* (1878), seen by many others at the time to champion an extreme, empiricist version of the dialectic.[60] Sorel is preeminent in the contiguous effort to extract a "new real metaphysics" out of the ruins of Marxism by returning to the scene of the dialectic through a set of "methods which alone deserve the name philosophical" (even if he says so himself).[61] Next, apprehending metaphysics as the decisive appropriation of the realm of spirit for the human subject, *belle époque* asceticism intervenes against the threatening ascendency of things primarily on behalf of endangered subjectivity.[62] Its purpose is to refashion the subject not as the mild-mannered Kantian advocate of the unity of apperception, whose action ceases upon the "I think" of armchair philosophers, but as the elite and virtuous "hero" of revolutionary antimaterialism, whose "philosophy is closely bound up with the apology for violence."[63] In other words, if materialism conceived as antimetaphysics posits a world where, as Sorel puts it, "there is no more opportunity for heroism," then a rightful victory of metaphysics over the object world yields a race of heroes, superior and righteous men standing high amid the common syndicates negotiating "the price of guano with manure merchants."[64]

In contrast to this project, the bearers of a loosely guild socialist eudaimonian politics arrive at the scene of metaphysics by a more circuitous route. They present materialism as the adverse side effect of unrestrained philosophical idealism: an outlook that they blame for the progressive spiritual impoverishment of the objective world (that is, for its relegation to the status of mere matter). Here, reconceived as a remedial program for inspiriting dead matter and a means to restrain the spiritually voracious subject, metaphysics manifests as radical empiricism and as a poor philosophy on two counts. First, it identifies as the field for its disciplinary enrichment the abandoned and pauperized realm of onticity that is discernible, variously, in the thing, the common, the quotidian, the ordinary. R. H. Tawney aptly names this endeavor "materialist utopianism," and T. E. Hulme (1883–1917), a leading poet-critic and philosopher-columnist for *The New Age,* finds it exemplified in "ordinary human expression" for the reason that "the simple man is in the best position to write metaphysics."[65] Second, to undertake such labor and enter into the spirit of reparative empathy with the toxicity of matter, the socialist-philosopher must be well trained in the methods of Heideggerean *Gelassenheit,* negatively capable of taking the stuff of onticity as given. She must then be willing also to renounce the mediating props of personality for an effect best explained with reference to Jerzy Grotowski's notion of "a poor theatre," wherein, "by a complete stripping down, by the laying bare of one's own intimity— all this without the least trace of egotism or self-enjoyment, . . . the actor makes a total gift of himself."[66] It is in this vein that Hulme redefines antimaterialism as a "metaphysics" contingent upon the subjective/psychic and epistemological dispossession to be performed, sacrificially, by "a race of naked philosophers."[67] Let us turn in the following two sections to the metaphysical elaboration sought by these discrepant paths and, in that regard, the translation of socialist asceticism and eudaimonism into two competing tenders submitted by the men of exemplary quality and without property for the political palliation of their troubled times.

Metaphysics: Two Types of Potentiality

Early twentieth-century socialist antimaterialism turned almost exclusively to the influential French philosopher Henri Bergson to substantiate its own internally divergent metaphysical ambitions. Sorel famously claims Bergson as a crucial source for his syndicalist program. The latter was, likewise, available to the scene of British guild socialism through various reviews, synopses, and translations of his work in *The New Age* and adjacent publications from 1909 onwards.[68] We do not have the space for a comprehensive account of Bergsonism within *belle époque* radicalism. But we can certainly note the appeal to the amateur metaphysicians at this scene (all seeking the creative revolution of a jaded world) of Bergson's audacious inauguration of metaphysics as an altogether new science that did not need to be thought so much as done or practiced as *askesis*, as an art of living. An example is the tenor of his exquisitely unreliable 1903 essay, "An Introduction to Metaphysics," which neither introduces readers to *prima philosophia* nor gives any account of its disciplinary history or basics, and thus merely marks the metaphysical as a significant stranger in the gathering crisis, to be befriended and treated with due hospitality.[69] What, then, is Bergsonian metaphysics? Or rather, how did its early twentieth-century socialist hosts accommodate it?

Let me summarily propose the following schema: neo-empiricist eudaimonism and neo-idealist asceticism play out their metaphysical differences through two misreadings—strictly, two contradictory, interested readings—of the theme of "potentiality" in Bergson's oeuvre.[70] Potentiality comes into view apropos the philosopher's strenuous rejection of philosophical finalism, a trait of thought that he finds common both to metaphysical and mechanistic (or positivist) accounts of the world, even though these systems seem at first sight to be mutually antithetical. How so? Metaphysical finality is, in effect, teleology: the argument that all things and beings are in stages of impartial development en route to a final destination or realization of perfected form. In other words, so long as they are enmeshed in material existence (that is, in a state of becoming), subjects/objects do not embody or exemplify the truth of their own being, which remains tantalizingly outside or beyond them. In fact they are constitutively negative in relation to it: not-yet, not-quite, not-really the real thing. As Bergson complains, "How, then, having postulated immutability alone, shall we make change come forth from it? Not by the addition of anything, for, by the hypothesis, there exists nothing positive outside Ideas. It must therefore be by a diminution . . . . It is therefore something negative."[71] In a similar register, mechanism also participates in finalist thought, albeit through the secular conviction that the existence of things and beings consists in conforming, with varying skill and success, to a previously arranged program or to pregiven laws. "The essence of mechanical explanation," Bergson writes, "is to regard the future and the past as calculable functions of the present, and thus to claim that everything is given. On this hypothesis, past, present and future would be open at a glance to the superhuman intellect capable of making the calculation."[72]

Bergson's critique of finalisms (whether metaphysical or mechanistic) is effectively a defense of potentiality, which he believes we can liberate through two remedial methods. The first of these, immanentism, takes the view that any knowledge that lies outside of its object is false. True or intuitive knowledges are those that install themselves right inside the imperfect thing itself. "One places oneself within an object," as Bergson puts it, "in order to coincide with what is unique in it and constantly inexpressible."[73] By a second route, we can also release potentiality from the icy grip of finalism by refusing to treat processual life as the negative or lesser version of perfect forms and ideals. This stance of anti-negativity asserts that there are no differences of degree (better, worse, best, less), only those of kind (apples, professors, harem pants). To resume our main themes, neo-empiricist eudaimonism intercepts Bergsonian immanentism to suit its particular project. It posits an expansion of the object world at the cost of the subject of metaphysics, which it pronounces merely latent because it is self-limiting (on conscientious grounds). In sharp contrast, neo-idealist asceticism intercepts Bergsonian anti-negativity to defend its particular investments in the sovereign limitlessness of consciousness—which it declares potent, as in possessing potency—against all materialist constraints (the threatening world of things).

In its elaborated version, then, eudaimonian empiricism picks up on Bergson's critique of supersensory philosophies, wherein the transformation or amelioration of the material/manifest world is always beyond, or external, to itself. Bergson counters this assumption through the dazzling semantic trick whereby the metaphysical is shown to be entirely immanent to existence and visible whenever the material-physical realm (*phusika*) is altered temporally through kinesis, mutation, or decay. As a result, the received metaphysical law of teleology is now displaced by a new law of change, in and for itself, neither for better nor worse. Additionally, material existence itself reveals a profusion, suddenly, of metaphysical objects (the *Überding*) that are always accretive, in excess of themselves. In the very gesture through which this heterodox metaphysics reanimates and respiritualizes the realm of matter (thus giving the world back to itself), however, it also takes something away from the (former) subject of orthodox metaphysics. Structured now by the modalities of change-without-telos (like every other thing) the subject of *prima philosophia* is bereft of any fixed properties of self and will never experience the full realization of personality. In Bergson's words, variously: "Our personality . . . changes without ceasing"; "each of our states . . . modifies our personality"; "individuality . . . is not fully realized anywhere"; "it is often difficult, sometimes impossible, to tell what is an individual"; "reality is mobility, . . . not things made, but things in the making, not self-maintaining states, but only changing states exist"; "All reality . . . is tendency, if we agree to mean by tendency, an incipient change of direction."[74] Thus, it could be said that potentiality—*contra* actuality and in the sense of the mere tendency or latency of personality—is the distinguishing mark of the new metaphysical subject. To participate entirely in metaphysicality—that is, to comprehend the continuous self-excession of the *Überding*—however, this subject must engage actively in further epistemological self-reduction. The "mind" as Bergson tells us, "has to do violence to itself, has to reverse the direction of the operation by which it habitually thinks, has perpetually to revise . . . [and] recast all its categories," so as apprehend "the very movement of the inward life of things."[75] In brief, an empiricist reading of Bergsonian immanentism condones the enforcement of certain constraints upon the subjectivity of the subject of metaphysics for the sake of world-enrichment. Bergson, it would appear, thinks highly of such a subject: "It will have contemplated itself in a mirror which reflects an image of itself, much shrunken, no doubt, but for that reason very luminous."[76]

In the second philosophical declension we are tracking, ascetic neo-idealism develops Bergson's critique of finality solely into a type of anti-materialism or antimechanism, upon the philosopher's own insistence that "Finalism . . . is only inverted mechanism."[77] To recapitulate, in a setting where finalism prevails, and the universe is believed to be carrying out a preformed plan, both beings and things are robbed of their agentive worth. They find themselves in place of a futility, marked by passivity and inhabiting, in existence, the prison house of "a metaphysical zero."[78] Socialist neo-idealism excises Bergson's beloved things from the equation and refashions his momentous "critique of the negative"—perceived by a later thinker like Deleuze to be *the* "single theme" of Bergsonian philosophy—against the curbs of objectivity alone.[79] From this modification, two consequences follow. First, Bergsonian anti-negativity appears as an animated discourse directed against any attenuation of subjectivity; to use his own terms, as one poised, variously, against "void," "interval," "fall," "losing," "insufficiency," or "deficit."[80] Second, it seems to make available to the temporalized subject of consciousness a new jargon of capacity. Liberated from the confines of finality, this subject can now enjoy the limitlessness of her own consciousness without any inhibition—that is, as a potency never exhausted by prior calculation; an "inexhaustible enumeration" or "indefinitely enlarge[d]" domain; the indefatigable "possibilities of action"; a field of "several possible actions."[81]

The concluding section briefly maps these accounts of Bergsonian potentiality, variously for and against the reduction of the subject of metaphysics (and so for and against the material world), upon two competing programs for the political.

Politics: Competing Exceptionalities

Toward the end of a corpus based on intense engagement with the work of Henri Bergson, the English amateur philosopher and anarcho-syndicalist, Ernest Belfort Bax (encountered earlier in this discussion) complains somewhat bitterly about the former's insufficient idealism—specifically, Bergson's failure to connect his doctrine with another that sees in reality simply the modifications of consciousness. Hard though it is to live with Bergson, however, it is much harder to live without him. An age beset by the perils of dialectical materialism and everyday hedonism demands a more muscular Bergsonism, or so Bax contends. This requires that metaphysics be reintroduced as a science of illimitability that lifts all curbs that objectivity imposes upon consciousness, whether philosophically, through a finalist lexicon (stasis, hypostasis, *terminus ad quem*, *summum bonum*), or existentially, as the ennui that drains the capacity of the pleasure-seeker, the self-exhaustion that haunts the consummation of desire.[82] A combination of Bergson and Sorel delivers the desired results. In particular, syndicalist thought supplies four sequences through which a skillful revision of Bergson resolves itself into a discourse of "sovereignty."

1. *À rebours*. In *Reflections on Violence*, Sorel dramatizes the limit of materiality in his account of the "relapse" into that barbaric state of nature to which men are eter-

nally prone, exemplified in contemporary bourgeois decadence.[83] Having risen from sensation into the realm of rationality, the mind inevitably retraverses its course into the indolence of what the Sorelian Eduard Berth describes as a *"liberté végétative et animale."*[84]

2. *Ricorsi.* Yet history bears witness to the renewal in human life of an upward movement subsequent to decline. In the present time our recommencement or spiritual reflux will begin through work (as in the working over of matter) and the world of production. For the Sorelian George Valois, especially, work is "the counterpoint of decadence," and prophylaxis against the enfeebling contagion of material comfort.[85] Accordingly, a new redeemer for the times emerges in the figure of man-as-worker, or *homo faber*, "at the service of the immemorial interests of civilisation."[86]

3. *The Man of Exemplary Properties.* Counterposing an energetic law of fabrication against the indolent consumption of given objects, the Sorelian *homo faber* is not a maker of goods so much as the producer of his own excellence. Like the great Gothic cathedral builders, he does not care about material remuneration or the imperishability of his works. His sole interest is in the slow accumulation of ascetic virtue: "This striving toward excellence, which exists in the absence of any personal, immediate or proportional reward, constitutes the secret virtue that assures the continued progress of the world."[87]

4. *Sovereignty.* Never entirely secret, however, the goods of excellence are structurally comparative. To "excel," as Arendt tells us in another context, is "to distinguish oneself from all others."[88] Thus conceived, most clearly in the thought of syndicalist royalists such as Valois and, later, Henrik de Man, excellence is the property of the superior or exceptional man: *le chef* or, more precisely, the *chef national.*[89] These are the themes that Carl Schmitt, whom we encountered in the introduction, sharpens in his *Political Theology* (1922) as the irrefutable symbiosis between exceptionality and sovereignty. To recall, with regard to the logic whereby only those perceived to be exceptional attain to sovereignty, only those who are sovereign can lay claim to, or command, the prerogatives of exceptionality, namely, sole access to exception or exemption from the limits either of law or of nature. To put this differently, we could say that sovereignty is founded on an ideology of idealist potentiality.[90] Where those under his jurisdiction are alike standardized and condemned to normativity, only the exceptional sovereign has the potential (strictly, *potenza*) to become other, to escape from, to be taken outside (*ex-capere*) and alter what prevails. So too, as the figure of singularity in the general mass—the one whose claim to the exception demands that all others submit to regimen, regularity, routine, and rule—only the sovereign has the potential also to become himself, to come into his own, to possess his own properties of self.

One last time, and this time in the spirit of manifesto, let us glean from the scattered archive of empiricist antimaterialism four contrary derivations of Bergsonism that resolve themselves into something like, but not quite, equality.

1. *The Myth of the External Limit.* Writing in the timbre of the anti-utopianism and antihumanism characteristic of *belle époque* radicalism, the socialist T. E. Hulme fulminates against the myth of external constraints (the evils of society, the temptation of worldly goods, the contagion of matter) from which the modern cult of personality obtains its sustenance. A politics founded upon the logic of this myth, Hulme writes, pursues the following, erroneous, reasoning: "Under ideal conditions, everything of value will spring spontaneously from free 'personalities.' If nothing good seems to appear spontaneously now, that is because of external restrictions and obstacles. Our political ideal should be the removal of everything that checks the 'spontaneous growth of personality.'"[91] Nowhere does this logic obtain more readily than in the austere texts of antimaterialism prescribing a recoil from matter as the only recourse against the retardation of "that bastard thing Personality, and all the bunkum that follows from it."[92]
2. *A Fellowship with Things.* In the writings of R. H. Tawney we can discern the shape of an antimaterialist manifesto prohibiting the pious renunciation of material goods for the sake of subjective immaculacy. The malaise of *belle époque* consumption, Tawney argues, does not consist in property so much as the amassment of "functionless property"; that is, it consists not in possession but in the waste or violence of what we might call a disowning possession: the enshrinement of "propriety rights . . . entirely separated from the objects over which they are exercised."[93] Neglected or nonrelational property, Tawney clarifies following his traumatic service in the war, bears a wound of materiality akin to the experience of untouchability and abandonment in the vortex of violence when men are turned into mere things.[94] "I hate touching wounded men," he confesses in an account of his own experience of abjection after being shot with rifle bullets through the chest and abdomen: "A man badly knocked out feels as though the world has spun him off into a desert of unpeopled space. Combined with pain and helplessness, the sense of abandonment goes near to break his heart. I did so want to be spoken kindly to."[95] In Bergsonian register, then, a truly reparative antimaterialism is the program of an owning nonpossession, wherein cultivated relationality to the thing serves as an order for manumission from its own wounded materiality. Through renewed intimacy with the subject, the object loses its status as property to become a prosthetic, as it were, to a cyborg: "so closely united to its owner as to seem almost a part of him"; "an extension of the personality."[96]
3. *The Man without Properties.* Without the opposition of materiality, Hulme writes, man is revealed as "an extraordinarily fixed and limited animal whose nature is absolutely constant."[97] Appropriate to this view is a philosophy "faithful to the conception of a limit," or rather one that yokes the revaluated concept of self-

limitation to the schema of empiricist potentiality (strictly, latency or tendency), available in Bergson and clarified, at its source, as the striking threshold concept in Aristotelian metaphysics.[98] Here, as the critical theorist Giorgio Agamben reminds us in his insightful gloss on Aristotle, wherein the potential for vision is at the same time the potential "not to see" (just as the potential "for darkness" is also the potential "for light"), the doctrine of potentiality subtly renders lack or incapacity to be as central to the fullness of being as ability or capacity.[99] In his words, "To be potential means: to be one's own lack, to be in relation to one's own incapacity. Beings that exist in the mode of potentiality are capable of their own impotentiality; and only in this way do they become potential."[100] Where, thus, do we arrive when potentiality is released from its task as the placeholder for sovereign exceptionality? Into the labyrinth, I submit, of Ulrich's personality disorder in Musil's, *Man without Qualities*, where "a certain lack of inner substance" is the means to the finding of other human beings; or into the heart of Narsinh Mehta's *vaishnava jana*, whose renunciations of his own renunciatory virtue enable him to praise the whole world.

4. *Not Quite Equality*. So it is that Tawney's sermon on the dispossession of subjective excellence resolves itself in the repossession of a "common humanity." In his words, "There are golden moments in the life of mankind when national aims seem to be bent for some noble purpose, and men live at peace in the harmony which springs from the possession of a common moral ideal, . . . the possibilities of joy and energy which every man knows to be in his fellow [*sic*] because he seeks them in himself."[101] On the face of it, this program for "the common," "commonality," "common-ness" looks very much like a program for equality, equity, or egalitarianism, and we could reasonably claim that the oppositions to which we have been bearing witness achieve their acme or reveal their true political content in a final antithesis between "sovereignty" and "equality." Yet, with regard to the detail whereby through his insistent recourse to an ethics of subordination the "man without qualities" rigorously exempts himself from the very project of equity that he wishes for the world, we need a truer set of antonyms arranged around the view that the man of exemplary and of occluded properties, respectively, exemplifies contrary types of exceptionality. Where the former is uniquely better than the rest, the latter is (once again, uniquely) lesser than the rest. The former is the only one who is not unequal; the latter, the only one who is not equal. The one is rare for the sake of his own dominion; the other, for the sake of the *demos*; the first seeks conditions for the display of his accumulated capacities, and the latter is unaware even of his own dispossession, unable to speak its name.

We have been plotting the antagonisms between two series: on the one side, *phusikaphobia*, the man of exemplary qualities, an ascetic credo for poverty and against the poor, neo-idealist Bergsonian metaphysics, the doctrine of subjective potency; and on the other side, *philophusikia*, the man without properties, a eudaimonian politics for the poor and against poverty, neo-empiricist Bergsonian postmetaphysics, and the credo of subjective latency or impotentiality. These antagonisms may well be distilled as a conflict between the competing claims of sovereignty and something without the precise properties of equality. If the first sequence relies upon that anxious and elite repossession of a good life that authorizes, once again à la Agamben, the consignment of most others to bare life, the second evacuates the good life of the possibilities of violent signification by reopening it to the promise of a radically inclusive, antihumanist democracy. Its projected eudaimonia is closer to the blessedness that Arendt finds at the heart of the term: "literally something like the well being of the *daimon* who accompanies each man throughout life, who is his distinct identity, but appears and is visible only to others."[102] To whom did this daimon appear? Was it able to stop some from performing the violence that was to come? Had it any comfort to offer countless others who experienced this violence? What did it look like? Could you touch it? Did it speak? In which language? By what signs? As with the fat lady of Bermondsey, perhaps it is sufficient to say that nobody saw her, but some, we can be sure, believed in her.

TWO

On Descent: Stories from the Gurus of Modern India

The American pragmatist philosopher William James, who was a regular contributor to *The New Age* and an important popularizer of Bergsonism among guild socialist circles, bridges the ethical worlds of the previous chapter and this one in unexpected ways. Toward the end of his Gifford lectures on natural religion, delivered between 1901 and 1902 at the University of Edinburgh and later published as *The Varieties of Religious Experience* (1902), James develops a connection between saintliness and egalitarianism through a counterintuitive argument in praise of voluntary spiritual defectiveness: a close cousin, as we will see, to antimaterialist *philophusikia*.[1] The figure of the saint especially designates the future of politics, or so James tells us, because her idiosyncratic goodness derives from the cultivated sickness of her soul. By a certain practice of infirmity (the whiff of "hospital purulence" ever fresh about her person) the saint heralds a millennial society "of true friends . . . on a large scale," in which "there should be no aggressiveness, but only sympathy and fairness."[2] This is a revolutionary stance, James avers, in an era of offensive good health and strong-mindedness. It counteracts the cult of excellence "so in vogue at the present day"; forever "offering its biceps to be felt, thumping its breast," or swooning before "heroic standards of life, . . . welcoming leadership, . . . glorifying the chief, . . . the actual tyrant, the masterful, overpowering man of prey."[3] Through the basic dictum "not to become pure . . . [and] not to be perfect," the saint also packages her egalitarian content in an egalitarian method, so simple and accessible that we could all be saints if we liked.[4] And we must like sainthood, I argue in the ensuing discussion, for the sake of democracy.

This chapter explores a prolonged encounter between the cultures of race ethnology (a source for early twentieth-century totalitarianism), on the one hand, and of heterodox modern Indian spirituality (a source for ethical democracy), on the other. Calling the former "a science of ascent," and the latter, "an art of descent," the discussion builds on the collective corpus of some gurus of modern India as developed in their cosmopolitan ashrams, and globally transmitted by their Western disciples across three successive historical contexts: interwar Freudian psychoanalysis; international pacifism during the Second World War; and, finally, the photojournalism developed by the French photographer Henri Cartier-Bresson during his association with Magnum photos in the postwar era.

Central to the argument is an understanding of "descent" as a democratizing spiritual exercise directed toward an anti-care of the self. To clarify, numerous ethical theorists working within Europeanist genealogies emphasize the nourishing and strengthening import of the spiritual exercise through the ages. This is certainly the view taken by the French philosopher of history Pierre Hadot, who points to the shared therapeutic nature of all (Western) ancient arts of living well. Whether they consist in "constant wakefulness of the moral conscience" or in "an invitation to relaxation and serenity," these arts, Hadot determines, converge in helping the subject of *askesis* to take care of himself so as to become better, bigger, stronger, and braver than the common lot or than is usual in the lives of ordinary people.[5] In contrast, I emphasize practices that responded to the historical contingencies we have been plotting by undoing the entangled connection between self-mastery and mastery over others. In the case of the gurus themselves, descent is a style of improper metaphysics and bad ontology that defends the admissibility non-value and nonbeing in daily practice, and is the crux of connection to everything (everyone) designated unfit for consideration or beneath contempt. In the case of their disciples, we consider three historical variants of descent: cosmophilia, or world-attachment consequent upon the cultivation of disillusionment; neutrality, or care for everybody consequent upon becoming nobody; and, contagious subjectivity, or the belief that self-work is always a work on others or for their sake.

The details enumerated above are scattered in the following pages. Since the guru-corpus vehemently declines its own mastery and authoriality, it is mixed in, below, with the life work of its interlocutors in a shared milieu of descent. However, any reader who finds this approach confusing may proceed by a sequential reading: first, of the sections "And Then the Saints Come Marching In" and "The Science of Ascent" (both context-setting in general terms of the scene of modern Indian spirituality and the *longue durée* of European race ethnology, respectively); second, of "The Democratic Sublime" and "The Art of Descent," which give an account of the reversals achieved by the guru-corpus; third, of the blog sections "Cosmophilia," "Neutrality," and "The Contagious Self," which account for some historical declensions of descent in chronological order.

And Then the Saints Come Marching In

In his examples of saintly politics, William James approvingly cites the modern saint, Sri Ramakrishna Paramahamsa (1836—1886), who developed his practice (or *sadhana*) in the latter part of the nineteenth century. Other contemporary observers also credited Sri Ramakrishna as the inventor of a new style of radical mysticism at the interstices of the Western and non-Western heterodoxies that had long thrived in modern colonial India. This was the view taken by the Oxford philologist Max Müller in his *Ramakrishna, His Life and Sayings* (1898), which highlights the surprising originality of "certain religious movements *now* going on in India."[6] A like chord is struck by the French pacifist and Nobel laureate, Romain Rolland (1866–1944), whose numerous writings on colonial Indian mysticism underscore its startling contemporaneity. Figures such as Ramakrishna and his kind, Rolland notes, deliver, "a new message of the soul," "the fruit of a new autumn," "a message for modern humanity" from "men who were living yesterday, our neighbors in the 'century,' and 'in our own time.'"[7] What was so pertinent about these saints?

The crux of avant-garde Indian spirituality consisted, commentators on the undertaking agreed, of a native antinomianism (strictly, against fixed laws and precedents, but especially with respect to those of one's own faith). In the main, this was an inwardly directed self-critique against orthodox Indian metaphysics as a privileged domain of nationalist sovereignty or superiority, and it resisted all attempts to build up or elevate anticolonial seekers through the more toxic steroids of spiritual life. It was also an outwardly directed anticolonial critique against overzealous Western iconoclasm/reformism, but chiefly it blocked invidious New Imperial arguments for the right to rule in places like South Asia by dint of a reasoning drawn from South Asian metaphysics itself: specifically, by way of the myths and rituals of Aryan origin. In these circumstances, Rolland and

Müller concur, the ecumenical mythopoeia of Indian antinomianism (in which there was equal commerce between gods of various faiths) and, no less, its hybrid *yogic* practices (tennis, spinning, the illegal manufacture of salt, English prosody, and French style-perfumery, to name a few) rendered orthodox metaphysics quite illegible and unavailable for antidemocratic misuse.

These appreciations of modern Indian mysticism generally followed the 1893 Chicago Parliament of Religions, where Ramakrishna, especially, was first introduced to Western audiences by his favorite disciple, Naren, or Swami Vivekananda. In an effort to globalize his master's ecumenism, Naren discoursed at large on how Sri Ramakrishna had practiced many of the world's religions with passionate intent: Hinduism, Christianity, Buddhism and Islam, and several other lesser-known creeds.[8] He had also spent significant portions of his life as a woman and as a monkey, wearing jewelry and living in treetops, sometimes at the same time.

In every way like those mediums who quickly become the message they bear, Sri Ramakrishna's disciple departed Bombay on May 31, 1893. Traveling on a ticket purchased by the Maharaja of Khetri and routed via Ceylon, Penang, Singapore, Hong Kong, Canton, Nagasaki, and Vancouver, Naren arrived uninvited at his destination in September, after an unplanned diversion through Boston. He carried little with him and wore, after consultation with female well-wishers, a robe (some say of glazed orange and others of blinding crimson) accessorized with an ochre turban of undisputed color. This ensemble was quite adequate to the mild Chicago fall that year (with lows of a mere thirty-nine degrees Fahrenheit), and entirely congenial to the Chicagoan eye. "Great crowds of people," *The Daily Inter-Ocean* noted, "pressed around the doors leading to the Hall of Columbus, . . . for it had been announced that Swami Vivekananda, the popular Hindoo monk who looks so much like McCullogh's Othello, was to speak."[9]

The World Parliament of Religions was conceived as a sideshow to that most colonial of events, the World's Columbian Exposition. Secured by the city of Chicago after stiff competition through the early 1880s with New York, Washington, and St. Louis, the Exposition commemorated Christopher Columbus's putative discovery of the New World through newly constructed fairgrounds sprawled across the green environs of present-day Hyde Park. Here Fredrick Law Olmsted's *beaux-arts* buildings made of white stucco and polychrome showcased the achievements of Western modernity with contrasting dioramas of backward cultures and peoples, for all those who failed to get the point. It was thought at the time, by the World Congress Auxiliary Committee, that a display of global religions convened

at the Art Institute would add to the ambient color, as in fact it did, exhibiting "strange robes, turbans and tunics, crosses and crescents, flowing hair
and tonsured heads, . . . strangely formed hats, somber cassocks of black,
and . . . ivory sticks carved with figures representing ancient rites."[10] For
a time the religious panoply rivaled the best efforts of the popular enter-
tainer Little Egypt, permanently stationed at a "Street in Cairo" upon the
Midway Pleasance, who was flown in to introduce the Western world to
that well-known Middle Eastern dance, the hootchy-kootchy. Yet, back at
the Art Institute, the desire for imperial pageantry was mixed, even in its
bureaucratic origins, with another charter for nonviolent collectivity. In
the words of the organizing committee, the chief aim of the Parliament
was, "to show . . . how many . . . truths the various Religions hold . . . in
common . . . [and] to bring the nations of the earth into a more friendly
fellowship, in the hope of securing permanent international peace."[11] If
not consistently, this latter impulse prevailed in some of the proceedings
and their historical effects thereafter, setting aside and parenthesizing the
sine qua non of colonial division to announce something like a floating
parity in adventures of the spirit: causeless, groundless, and gratuitous.
It was in this register that Vivekananda spoke. His unofficial, impromptu
remarks on spiritual inclusivity, especially, assumed the form of that singular universality—erupting from "the event," the "pure encounter," "addressed to everyone, without a condition of belonging being able to limit
this offer"—that distinguishes, if Alain Badiou is to be believed, the saint
from the priest.[12]

When he rose to speak on the afternoon of September 11, 1893, a date
whose coincidence can hardly be overemphasized, Vivekananda's opening
salutation alone drew applause for several minutes, according to several
eyewitness accounts: "When that young man got up and said 'Sisters and
Brothers of America,' seven thousand people rose to their feet as a tribute to something they knew not what. When it was over I saw scores of
women walking over to the benches to get near him, and I said to myself,
"Well, my lad, if you can resist that onslaught you are indeed a God!"[13]
Recently, in the fall of 2010, the South Asian artist Jitish Kallat transfigured
Vivekananda's address at the Parliament of World Religions into an art-
work called *Public Notice 3*, keenly attentive to the political ramifications
of the speech. This site-specific installation at the Art Institute converted
the words of the original text into LED displays on each of the 118 risers
of the museum's grand staircase, in the five colors (green, blue, yellow,
orange, and red) currently deployed by the US Department of Homeland
Security's alert system. Meditating on the ironic coincidence of a date on
which history failed to repeat itself, Kallat's work makes its point through

an aesthetic of escalation. The higher we ascend on the staircase, and the higher the level of security alert, the further we have moved from Vivekananda's intent. To get back to the beginning, we can observe Nietzsche's logic of eternal recurrence in laboratory conditions of controlled iterativity by going up, around the landing, down, and then up again; sometimes inhabiting a better world, sometimes a worse one, on and on. Alternately, we could follow a procedure that museum authorities might not recommend, yet one that is at the heart of saintly politics. Once upon the apex of the highest riser, we could undo the sequence of our ascent by feeling our way backwards—by becoming backward—the words all upside down and syntactically deranged now as we trip headlong over the textual fragments scrambling the joints of the museum's Women's Board stairwell, finding our way to the shared common ground level in the act, perhaps, of falling: "Sisters and Brothers of America, . . . I am proud to belong to a religion which has taught the world both tolerance and universal acceptance. We believe not only in universal toleration, but we accept all religions as true. I am proud to belong to a nation which has sheltered the persecuted and the refugees of all religions and all the nations of the earth. . . . I fervently hope that the bell that tolled this morning in honor of this convention may be the death-knell . . . of all persecutions with the sword or with the pen, and of all uncharitable feelings between people wending their way to the same goal."[14]

Some two and a half years after the Parliament of World Religions, on his second trip to the West in 1896, Vivekananda met Max Müller in Britain, and soon after, he met William James, on a Cambridge visit to give a lecture at the Harvard Graduate Philosophical Society entitled "The Vedanta Philosophy." Between 1902 and 1904, on a third trip to America, he sat in on several of James's lectures, in this period also declining academic offers from Harvard and Columbia for the reason that the tenure system was not congenial to the life of a wandering monk.[15] An American devotee from this time records the instant chemistry between Vivekananda and James in terms invariably more adulatory of the former: "After dinner, Professor James and the Swami drew together in intimate private conversation that lasted until midnight. When Professor James had left, Sara asked Vivekananda, 'Well, Swami, how did you like Professor James?' He replied, 'A very nice man, a very nice man!' The next day a letter came for the Swami . . . from Professor James, . . . addressing him as 'Master' and inviting him to his own house for dinner a few days later."[16]

These charged fin de siècle encounters had an enduring impact upon the mood and course of transnational spiritualism. In subsequent years the Ramakrishna movement achieved the global provenance so eagerly sought by Vivekananda, with multifaith, multicultural "missions" established across the world.[17] Vivekananda became the first popular guru in the West, and initiated numerous Western disciples into the collaborative style of the guru-disciple relationship. With characteristic generosity, James, too, continued to play a part in popularizing modern Indian mysticism to his wide constituency of radical socialists, spiritualists, philosophers, and psychologists in America as well as on the Continent. Meanwhile, in India, there appeared a series of new-style ashrams very similar in sensibility to the Ramakrishna movement and highly congenial to Jamesian saintly politics. Congregated around a great guru or two, these collectives—our primary text from here on in—quickly became a hub of spiritualist cosmopolitan exchange and negotiation, troublesome to the imperial administration as also to nationalist insurgency.

Three gurus, besides Sri Ramakrishna, are most representative of this milieu. Mahatma Gandhi (1869–1948), Sri Aurobindo (1872–1950), and Sri Ramana Maharshi (1879–1950). Sri Ramakrishna, who hailed from rural Bengal, was of a much earlier generation than his cohort. If conventionally unlettered, he still found his most devout following among the newly anglicized Bengali intelligentsia. The Gujarat-born and London-educated Mahatma Gandhi was not acknowledged as sharing the same spiritual stature as the others. Indeed, he was never a dedicated mystic, but he firmly held that his political and social experiments were but outward expressions of his *sadhana*. As he writes in his autobiography, "I should . . . like to narrate my experiments in the spiritual field which are known only to myself, and from which I derive such power as I possess for working in the political field. . . . The experiments are really spiritual."[18] Gandhi's many ashrams included Phoenix and Tolstoy Farm in South Africa and, later, the Sabarmati and Sevagram communes in India. Sri Aurobindo, also from Bengal like his precursor Sri Ramakrishna, founded his own ashram in former French India while on the run from imperial police for extremist activities in British India. He was educated at St. Paul's, London, and as a classicist at King's College, Cambridge. The youngest of the gurus, Sri Ramana Maharshi, of Tamil descent, ran away from home and dropped out of school well before the age of sixteen to establish an ashram beside the great mountain Arunachala, barely two hours or so as the crow flies from the Sri Aurobindo Ashram at Pondicherry. In his own lifetime Sri Ramana drew the largest number of Western disciples, many of them escapees from the miserable wars of the previous century. These included colonial personnel stationed in India, European refugees from the Continent, and Americans caught up in Asia during the Second World War—some through military service in the region and others as civilians interned in Japanese camps.[19]

BLOG 1: COSMOPHILIA

Somewhere at the outset of this chapter I'm writing on the gurus of modern South Asia, I find myself in the claustral bowels of the Regenstein Library at the University of Chicago, risking death by compression between moveable stacks. I'm searching through interminable maroon rows of dissertations past for a thesis by one William Barclay Parsons concerning a little-known correspondence between Sigmund Freud and Romain Rolland (henceforth SF and RR) between 1923 and 1937. Parsons's interest is in the positive influence that RR may have had on SF's reputedly inglorious view of religious experience, leading, perhaps, to the latter's erratic concessions to the paranormal (his developing interest in telepathy, and so on). These things interest me too. But most of all I want to get my hands on Parsons's first-time translation and collation of the correspondence in order to confirm an academic rumor I've heard about RR introducing SF to the gurus I'm working on.

There aren't many letters, but the available fragments are distractingly passionate, mainly from SF's side, whom I've always and wrongly supposed unsentimental. He praises RR tenderly as a man who knows "how to give presents," claims the latter's letters as precious "relics" he's reluctant to part with, and, in another missive, after an unsuccessful cancer operation, writes, "Aware that I am unlikely to see you again, I may confess to you that I have rarely experienced that mysterious attraction of one human being for another as vividly as I have with you."[20] These letters also hint, tantalizingly, at a shadowy interwar *ménage* between psychoanalysis, European pacifism, and Indian mysticism, which the two friends instantiate across an oddly collaborative oeuvre. During this process, RR sends SF his three-part study of the Indian gurus mentioned earlier, beginning with a volume on Mahatma Gandhi, and ending with one on Swami Vivekananda. "Mahatma Gandhi will accompany me on my vacation," Freud writes in June 1924; elsewhere, acknowledging the arrival of subsequent guru volumes with similar respectful bemusement, he writes, "I shall now try with your guidance to penetrate into the Indian jungle from which until now an uncertain blending of Hellenic love of proportion, Jewish sobriety, and philistine timidity have kept me away. I really ought to have tackled it earlier; for the plants of this soil shouldn't be alien to me; I have dug to certain depths for their roots. But it isn't easy to pass beyond the limits of one's nature."[21]

Although the two men seem to disagree prima facie on the uses of religion (especially its tropical Eastern varietal), sources besides these letters show how they met halfway even on this contentious subject through other shared convictions and the desire simply to please each other. This is what a collage of the available materials gives us. Early in 1923, SF made contact with RR, who was an important figure in the early twentieth-century continental antiwar movement. He was also one those rare thinkers who understood the late–fin de siècle crisis of Europe as symptomatic of the implicit accord between imperialism and fascism. Mindful of the intersecting components of this scene, RR put out a call for an equally complex and ideologically mixed-up mode of resistance that earned him not a few enemies, both from the left and the right. Here's a telling slogan from his writings: "If I am a pacifist, I am also an antifascist, and my pacifism is revolutionary. . . . Every fascist movement is based on a murderous ideology of racism or dominating imperialism, which leads to wars of conquest and the enslavement of other countries and other peoples."[22] Albeit on a smaller scale, SF, too, dabbled in like-minded antiwar/anti-imperialism/antifascism polemic. Especially notable is an essay he wrote before the contact with RR called "Thoughts for the Time on War and Death" (1915); and another, written at the behest of Einstein in 1932 called "Why War"? The first anticipates RR by claiming that the modern violence instinct is fueled by the partition between so-called inferior and superior races and by the translation of foreigners or aliens into enemies and scapegoats. In one of his earliest letters to RR on these themes, Freud writes movingly about the particular vulnerabilities that attach, in context, to his own Jewishness: "I, of course, have belonged to a race which in the Middle Ages was held responsible for all epidemics and which today is held responsible for the disintegration of the Austrian Empire and the German defeat. Such experiences have a sobering effect and are not conducive to make one believe in illusions."[23]

What's interesting but hard to make clear sense of at this stage is the way these friends agree that the solution to the European crisis lies in the quaint concept of a "love for mankind." This can only be achieved, they say, through a considerably less quaint commitment to "disillusionment." This proposed symbiosis between "love of mankind," on the one hand, and "disillusionment," on the other, is key to the SF and RR intellectual exchange.

Readers of SF will immediately recognize the disillusion theme as canonical in his work. It's also germane to RR's, and acknowledged as such in contemporary reviews of his anti-perfectionist and antiheroism novel *Liluli*. This work is described by one reader as "a triumph of disillusion" for its scathing critique of all great heights and pure ideals in human sociality on the grounds that "every 'uplifter' carries in the very heart of his teachings an Inquisition."[24] The love of mankind theme is a regular refrain in SF's letters and writings. Combined with the disillusion theme, it produces a theoretical compound or alloy that I'm inclined to call *cosmophilia* after a quotation from the *Didascalicon* of the great German theologian, Hugo of St. Victor, which Edward Said invokes consistently in his writing. This is what Hugo says:

> It is therefore, a great source of virtue for the practiced mind to learn, bit by bit, first to change about in visible and transitory things so that afterwards it may be able to leave them behind altogether. The man who finds his homeland sweet is still a tender beginner; he to whom every soil is as his native one is

already strong; but he is perfect to whom the entire world is as a foreign land. The tender soul has fixed his love on one spot in the world, the strong man has extended his love to all places; the perfect man has extinguished his.[25]

In Hugo's formulation, trebly underscored by Said, the lover of the world (or *cosmophile*) may well be better than the localist or nationalist but she is still notably one step short of perfection—and, Said might add, also of mature cosmo-politanism, whose subject must seek estrangement from all particular attachments—that is, from the narcissism of petty differences. Yet this is the very step (quite literally of arrested development) implicitly privileged by SF and RR when they ask their contemporaries to abandon illusions, ideals, heights, zeniths, and self-improvement projects so they can better learn to love the inhabitants of "every soil."

SF's take on *cosmophilia* is probably most clearly developed in *The Future of an Illusion*, which he sends to RR late in 1927. The arguments of this book are well known and work up themes from his earliest psychoanalytic hypotheses. (1) The civilizing process demands painful, first-order renunciation of our instinctual nature. (2) This is quickly followed by compensatory idealizations by way of religion, art, nationalism, and war, which give the names patriotism, heroism, valor, and piety (all synonyms for violence in the end) to the privations imposed by civility. (3) We're compelled to be high, in other words, precisely because we are forbidden to be low, and the higher we think we are, the less capable we are of compassionate coexistence. (4) The cure— whereby we might "humbly acquiesce in the small part which human beings play in the great world"—belongs to psychoanalysis, of course, and involves a second-order renunciation, this time of the first-order renunciation of instinctual life.[26] (5) There's no guaranteed outcome, but by learning to live with what is base in our nature, in the first place, we may just avoid the distorting pitfalls of substitutive self-idealization and, thence, along the way, learn to live more easily and peaceably with others who seem lesser or baser than ourselves. This is the short version of the path from disillusionment to world-love.

Acknowledging receipt of SF's "lucid and valiant little book," RR is all agreement with these claims. But he makes one crucial qualification. Certain kinds of mystical practice, specifically those he's currently researching for "a future book" on "contemporary" Asian mystics, in fact, best perform the double renunciation at the heart of SF's politico-therapeutic program.[27] It's very likely that SF lent RR the themes that helped him to read the mystics in question as exemplars of a love for mankind premised upon corollary renunciation of the material and immaterial perks of regular religious life: "all dogma, all credo, all church organization, all Sacred Books, any hope of a personal afterlife, etc."[28] Moreover, as RR's subsequent volumes emphasize, these figures are a bit like the Russian Christian-Marxist philosopher Nikolai Berdyaev's "aristocrats of the spirit," who, knowing too well their own capacity for top-rung perfection, "feel the necessity not only to rise but to descend"—to the second rung of world-love for the greater cause of social justice.[29] Their *cosmophilia*, we learn, is a nuanced, two-part affair. Part 1 (and Gandhi's really good at this, apparently) is the practice of commonwealth, or the view that religious, national, racial, and even individual peculiarities are not the basis for separation and hierarchy but are intangible resources that we merely hold in common as trustees or custodians on behalf of others; an idealistic notion, RR writes, "which the new democracies of the West were writing unconsciously and blindly."[30] Part 2 concerns the practice of common knowledge. This is a position against virtuosity, genius, and expertise (that is, against election by the "elect"). And it is realized in various disciplines of unlearning and decultivation: "a unique education," RR puts it, to achieve "a footing of equality with every man," as exemplified in the lives of Sri Ramakrishna, and Swami Vivekananda.[31]

All this detail is clarified example by example in the collected guru-corpus that SF only receives in toto in 1930, but it's sketched quite liberally in RR's letter of December 5, 1927, which was written in response to *The Future of an Illusion* and furnishes, in turn, the first chapter of *Civilization and Its Discontents*.[32] "Your letter of Dec. 5, 1927, containing your remarks about a feeling you describe as 'oceanic' has left me no peace," SF writes upon receipt of this missive. "It happens that in a new work which lies before me still uncompleted I am making a starting point of this remark; I mention this 'oceanic' feeling and am trying to interpret it from the point of view of our psychology. . . . I don't mention your name but nevertheless drop a hint that points toward you."[33] *Civilization*, accordingly, opens with a reverential tribute to Rolland ("The views expressed by the friend whom I so much honor . . .").[34] And although SF doesn't exactly acknowledge direct collaboration between RR's apologia for modern Indian mysticism and his own project, he places the two in dialogic relation to each other. What follows, at the very heart of psychoanalytic thought, then, is SF's surprisingly congenial reading of RR's guru volumes as a path toward a world-repairing, nonpathological, anti-care of the self. This is a practice or condition, SF tells us, of astonishing openness toward the world that sometimes requires a radical suspension of "normal" ego-protection/defense mechanisms. It posits a type of voluntary vulnerability or debility that is, nonetheless, quite outside the remit of treatment or cure because it looks like a bad case of love[35]—or, more precisely, of *cosmophilia*. In Freud's words, "The views expressed by the friend whom I so much honor . . . caused me no small difficulty. I cannot discover the oceanic feeling in myself, . . . [but] if I have understood my friend rightly, he means the same thing by it as the consolation offered by an original and somewhat eccentric dramatist to his hero who is facing a self-inflicted death. 'We cannot fall out of this world.' That is to say, it is a feeling of an indissoluble bond, of being one with the external world as a whole."[36] To attain to this state of ontic un-fall-ability, though, we first have to let ourselves fall into the world, perhaps by falling for others. That we might learn these preliminaries on the analyst's couch or in the lotus position and contradict the hatred of democracy in so doing is, at the very least, food for thought.

The Science of Ascent

Anticolonial antinomianism found a curious adversary in evolutionary race ethnology. This discipline was characterized by all the usual presumptions of rank and so forth in relation to colonial worlds. Nonetheless, it relied substantially upon Indian data not only to make a case for the comparative evolutionary superiority of Western individuals but also, as historian Susan Bayly argues, for the emergence, over time, of advanced political institutions in "Aryan" Europe.[37] From the mid-1860s onward, following a split between the Ethnological and Anthropological Societies of London, leaders of the latter camp sought a direct hand in colonial governance. They argued that racial ethnology could supply incontrovertible evidence for the inevitability of European conquest by showing modern European imperialists their sole claim to the ancestry of an Aryan/Caucasian race of proto-colonizers. To make this case, it would be necessary to take on the conflicting evidence provided by contemporary Sanskritists and comparative philologists. It was also vital, as the colonial anthropologist (and Scottish anatomist) Robert Knox put it, to contest "the ultra-liberal and democratic party in politics [proceeding] on the assertion, that of one blood God made all the nations of the earth."[38] Handled correctly, these quarrels could disarrange the prime signifiers of democratic thought and surgically excise from modern politics the bad influence of following tradition: "Jeremy Bentham, . . . Helvétius and the French Encyclopedists, who were again but a far-off reverberation of Democritus and Epicurus."[39] How did racial ethnology achieve these ends? And how might we regard ethnological political theory as a key source for new imperialism's science of ascent?

We can focus almost immediately on a single shared feature of late nineteenth-century ethnology, namely, an overvaluation of the political virtues of liberty combined with an assault on the two commonly associated concepts of equality and fraternity. As Knox has it, "Equality and fraternity are but the sinister yet legitimate progeny of the principle of primal and organic unity."[40] The consequent solitariness of liberty in ethnological politics is the result of a violent disruption of the delicate nature/obedience index once considered integral to political idealism by Jeremy Bentham and his generation—those campaigners for the widening of franchise across Europe, critics of imperial prejudice, and curators of the various Bills and Declarations of Rights.[41] Let me explain.

Bentham's *A Fragment on Government* (1776) argues—in keeping with the mood of his intellectual cohort—that if nature fuels the liberty with which individuals serve their own interests, then obedience secures its necessary curtailment for the sake of equality and in order to safeguard the greatest happiness of the greatest number. To this harmonization of nature/obedience on behalf of the multitude (which Bentham, of course, calls utility), Étienne Balibar has more recently given the name "equaliberty." This is "the proposition," in his words, "that equality and liberty are inseparable."[42] But a few decades before the interventions of racial ethnology, these enlightenment adjustments favoring obedience over nature and, accordingly, the compound concept of equaliberty had come under siege by various broad-spectrum, antidemocratic movements. Opponents included a new, pan-European generation of liberal-romantics (G. W. F. Hegel, Wilhelm von Humboldt, Alexis de Tocqueville, J. S. Mill) impatient to modify the all-too-righteous morphology of the political inherited from their intellectual forbears. Their angry repossession of politics as the domain exclusively of nature-liberty is apparent even in the work of a thinker as supposedly salubrious as J. S. Mill. In various antidemocratic writings (*On Liberty*, recommending despotism for India, and *Considerations on Representative Government*, advocating plural votes for educated citizens, at home), Mill neatly fractures Bentham's nature/ obedience index into a nature-only index, on the one hand, attentive to the liberty exclusive to superior men, and an obedience-only index, on the other, apposite to the flatness, commonness, and equalization proper to inferior or mediocre men. "Strong impulses," Mill writes in defense of nature-liberty, in *On Liberty*, "are but another name for energy. . . . It is through the cultivation of these that society does its duty and protects its interests, not by rejecting the stuff of which heroes are made, because it knows not how to make them."[43] In contrast, he observes in the same text, untrammeled obedience-equality is deleterious to political culture and social life. As he puts it, "In our times . . . the individual or the family do not ask themselves, what do I prefer? . . . They ask themselves . . . what is usually done? . . . Thus the mind itself is bowed to the yoke, . . . until by dint of not following their nature they have no nature to follow."[44] Mill, and fellow thinkers such as Alexis de Tocqueville, agreed that democracy, especially, exemplifies the crisis born of the defeat of nature by obedience. It is, in their combined words, a "law of descent [which] constantly levels men to a common point" and requires a reparative effort of ascent: "to rise," as Mill puts it, "above mediocrity."[45]

By the time racial ethnologists appear on this scene, the tropes of liberty and freedom already belong to the critique of democracy as emblems of the superior man of nature. All that is needed to make them fully conversant with New Imperialism is their concerted racialization: first, by gathering nature-liberty within the etiology of racial conquest and, second, by consigning obedience-equality to the rubbish heap of racially conquerable peoples of the world. Thus, we learn from Knox, if the historical degradation of inferior races, "consists in [their] unquestioning obedience," the freedom-loving tendency of superior races is confirmed not only in current imperialist autocracy (imposing rather than following law) but also in its genetic derivation from the prior ascendancy of ancestral Aryan invaders.[46] Securing this confirmation proves more difficult than the vandalizing of modern political thought that we have been tracking. How so?

In its original elaboration, both by eighteenth-century Sanskritists, such as William Jones, and nineteenth-century comparative philologists, such as Max Müller, the Aryan hypothesis was arguably quite favorable to anti-imperial democratic thought. Conceived as a conjecture about the global migrations of a benign, xenophilic, exogamous (and possibly Caucasian) race, it was conjured, as is very well known, to explain the strange kinship of Indo-European languages. As such, the myth of shared Aryan origin supplied, in William Jones's reading, sound evidence for the originary monogenism of all races and, in Max Müller's iteration, a reasonable basis for their consequent cultural and social parity. We "must all have proceeded from one pair," as Jones concludes, or we all "hold coordinate rank [as] members of one and the same class," according to Max Müller.[47] In order to extract from this prior scholarship the desired rendition of the Aryan as conqueror rather than wanderer, eugenicist rather than miscegenist, and captain rather than communist, racial ethnology hit upon a double manipulation of the South Asian caste-system. First, it argued that the contemporaneity, more or less, of Aryan invasion with the codification of caste hierarchy in the texts of high Hinduism attested the Aryan's will to racial and social domination and was proof positive of his aversion to contamination and admixture with conquerable entities.[48] Second, however, if caste indeed confirmed the Aryan's originary hierarchy, the decline of this institution over time (through careless interbreeding) also confirmed that there were, in fact, no extant "Eastern Aryans"—no living nightmare, that is, of Max Müller's "Aryan brother."[49]

It was with this charter in hand that racial ethnology insinuated itself into colonial governance, and its influence is registered most plainly in the growing obsession with caste-data that marks Indian census operations between 1881 and 1901.[50] The first formal 1881 census enumerated but a chaotic assortment of Indian castes and tribes accompanied by numerous emendatory reports emphasizing the functionality of caste (as an occupational division of labor). In sharp contrast, the epochal census of 1901, which was supervised by the ethnographer Herbert Hope Risley, declared the caste system a community of race first formulated at the putative scene of Aryan invasion.[51] At this moment in 1901, India became a veritable carnival of ascent.

Four groups or movements are implicated in the unseemly scramble for rank provoked by Risley and others. (1) Western ascent: This concerns the efforts of ethnology proper to establish once and for all the decisive attrition of the Indian caste system and thus the sole claim of European races to pure Aryan stock. (2) Intra-Western ascent: At the scene of New Imperialism, Europeans competed among themselves to claim the purest Aryan quality of their own national ancestors. That this project entailed the systematic exclusion of Semitic culture and language and of the Jews of modern Europe is the stark testimony, of course, to the imperial-fascist collusions under analysis. (3) Eastern ascent: Rejecting the caste inflections of ethnology in favor of its racial analysis, many Indian cultural nationalists invoked collective autochthony to declare South Asia the conclusive racial home or natural habitat of the Aryan. However, since Hindus alone were true descendants of the original stock and faithful custodians of Aryan scripture, a foundational xenophobia was exigent for national recuperation in fallen colonial times—as the basis of "Hindu superiority" and for the progressive purging from the body politic of Muslims and other late-coming European foreigners.[52] (4) Co-ascent: Within some quarters of colonial administration a reflux of affection for the (younger) "Aryan brother" yielded marginal interest in helping authentic Indian races recover their Aryan aboriginality. To this end, while compiling caste data for the 1901 census, Risley subjected random samples of the population to a series of race-determination tests. Aimed to weed out imposter castes falsely imitating Brahmanic ritual, Risley's procedures enlisted colonialism in the eugenic purification of South Asia. "Those methods," he writes, "might . . . enable us to detach considerable masses of non-Aryans from the general body of Hindus, and to refer them, if not to the original tribes to which they originally belonged, at least to the general category of non-Aryan."[53] And so they did, giving new life to entrenched domestic prejudice and overlordship over putative non-Aryan castes, tribes, and outcastes.

These events are familiar and painful to recall. The particular, if simple, inflection of my retelling is as follows. The ethnological Aryan myth was built upon preliminary damage to the most profound fibers of modern democratic thought, so that the tropes liberty and freedom can no longer claim innocent access to the eighteenth-century Declarations and Bills of Rights and their corroborating revolutions. We are heir also to their distortion by a mediating science of ascent that was responsible for attempted theoretical ruination of the series obedience-equality, equality-fraternity,

parity-artfulness, and justice-unnaturalness. To recycle these waste materials for present usage, we may well have to rehabilitate what Tocqueville
once negatively identified as democracy's "law of descent." Some individuals and subcultures, I am claiming, may already have gone a long way toward salvaging this law on our behalf from the ruins of imperial-fascism.[54]

BLOG 2: NEUTRALITY

I have Quaker pamphlets to read in the Law Library, civil rights comic books on PDF, reels
of vertigo-inducing microfilm on conscientious objection, stacks of homosexual-pacifist
desiderata textured with Californian great weather, deadly war testimonies from the
Pacific Rim, and more and more retellings of the gurus in well-thumbed, 1950s, small-
sized editions ("Good. Slight damage to spine.") arriving in droves from vendors of
used books. Diverse though the material is, it adds up to the single word *neutrality*—
easily obscured by the surrounding din of the Second World War.

Many years ago, on a trip to consult archives at Gandhi's Sabarmati Ashram in
Gujarat, I was delighted to find Christopher Isherwood's gay volumes on the gurus of
modern India prominently displayed in the ashram bookshop, alongside a *variorum*
on nature cure and sexual restraint. As it happens, there's not a great deal about
Gandhi in these books—*Ramakrishna and His Disciples*, *My Guru and His Disciple*, *Christopher and His Kind*. Yet, taken together with Isherwood's other writing, especially
his candid dairies between 1939 and 1960, they share Gandhi's anarchist distaste for
authority figures (himself included). They also enthusiastically endorse his vision, the
kingdom come, for everyone to inhabit their own mobile guruhood through those
very personal materials where we seem least worthy of sanctification.

Isherwood's Ramakrishna book (bright pink in the forty-rupee edition on sale in
Sabarmati) is gleeful anti-hagiography. It presents this inaugural figure as a "phenomenon," in the Bergsonian sense of the phenomenal object to be intimately experienced by the devotee, rather than an awesome subject to be reified by same.
There's more affectionate quibbling with authority in *My Guru and His Disciple*, and
then, in *Christopher and His Kind*, the appearance through a coming-out memoir of an
irreverent sequence wherein the chronic interchangeability of guru and disciple gains
an additional twist with the title's replacement of the proper coordinates of spiritual
community with the quite improper coordinates of homosexual dissidence, implying
the congeniality of each to the other. Christopher is his own guru, is Ramakrishna, and
never more so than among his objectionable kind.

This makes for noteworthy cultural interpolation in the hitherto fairly Western
project of queer/perverse hagiography, drawing the gurus of modern India into a
shared genealogy, perhaps, with *Saint Genet*, *Saint Foucault*, *Saint Wilde*, and the Sisters of Perpetual Indulgence. There's a fair amount of generalized queer hagiography
in *Christopher and His Kind* in the detail of Isherwood's interwar years in Berlin, when
he played heretic to a vast heterosexual dictatorship—as he calls it—from the fragile

environs of Magnus Hirschfeld's institute for the third sex. Even here, however, Isherwood betrays a telling reticence about polemic and its tactical double, the politics of oppositionality (call it dissidence, alterity, even revolution). The margins, we often hear from him, turn too quickly into venues of hair-splitting fission within the ranks: homosexuals against communists against pacifists, and not a woman in view. "I shrink from the duty of opposition," he will write in years to come. "I am afraid I should be reduced to a chattering, enraged monkey. Screaming back hate at . . . hate."[55] Far better, Isherwood avers, to opt for a manifesto for everybody, which supplements the outside/inside battleground with two options: for radical insideness (we are all within), and radical outsideness (we are all without), respectively. From the example of Vivekananda, Isherwood learns the practices of mindfulness appropriate to this program. "All beings," he writes, "north, south, east and west"—and then falters— "the points of the compass bother me; . . . where is everybody?"[56]

The trouble really sets in with the realization that in order to embrace everybody, it's necessary, perhaps inevitable, to become nobody. You have to lose position, not only in the sense of single-minded revolutionary objectives but also in the sense of the importance customarily attaching to them. "The whole essence of my 'position,'" Isherwood observes, "is not to make statements. I am the only silent member of a community of all-too noisy prophets. My motto: *Nescio, Nescio.*"[57]

Isherwood's *mantra*, "everybody-nobody," gains its charge from an *askesis* of neutrality that was being practiced within many subcultures of American interwar pacifism, with a little help from the gurus of modern India. Isherwood and his friend, the poet W. H. Auden, fled into this fold in 1939 to escape conscription into the second European war. It was complicated to be neutral in this war, and their flight from active service was severely criticized by friends and enemies on both sides of the Atlantic. Playing on the title of Isherwood's novel *Mr. Norris Changes Trains*, a doggerel from the time puts it sharply: "The dog beneath the skin has had the brains / To save it, Norris-like, by changing trains."[58] It was precisely such invective against neutrality as cowardly fence-sitting that American pacifism turned on its head; transforming the neutral into a way of life requisite to the onset of global egalitarianism.

The philosopher-essayist Roland Barthes has written movingly about the neutral as an ethical stance concerning the ameliorative uses of depression: how to do good out of feeling flat and low (or, conversely, how to achieve such flatness in order to do good). This condition, Barthes insists, is chemically adverse to authoritarianism. Impervious to distinctions in the outlying landscape, it effortlessly squanders the distinct boundaries of the self as well. In Barthes's words, "I propose that the desire for the Neutral is desire for—first, suspension (*épochè*) of orders, laws, summons, arrogances, terrorisms, puttings on notice, the will-to-possess—then, by way of deepening, refusal of pure discourse of opposition. Suspension of narcissism: no longer to be afraid of images (*imago*): to dissolve one's own image."[59] A famous Quaker pamphlet from the annals of American conscientious objection puts the case in strikingly similar terms, emphasizing that neutrality in wartime is sometimes the exact opposite of self-regard. Thus, there's no permission, we learn, "to withdraw into some calm retreat, assume for ourselves a holier attainment, . . . to wait in security until the storm rolled by . . . . We wanted to show our faith . . . in a way that would . . . take us out of self."[60]

The conscientious objectors (COs) practicing this credo substantiated their thinking from various sources born of multiple convictions. Bodies as diverse as the American Friends Service Committee (AFSC), the religious-minded Fellowship of Reconciliation (FOR), and the socialist-atheist War Resisters League (WRL), combined in committees on Africa, Leagues for the Freedom of India, and fostered programs against US intervention in Asia and in Central and South America, petitions seeking independence for the Philippines, demands for the revocation of the Chinese Exclusion Act, the founding in 1942 of CORE (Congress of Racial Equality) and, earlier, the Conference for Progressive Labor Action, to name but a few items.[61] Informing this agenda was the belief, best articulated by the pacifist-socialist-civil rights activist A. J. Muste, that war conceals the "integral connection" between "economic exploitation, fascism, racism, Jim Crowism."[62] So pacifism must expose this connection and undo it through a countering alliance of socialism, anti-fascism, and racial harmony.

There was another unexpected prompt to the inclusivity of this culture. In 1940, President Roosevelt authorized the Selective Training and Service Act. The act provided alternative service options for COs who refused to serve as combatants. It also significantly widened the denominational scope of religious objection beyond traditional provisions for Christian groups like the Quakers, Mennonites, and Brethren. The result was a platform for unprecedented religious ecumenism at the already diverse scenes of CO action. Many on this platform (even the most nonreligious) turned to the materials of modern South Asian antinomianism—already familiar in America following Vivekananda's runaway success at the Chicago Parliament of Religions, barely four decades before the outbreak of the Second World War. Numerous COs, amongst them Bayard Rustin and Richard B. Gregg, visited India in this period. Many wrote with particular interest about Gandhi and his methods, and founded pacifist ashrams in Harlem, Newark, Trabuco—and one on Ivar Street in Hollywood, dearly beloved to Christopher and his kind: homosexuals, expatriate war-resisters, and their domestic counterparts, organized around the figure of the Indian Swami Prabhavananda and the journal *Vedanta for the West*. All these enterprises emphasized the disciplinary nature of neutrality in wartime as a preparation and training in which, we learn from Roy Kepler of the WRL, "power comes in giving up power."[63]

With historical hindsight, we can see this as an experiment in perpetual democracy. Isn't that what you get if everyone is always, simultaneously, represented on a political terrain in which victory per se or being victorious, as a leader, is suspended? We abide democracy because of the consolation of its iterativity: everyone notionally gets a serial shot at power for some time (classically, fifteen minutes). Maybe this is wise. But there's so much to like also in the unwisdom of this messy pacifist scene we're talking about, with its perverse redactions, whereby the potential somebodys of politics choose, à la Barthes, to dissolve their own image even before they enter the *polis*. Grant "merit to the opponent," the CO Dave Dellinger writes, after Gandhi; seek "no special privileges"; refuse "a selfish victory based on the power of one side to impose its will on the other."[64] Or, as the comic book *Martin Luther King and the Montgomery Story* explains, nonviolent neutrality is the unusual practice where, "nobody is defeated, everybody shares in the victory."[65] Here are three topics for further consideration.

1. *The Least Important People.* During the Second World War, COs deputed to civilian public service (CPS) camps consciously saw themselves as giving harbor to the most neglected groups in modern postwar society. Many spent the length of the war doing relief and rehabilitation work in refugee camps. "You had to give all your time, confidence, faith, courage," Isherwood writes, "to those badly rattled middle-aged people whose lifeline to the homeland had been brutally cut, and whose will to make a new start in the new country was very weak."[66] COs also served as attendants in mental hospitals, publicizing the execrable conditions in these forgotten institutions, and offered their services as human guinea pigs in medical experiments conducted in leading national universities. Here they were infected by hepatitis, malaria, pneumonia, and other parasites, and subjected to extreme temperatures and semi-starvation diets to test the endurance of the human body. Many participants regarded the program as an important exercise in principled self-enfeeblement. There was no remuneration for this work.[67]

2. *Diffusing Antagonism.* Nonreligious COs serving prison sentences throughout the country took their work to be the reform of the segregated prison system. To this end, they refused nonviolently to cooperate with prison authorities, never responding with violence even to the most brutal recriminations. Famously, in 1943, the white COs being held at the Danbury "correctional facility" maintained a hunger strike against prison apartheid for nearly twenty-three days before being force-fed through tubes amid something of a public outcry. As a result, Danbury became the first federal prison to abolish Jim Crow seating.[68]

3. *Changing Places.* In the 1940s, well in advance of the freedom rides of the 1960s, several "journeys of reconciliation" were undertaken by white and black pacifists. To prepare for these journeys and train themselves against violent retaliation, the activists participated in complex sociodramas in which each would play the part of a potential antagonist so as to achieve intimacy, in advance, with the aggressors they would necessarily face: "Participants would act the roles of bus drivers, hysterical segregationists, police—and 'you.'"[69] Isherwood describes such exercises of complex self-identification at length; they required the ethical subject of neutrality to settle his mind, alike, on "British and Nazi airmen, . . . Hitler, Churchill, . . . Teddy, our dog in Portugal. T. Y. Liu. Admiral Byrd. The ocean with all its fish."[70]

Refusing, thus, to be goaded into antagonism/heroism by the hostilities provoked by his occupation of a front seat on a bus from Louisville to Nashville, in 1942, the gay, African-American, pacifist, Gandhian, and *sadhaka* Bayard Rustin was brutally beaten. "There is no need to beat me," he recalls saying, "I offer you no resistance."[71]

The Democratic Sublime

The stories I'm narrating demand due acknowledgment of a rapprochement between democratic thought and modern mysticism in the age of empire. It doesn't help that such rapprochement is expressly forbidden for postcolonial criticism in the first and last commandments (for worldliness and against religious disposition, respectively) of Edward Said's *The World, the Text, and the Critic* (1983). What's more helpful, curiously, and as we'll see, is the Weberian analog to Said's thought, wherein the betrothal between religion and democracy isn't forbidden but rendered impossible by a third term—*disenchantment*—that stands between the former two. Closer inspection reveals that, much like the illusory brick wall that's Platform Nine and Three Quarters of J. K. Rowling's *Harry Potter* series, Weberian disenchantment is a portal rather than the barrier it appears to be. But unlike Rowling's platform, it doesn't transform mundanity into a scene of magic so much as the reverse. Modern religion, Weber tells us, contra Said, can certainly enter the domain of democratization. It can only do so, however, at a cost. By passing through the destructive alchemy of disenchantment on the way to equality, it must forever lose its distinctive medium, idiom, and properties to become an altogether different entity, unrecognizable even to itself. Thus Protestantism morphs into capitalism upon its passage into the brave new world, and charismatic power, likewise, is reconfigured as routinization upon the delegation of authority.

We could say that disenchantment is the correlate of democracy in the modern world about which Weber writes, in the early years of the twentieth century, with such an air of bereavement about him. It is also the necessary solvent of religious culture. It arrives uninvited on the scene whenever/wherever the recognition of others becomes the basis for legitimacy rather than merely its consequence. This is not to say that disenchantment has a taste for virtue. Indeed, the shifting locutions of legitimacy are as often instrumental as they are altruistic, born of the insecurity and anxiety of great men more than of their goodwill. Either way, just sociality is accompanied by the decline of magic. Let's follow an example from Weber more closely. Over time, he tells us, even the most devout disciples of a religious or charismatic leader will start to crave the quiet life, a stable job, reliable forms of leisure, and worldly connections—seeking by degrees to become faculty or officials instead of the constantly rattled vessels of *esprit*. So as to secure the loyalty of these subordinates, charismatic authority submits to a process of normalization. Objective criteria are established to ensure the smooth recruitment of subsequent leaders, and charisma is slowly displaced from the rare individual to the endowed office, which is generally better served by efficiency, punctuality, and reliability than by random bursts of divine inspiration. In other words, even as she becomes a servant of those under her authority, the charismatic leader's heroic powers and magical means undergo a fatal banalization.[72]

How are these Weberian declensions possibly congenial to a rapprochement between religion and democracy? In which way does disenchantment's impossible interval reengage retreating spirits in the public sphere freshly cleared of religious residuum? Are we even looking for what remains of the gods? We could do much worse than return to Weber at this point, for what's helpful to our concerns is his own subtle distinction between two orders of disenchantment that we might call a "Type A form of regulatory disenchantment" and a "Type B form of voluntary disenchantment." Type A, or regulatory disenchantment, describes the structural and abstract forces of democratization (bureaucracy, routinization, popularization), which enforce a leveling action upon everything that seeks and possesses a presence in modernity. But this scene also accommodates the antigenic practices of the Type B, voluntary style of self-leveling, which Weber elaborates most clearly in his various musings on vocation and calling.

A calling or vocation, according to Weber, gives "every-day worldly activity a religious significance" because of its high moral valuation of secular labor as "a task set by God," no less.[73] In so doing, it yields a new form of antimonastic asceticism whose subject must undertake a signatory self-attrition. The subject of a calling must disregard spirit for the sake of the world, but once in the world, she must disregard her own advancement for the sake of spirit. These are the exacting themes that Weber develops over two lectures first presented at Munich University during the winter semester of 1918–19. The ideal type of vocational politician, he tells his audience, willingly exposes himself to the contaminants of power and the accompanying risks of corruption for the sake of the cause. Such is his "acosmic love" for the humanity he serves.[74] He will permit the world to disrupt his own salvation, especially when the world is lacking in comparable value. More than the politician, though, the scientist comprehends vocation as "a personal attitude" requiring volitional abandonment of one's own flair and originality for the common good.[75] The scientist favors anonymity over celebrity and the labor of trivial computations over the hubris of the impresario, and always manifests the ardent hope (for praying isn't appropriate here) that his own work be surpassed by that of others. As Weber puts it, "Every scientific 'fulfillment' . . . *asks* to be 'surpassed' and outdated. . . . It is our common fate and, more, our common goal. We cannot work without hoping that others will advance further than we have."[76]

To put all this more plainly, Weberian vocation is the footnote that complicates the otherwise compulsory alignment between democracy and secularism with which we began these digressions and which is, arguably, the main hypothesis of Weber's larger oeuvre. Through this footnote, we learn the following: whenever disenchantment is transformed into a voluntary practice sensitive to changing times—rather than a historical inevitability merely to be suffered—democracy proves irreducible to secularity (and ongoingly amenable to religious thought).[77] Indeed, Weber observes, the practices of self-miniaturization or reduction that attach to a calling supply an altogether new terrain for the sublime in the age of democratization. Their intervention ensures that in the wake of the departing gods sublimity does not vanish so much as change style and scale, leaving behind grand scenes of monumentality to take up residence "in *pianissimo*." It can be found, henceforth, "only within the smallest, most intimate circles."[78] These small circles of Weber's democratic sublime are also the theater proper to the gurus of modern India.

The Art of Descent

We know a great deal about the gurus of modern India because of their active participation in the print cultures of colonial encounter. The cultural historian Isabel Hofmeyr evocatively describes the global exchanges facilitated by the various small printing operations of the era: "Hindu reformist, Sikh transnationalist, African nationalist, or pan-Islamic or white laborist. Central to these repertoires of transoceanic communication were streams of print culture: blizzards of periodicals, pamphlets, leaflets, and tracts setting out the programs and principles of their makers."[79] Amid these streams of transnational media, an ecumenical "maritime market of faith" commanded unexpected attention and included, among diverse religious material (cures, propaganda, miracle narratives), writing by and about the leading Indian gurus of the time.[80] Most ashrams had their own presses and publication departments, whose output came into local and international circulation through the early decades of the twentieth century.[81] In addition to the fin de siècle commentaries on Sri Ramakrishna by Max Müller, William James, and Vivekananda, an authoritative record of this guru's conversations with disciples—the *Sri Sri Ramakrishna Kathamrita*—was serialized in Bengali between 1897 and 1932 and translated into English in 1942 by Swami Nikhilananda and Margaret Wilson, daughter of the American president Woodrow Wilson. The first collection of Sri Ramana's teachings, the Tamil *Nan Yar* or *Who Am I?* was compiled in 1901. It reported the findings of a government official, Sivaprakasam Pillai, who had sought out Ramana in a mountain cave and recorded on a slate the young saint's cryptic answers to fourteen questions concerning how to know one's true identity.[82] Despite Sri Ramana's early appeal to a cosmopolitan constituency of disciples, the Western world was formally introduced to his philosophy much later through Paul Brunton's *A Search in Secret India* (1938), a guru-quest in the East, hailing Sri Ramana as "the Master . . . I seek."[83] In the early years of the century Gandhi also began to write up his discoveries about the symbiosis of spirituality and politics in the pages of the multilingual newspaper *Indian Opinion* (founded in 1903) and in writings such as *Unto This Last* (1908) and *Hind Swaraj*. Sri Aurobindo refined his philosophical position in a series of essays between 1914 and 1921 for the new monthly periodical *Arya: A Philosophical Review*.

The explication below showcases the gurus in an incorporated account of their varied teachings, mixed into a dialogue with Western metaphysics. In this account their intimate biographies remain elusive. Our aim has been to animate the transnational encounter with antinomian, modern South Asian spirituality in a range of surprising contexts and in forgotten registers. Moreover, the gurus' own commitment to personal anonymity and obscurity was an integral aspect of the art of descent. Gandhi wrote his now famous autobiography, *The Story of My Experiments with Truth*, under duress, imploring readers not to take his advice as authoritative and supplying guidelines for treating his life as common property, "in the light of which every one may carry on their own experiments according to his inclination and capacity."[84] Sri Aurobindo puts the matter more plainly in a letter to a disciple: "I am not interested in my own biography. . . . This idea of a Life going into details and Personalities is itself an error."[85]

I've selected Sri Ramakrishna, Mahatma Gandhi, Sri Aurobindo, and Sri Ramana from the ocean of their peers because their corpus (literary and practical, printed and impalpable) was believed to constitute a new mystical style and a cohesive metaphysical typology by numerous disciples and interlocutors—one that provided a timely prophylactic against the terrifying collusion of imperial-fascism and antidemocracy.[86] In these accounts and their own writings, it is clear that the gurus of modern India were allied in a *sadhana* that posits something very like Weber's Type B voluntary disenchantment as a core practice favorable to democratization, if less so to standard procedures of spiritual immunization. Marked by a refusal to retreat from the world and by low estimation for projects of salvation and salvability, generally, this *sadhana* betrays additional interest in spiritual technologies that are actually disruptive of liberation projects. It does not express the view that the path of liberation should be set aside provisionally or even abandoned so as to engage more pressing secular concerns. Rather, it is engaged with exercises of undoing, whereby an aspirant who has already embarked on procedures of perfection and realization may successfully reject the path of ascent for another of descent. In these cases, as with Icarus, the proper measure of falling is precisely capacity for or proximity to the light. To understand this art of descent, apropos Weberian disenchantment and as countermand to the antidemocracy of racial ethnology, we must consider it in context of its own disciplinary terrain, under the following subheadings: first, as a mode of improper metaphysics that tends toward the negativity of others; second, as a form of bad ontology concerned with the cultivation of self-negativity. The former critiques Western misuses of Indian scripture, and the latter discloses invitations for such misuse encoded within Indian scripture itself.

Improper Metaphysics, or the Negativity of Others

Sometime toward the end of 1864 there arrived in the gardens of Dakshineshwar a wandering ascetic from the Punjab by the name of Totapuri. The ascetic was enlisted to teach the local guru, Sri Ramakrishna, the path to radical spiritual perfection: *nirvikalpa samadhi*, a state in which the seeker rises above the limitations of everyday empirical existence to achieve full union with the divine. "A man who enters that state is bound to lose all his me-ness—his petty desires, lusts, hopes and weaknesses. When he emerges from it he is a bridge to Immortality!"[87] With characteristic spiritual virtuosity, Sri Ramakrishna quickly attained the heights extolled by Totapuri. As soon as he had done so, however, he turned his face symbolically back toward the world and descended. In the words of a recent commentator, "Voices commanded him to descend, to come back, or at least to keep looking back."[88] Thereafter, he occupied a messy threshold zone that experts call *bhavamukha*, or the face/place of affect: "the border line between the Absolute and the Relative."[89] Many hagiographies skip over this curious episode of self-interrupted ascent in Ramakrishna's otherwise exemplary career. Others explain it away as the credo of "a new generation" committed to a "compromise between God and the world."[90]

We get a more detailed gloss on this event from a related epiphany recorded by the French-Jewish mystic Mirra Alfassa, another a guru of modern India who was Sri Aurobindo's spiritual collaborator. This is how she describes the experience in a conversation with a disciple: "The state I found myself in was like . . . a descent into the most total negation of the Divine. . . . And this corresponds to a state in which one is so *perfectly* identified with all that is, that one becomes all that is anti-divine in a concrete way. . . . Basically, this kind of will for purity, for good, in men—which expresses itself in the ordinary mentality as the need to be virtuous—is the *great obstacle* to true self-giving. . . . Take your share of the burden, accept yourself to be impure and false, and in that way you will be able to take up the shadow and offer it."[91] Alfassa's engagement of the negative imports into the customarily rarefied and solipsistic domain of spiritual life a telling idiom of labor and service, toil and cooperative endeavor. These tremors of meniality and collectivity in matters of spirit look a great deal like the work of Weberian calling, abandoning the gifted seeker's state of grace for the sake of an arduous common purpose. The result is not the relinquishment of metaphysics so much as the reversal of its customary direction.

We can clarify the stakes with a little help from Jean-Paul Sartre and in the context of a wider field of Western, post-Kantian, antimetaphysical philosophy. In his *Saint Genet* (1952) Sartre draws attention to a perverse metaphysics that seeks to bring consciousness to forms of social negativity that are consigned to nonexistence or rendered unspeakable by unjust historical circumstance and the order of ruling preferences. In his words, "We ignore the negative moment of our activities . . . [and] mark in the name of cleaning up, the destruction of the day before. We . . . arrest spirit by ejecting its springwork of negativity . . . [and identify] forever Good with Being, hence with what already is. As Being is the measure of perfection, an existing regime is always more perfect than one which does not exist."[92] In context, the dark saint (Genet: thief, bastard, homosexual, convict), who undertakes a reinvestiture of nullity and, accordingly, a revolutionary presencing of the negative, must first situate himself outside it—in the realm of the positive—and then breach the division/hierarchy of Being and non-Being by means of an "involution" or "downward ascesis." As Sartre puts it, "The ascesis takes place in the opposite direction of the metaphysical hierarchy, that is, in the direction of lesser being. Being serves as the springboard for leaping into Nothingness. . . . It is a matter of wresting oneself from God, of settling into one's own finiteness."[93]

Sartre's accent on descent departs significantly from other modern negotiations of Nothingness or non-Being. As is well acknowledged, with the disciplinary displacement after Kant of metaphysics by epistemology, the antique problem of non-Being was reconfigured (in Western philosophy) as a new problem about the limit of thought itself. Or rather, it was experienced anew as the sheer intolerability of the unthinkable or the unknowable. This was increasingly, to cite the social theorist Robert Pippin, "the problem of *theorizing* what was historically missing, absent, simply not, in this historical moment, and understanding the nature of its claim on our attention."[94] Among many efforts through the nineteenth century to deal with non-Being, Hegel's resolution offers the most useful foil for our thematic. Briefly, Hegel rescues non-Being for secular epistemological use by reconstituting it as the "not-yet" (rather than the nothing) of any historical community's relation to its own ideals. Pippin is apt again: "The lack or gap or failure in question is initially the obvious one: a community is not living up to its ideals. . . . This is then said to have unavoidable existential consequences. . . . And then the most difficult claim: the status of the ideal not being lived up to is something like 'the best we have been able to do so far.'"[95] In his strictly teleological rehabilitation of non-Being as but a stage of forgetfulness or failure en route to the otherwise guaranteed realization of ideals and actuals, Hegel arguably eliminates its terminal negativity. The process we are tracking is quite different. In the art of descent what is eliminated is not the negativity of non-Being but something like the non-Being of negativity—that is, the latter's interdiction and trashing. This enlists the negative to be: to take place, occur, participate, and obtain representation. And so, I submit, the work of radical democracy is inaugurated.[96]

Nowhere are these conjectures better mobilized against the science of ascent than in Sri Aurobindo's writings for the journal *Arya*, which he co-founded with Paul Richards and Mirra Richards (née, Blanche Rachel Mirra Alfassa), both French nationals with a strong interest in modern spirituality. Devoted to comparative religion and epistemology (besides "the highest problems of existence"), the journal took on its controversial name consciously so as to wrest the concept "Aryan" from current racist distortions and reclaim it as an inclusive ethical and social ideal.[97] An essay published in the journal is at pains to make this point: "Western Philology has converted it [*arya*] into a racial term, an unknown ethnological quantity on which different speculations fix different values. Now . . . some are beginning to recognize that the word in its original use expressed not a difference of race, but a difference of culture. For in the Veda the Aryan peoples are those who had accepted a particular type of self-culture, of inward and outward practice, of ideality, of aspiration."[98] The editors' combined desire for a global platform for their ecumenical message—"a vast synthesis of knowledge harmonizing the diverse traditions of humanity, occidental and well as oriental"—was answered by an unexpected turn of events.[99]

As Sri Aurobindo was developing the prospectus for *Arya*, Archduke Franz Ferdinand was assassinated in Sarajevo, and by the time the first issue appeared in print Europe was at war. By September 1914 India and Indians too would be drawn into battle as contenders and stakeholders in the conflict. Responding to this challenge, Aurobindo renewed his commitment to clarify India's role in "the general life of humanity" as one of "generous emulation and brotherhood with all men and all nations."[100] When the Richards left for France in February 1915 (Mirra Alfassa would return to Pondicherry forever in 1920), Aurobindo dedicated himself to a prolific output for the magazine.

Most pertinent for our discussion are essays engaged in reinterpretation of the Vedas—held to be the codified scripture of early Aryan settlers in South Asia. Progressively revised and gathered into *The Secret of the Veda*, these essays instigate an anticolonial objection to the insinuation of European imperialism into the myth of an antique encounter in South Asia between a conquering master race (the Aryans) and an indigenous slave race (Dravidian or Dasyu) that was resolved in favor of the former. Directly rejecting the racialization of the Arya-Dasyu encounter as the work of hack ethnology, Sri Aurobindo declares that the Vedas represent the collaborative or "integral knowledge" of "the so-called Aryans and Dravidians as one homogenous race."[101] The Vedic literature, he advices, only deploys the terms *Arya* and *Dasyu* as symbolic-allegorical markers of a complex spiritual field. This describes a work on the self in which judicious inversions along the vertical axis of metaphysics proper yield an eminently desirable symbiosis of positive and negative value. In such a reading the Dasyu-signifier, characterized in the literature by darkness and depth, is the secret of the Vedas. It renders negativity and non-Being the foundation of spiritual knowledge: "The world as we see it has come out of the darkness concealed in darkness. . . . This non-existence of the truth of things, *asat*, is the first aspect of them."[102]

Against this setting, the Arya-signifier designates the subject of the quest. She is a naive beginner initially familiar only with the modalities of ascent: "Whoever . . . ascends the hill of being is the Aryan. . . . The Aryans are the desirers of the godheads, *devayu, usij*; they seek to increase their own being and the godheads in them by the sacrifice, the word, the thought."[103] As for Icarus, though, light, height, and divinity prove pathological for the Arya-beginner and therefore preparatory for the remedial work of involution. To put this differently, the Arya's extremist and clois-tered positivity is the precondition for its own undoing. In this disman-tling lies the course of true awakening. The spiritually fledged Arya is the one who willingly flees from the gods to undertake a descent toward the scenes of Dasyu; in the opposite direction, that is, from priority and self-increase. Here's Sri Aurobindo on the (reformed) Aryan path:

> We become as men blinded by a light so that we can no longer see the field which that light illumines. Such is the teaching, calm, wise and clear, of our most ancient sages. They had the patience and the strength to find and to know; they also had the clarity and humility to admit the limitation of our knowledge. . . . However high we climb, . . . we climb ill if we forget our base. Not to abandon the lower to itself, but to transfigure it . . . is the true divinity of nature, . . . integral and all-embracing.[104]

In these elaborations, then, the art of descent emblematizes its anti-elitism through a self-complicating fidelity to the negative, or the space/place of metaphysical rejects. We have considered ways in which the per-formance of such fidelity involves (politically redemptive) collateral dam-age for the *sadhaka* (or the subject of the quest). Let's briefly catalogue at-tending strategies of preemptive self-ruination; exercises whereby seekers might train themselves, in advance of the act of falling, to feel at home in negativity and to bear up against the costs of so doing.

Bad Ontology, or the Cultivation of Self-Negativity

Sri Aurobindo's *The Secret of the Veda* makes its case against the adverse culture of New Imperialism by recuperating native scripture as the origi-nal source of a politics of equality and coexistence. There is great surprise, therefore, in his nearly simultaneous recantation in another set of essays of indigenous tradition as the locus classicus of philosophical totalitari-anism. Gathered into *The Life Divine*, these essays were serialized in *Arya* between August 1914 and January 1919, almost the entire length of the Great War. They were revised into a thousand-page magnum opus in 1939 and 1940, during the early phases of the Second World War. Energized by a bold new emphasis on the "revolutionary individual effort" of spiritual life (available to all seekers) over and above the received content of canoni-cal Indian traditions, *The Life Divine* takes issue with a post-Vedic ontologi-cal system formalized in and as the school of *Advaita Vedanta*.[105] Opposing as illusory all antinomies of spirit/matter, mind/body, and words/things, the philosophers of *Advaita* famously expounded the sole reality, like Hei-degger after them, of an ontic-ontological accord in which contradictory elements combine and are unified.[106] And here lies the complication. *Advaita*'s theoretical pull toward mastery, Sri Aurobindo demurs, is encoded precisely in the secret arithmetic of ontological synthesis. Its disciplinary war on contradiction and crusade for reparative unity is formalized in a seemingly benign valorization of the number one, as in "I am at one with the universe," or "We are as one," and so on. Yet, insofar as the one of ontological harmony is postulated as the only reality and therefore the best—the place, in Sri Aurobindo's words, of, "no deficiency, . . . no failure of Force, . . . no negation of delight, . . . all illimitableness, all infinity, all absoluteness"—these warm and fuzzy numerics start to show their steel.[107]

To clarify, when observed closely, the one of *Advaitic* philosophy gains its true import via the old Sanskrit formula, *ekam evam adwityam*, or "One without a second," meaning irreducible and indivisible but also incomparable, unbeatable, unmatched. Here are some illustrative phrases from Shankara, the great master of the school under review: "The supreme, pure, self-existing, uniform, unmixed bliss . . . is . . . the only one. . . . Nothing remains but this, . . . the one reality without a second, . . . eternal, fixed, without stain."[108] The principles of purity (unmixedness) and perfection (stainlessness) secreted within Shankara's "one without a second" are by no means intrinsically antidemocratic. Yet, Sri Aurobindo contends, they can be made to serve the desires of modern tyranny. In his words, "[This is] to seek unity by reducing all ruthlessly to the terms of one, [and] in order to assert this one, [we must] get rid of the others."[109] Nowhere, he adds, do these derivations apply more starkly than in the discourse of a master race, and through the concatenation of collectivities under the sign of a singular, authoritarian, and canonical state, both in vogue in the first half of the twentieth century. As he puts it, "But where was that vague thing, the collectivity, and how could it express itself as . . . an organized . . . will? Let the State be perfect, dominant, all pervading, all seeing, all effective; so only could the collective ego be concentrated . . . and the survival of the best . . . secured by the elimination of the unfit and the assimilation of the less fit."[110]

Premodern South Asian ascetic texts forewarn practitioners that the integrity of the ontological one is always threatened by scenes of relationality (minimally, a gathering of two and, maximally, of all). More so, the sages of *Advaita* advise, the distorting multiple-vision of relationality accrues from the false attachments of the subject/ego. In consequence, its reparation calls for rigorous practices of ego-dissolution. As we learn from a substantive commentary on Shankara, "He is 'liberated while yet living,' who . . . is freed from all bonds through the removal of Ignorance. . . . Freedom from egotism . . . will . . . free [such a one] from every semblance of difference."[111] And here is an apposite critique of this attitude from *The Life Divine*: "By getting rid of the ignorance of the ego and its resultant limitations, we do indeed eliminate dualities, but we eliminate along with them our existence in the cosmic movement."[112] Thus we arrive at another crucial juncture in the art of descent. To resolve their numerical dispute with *Advaita*, the gurus of modern India redress the mastery-producing techniques of ego-dissolution with a counter-*askesis* consolidated around weakness-producing techniques of ego-retention. In this schema the ego is understood doubly as arrearage to contradictions (pleasure/pain, success/failure, love/death) but also as the ethical locus of falling for others. Below are compatible lessons from the other gurus in our roster.

Gandhi's project, we saw in the introduction, is enlivened by a revolutionary subject of *swaraj* whose freedom from subjection to the unjust external/foreign laws of imperial governmentality begins as a program of stringent self-governance or self-mastery, simultaneously political and ethical. The aforesaid subject is enlisted to transform the arena of subjectivity into a battleground wherein she must dispose herself against herself, heautocratically, in an antagonistic relationship.[113] Yet, however such *askesis* militates against the desiring self/ego, it never resolves into indifference to or detachment from the rest. In its Gandhian intonation, self-mastery is principally a means to master mastery over others. While curbing the territorial extension of the ego, it pulls back upon the slightest contingent annulment of the world. The most meaningful liberation is thus from oneself (or from mere self-interest), preparatory to becoming irreducibly bound to the multitude. In this way Gandhian *swaraj* is an appeal for the importation into politics of a soul-force or love-force: that carefully tended residuum of attachment that brings with it the complicating yet certain knowledge that it is better to suffer than to cause suffering. A circular logic ensues. Without the cultivation of "immeasurable pity" or "love," it is not possible "to sacrifice yourself."[114] And "love" (we hear in a familiar refrain) is itself borne of self-extinction—"it can only be expressed fully when man reduces himself to a cipher."[115]

These modifications are well registered in Gandhi's gloss on his predilection for various self-mortifying practices (fasting, continence, vows of silence) in the face of social catastrophe (riots, outbreaks of violence). He insists that such exercises do not tend toward mere purification and detachment—namely, the desire for spiritual rarefaction as its own end. Rather, as methods of self-forgetting, they assist the practitioner to focus more keenly upon the crisis at hand by "reaching the heart of things."[116] There can be no political or social merit, Gandhi emphasizes, in a spiritual program that simply releases the spiritual subject from the world. In his words, "All our prayers, fasting and observances are empty nothings so long as we do not feel a live kinship with all life."[117]

Sri Ramakrishna's explicit objections to the non-ego of ontology (more in line with Sri Aurobindo's conclusions in *The Life Divine*) can be gathered as *bhavamukha* variations. They build upon the formative interruption of prodigious spiritual flight early in his *yogic* career. The amanuensis who recorded the *Sri Sri Ramakrishna Kathamrita*, comprising the master's life and words to followers, notes that the experience of descent left Ramakrishna with a symptomatic "trace of ego" that equipped him "to work for the welfare of humanity."[118] In subsequent teachings, Sri Ramakrishna frequently recommended this condition (with attending practices) to aspirants who were overzealous for yogic excellence. So, for instance, in conversations with a devotee—a busy physician called Dr. Sarkar, who worried a great deal about his own spiritual shortcomings—Ramakrishna is at pains to extol the uses of deficiency in certain forms of *sadhana*, his own included. An important exercise, he clarifies, calls for the distinction (and variant treatment) of two egos. The first "unripe," or "green," ego is certainly an obstacle on the path of liberation and must be vanquished. This ego of rampant self-regard, Sri Ramakrishna explains, "makes me feel: 'I am the doer. I am the son of a wealthy man. I am learned. I am rich. How dare anyone slight me.'"[119] An altogether different attitude holds for a secondary ego, the "ripe-ego," or "servant-ego," which is the scene of reattachment to the world, and which the seeker must earnestly retain and recall "after attaining *samadhi*."[120]

As a reservoir of conscious or cultivated defectiveness, Sri Ramakrishna's own secondary/affective ego reportedly provoked acute sensitivity to existential suffering at large. "A monk who knew him," we hear from a somewhat lugubrious follower, "has said that during the first days of his return from ecstasy to the bosom of identity, he howled with pain when he saw two boatmen quarrelling angrily. He came to identify himself with the sorrows of the whole world, however impure and murderous they might be, until his heart was scored with scars."[121] Such agonies notwithstanding, Sri Ramakrishna upheld world-attachment as the crux of his teaching and tried to explain that to his favorite disciple, the adept Swami Vivekananda, or Naren, who was always importuning his master for the secrets of liberation. In a tutelary dream about this beloved pupil, the guru reports envisioning Naren as a great renunciate and sage lost in meditation until a child is entrusted to draw him back into the world. Here is one rendition of the dream: "The child . . . tenderly clasped his neck with his lovely arms, and addressing him in a sweet voice, tried to drag his mind down from the state of Samadhi. That magic touch roused the sage, . . . and he fixed his half-open eyes upon the wonderful child. . . . In great joy the strange child spoke to him, 'I am going down. You too must go with me.'"[122] In the dream the sage readily descends, though its communication in waking time allegedly leaves Naren irritable and all the more rebellious.

The Ramakrishna hagiography abounds with such prickly exchanges between master and disciple in the context of a dissonant pedagogy wherein true knowledge entails the gift of inadequacy: a willingness to know less and be less successful in the quest. "O Mother," Ramakrishna is said to have prayed, perversely, "give Naren a little of Your Illusion."[123] In a classic exchange toward the end of the guru's life, Naren comes to his bedside to report on a superlative pilgrimage to Bodh-Gaya, the garden in which the Buddha attained final release from the false attachments of earthly life. In the resulting conversation on the merits of Buddhism over Hinduism, the disciple is defiantly rapturous about the Buddhist credo of renunciation: "How great his renunciation was," he recalls from the legend of Siddhartha Gautama. "Born a prince he renounced everything. . . . After attaining Buddhahood and experiencing Nirvana, Buddha once visited his home and exhorted his wife, his son, and many others of the royal household to embrace the life of renunciation. How intense his renunciation was!"[124] Ramakrishna (palpably sulking) immediately calls an impromptu symposium to reveal Buddhist renunciation as a preliminary exercise—but a first step toward the greater aim of Buddhist compassion. Vivekananda concedes the lesson eventually, albeit wryly, also as the chief theme in his own master's work. "Great souls," he paraphrases for the benefit of Ramakrishna's gathered disciples, "even after their own liberation, retain the ego and experience the pleasure and pain of the body that they may help others to attain liberation. It is like coolie work. We perform coolie work under compulsion, but great souls do so of their own sweet pleasure."[125]

Similar adaptations obtain within Sri Ramana's practice. Extremely popular amongst Western followers, this South Indian guru was regarded as a textbook example of detachment; everything that a realized person or renunciate should be. The European writer and seeker, Paul Brunton, reverentially describes Ramana's signatory style in these terms, as an enviable disregard for existential noise: "I seize the opportunity to plague him with further questions, which he patiently answers in terse epigrammatic phrases, clipped so short as rarely to constitute complete sentences. But once, when I propound some fresh problem, he makes no answer. Instead, he gazes out toward the jungle-covered hills which stretch to the horizon and remains motionless. Many minutes pass, but still his eyes are fixed, his presence remote."[126] Indian followers encountering a living guru for the first time, such as the disciple Viswanatha Swami, reinforce this impression as well. Here is the Swami's reminiscence of life with Ramana: "He seemed to live apart from the physical frame, quite detached from it. His look and smile had remarkable spiritual charm. When he spoke, the words seemed to come out of an abyss. One could see immaculate purity and non-attachment in him and his movements. I sensed something very refined, lofty and sacred about him."[127]

Their awe for Ramana's apparent disconnection aside, Brunton and Viswanatha Swami also underscore the guru's paradoxical disinterest in *mukti*, or liberation, and his insistence that followers should pursue their quest in the midst of the most mundane tasks.[128] Indeed, more than a path to ego-extinction, his practice incorporates a noteworthy accent on befriending and accommodating imperfections. The moral is underscored in his favorite parable concerning a world-conquering emperor—much like the Alexander of Cynic narrative—who fears only his own shadow, for it reminds him constantly of the insubstantial nature of majesty. The emperor orders palace guards to throw the offending shadow into a moat to be devoured by alligators. On one occasion he even digs a grave in which to bury the dark double. Yet he cannot be rid of his shadow. So Ramana says, "If you are afraid of your shadow falling across your path, and think of it as a curse, take your mind off it. Turn toward the sun, and your shadow will be behind you, ready to follow you like a friend, not confront you like an enemy."[129]

Devotees clarify that Ramana's path of organic realization requires an idiosyncratic yoga of the heart. This heart—or *hridayam*—is foregrounded in the *Sri Ramana Gita*, comprising the guru's key teachings in dialogue with a disciple-amanuensis between December 1913 and August 1917. Nothing in the dialogue, we learn at the outset, derives from "scriptural learning, nor *anumana* (logical inference) and *pramana* (precedent authority). He has taught only what he has himself experienced or seen with the inner eye of meditation."[130] The vital instruction is delivered in 1915 during the monsoonal season, when monks were compelled to remain cloistered in "one and the same place."[131] Unprovoked by a query, the guru utters the following cryptic verse: "In the interior of the Heart-cave Brahman alone shines in the form of the Atman [the divine in the form of the aspiring self] with direct immediacy as I, as I. Enter into the heart with questing minds, or by diving deep within or through control of breath."[132]

Ramana returned to the credo of the heart again and again, sometimes citing obscure texts in support of his emphasis or insisting that the doctrine required no authoritative support, as it was borne of direct spiritual experience.[133] Numerous followers claim to have shared the experience in subsequent practice. It has been recorded that a devotee received initiation in a dream-vision, in which Ramana touched him on the chest with a forefinger. Another follower notes that the heart-region was typically animated when meditating in the guru's presence: "Suddenly, his eyes emitted light, spat fire, and when he looked at me, his look went straight into me, physically into my chest. The heart center, very often felt in his presence, began to get warm, became hot like fire, and then started to spark as if an electric machine were installed into my heart."[134] Sri Ramana, he concludes, "opened my heart."[135] But what and where is Ramana's heart? In fact (much like Sri Ramakrishna's ego hypothesis), there are two of these. The biological heart, on the left side, must be ignored by the *sadhaka*, for it is but the site of embodied or solipsistic subjectivity. Instead, all meditative focus should fall upon another spiritual heart, the locus of a relational subjectivity to be derived from and with others, namely, alter egos. The spiritual heart is very different from the physiological heart in its constitutively flawed poetic anatomy. Located "on the right side of the chest, not at all on the left," this heart "hangs upside down" and has "a subtle hole in its center."[136] Identified as the first point of consciousness for one who "returns [when] the transcendental experience drops away and the ego again takes possession," Ramana's damaged heart is also "the common center . . . for all humanity."[137] It is the level ground upon which we are gathered into the company of undifferentiated fellow creatures—or the seat, we might add, of a disenchanted world awaiting the *pianissimo* of postdivine sublimity.

To summarize our main themes, if the preemptive self-leveling encoded in Weber's voluntary disenchantment effects an accord between religion and democracy, the combined work of the gurus of modern India quite literally redoubles that effort. Elaborated in a milieu where new imperialism's antidemocracy was exacted as a science of ascent by dint of Indian scripture, the countermanding art of descent posits itself as an occult reversal—not only toward democracy but insistently against its detractors. Premised on inversions along the vertical axis of metaphysics proper and as the preparatory work of self-ruinance at odds with the perfect one of ontological unity, it cleaves to small people and large numbers, anybody and everybody.

There is significant recognition of this project in Arthur Koestler's 1942 essay "The Yogi and the Commissar," first published in the British literary magazine *Horizon*. Drawing on his own interest in Indian spiritualism and wider community with Western disciples of the gurus of modern India, Koestler argues that the various crises of the first half of the twentieth century gave rise to two opposing political futures: the way of the Commissar and the path of Yogi. The Commissar is a strong-willed subject of perfection who is willing to do anything and sever any ties for the sake of the ideal revolutionary end. The Yogi, on the other hand, is a self-endangering subject of connection always willing to botch or defer revolutionary objectives so as to sustain the links between self and world. Tending—like William James before him—toward the latter, this is what Koestler writes about the Yogi's yoga: "He believes that each individual is alone but attached to the all-one by an invisible umbilical cord . . . and that his only task during his earthly life is to avoid any action, emotion or thought which might lead to a breaking of the cord. This avoidance has to be maintained by a difficult, elaborate technique, the only kind of technique he accepts."[138] This product may have harmful side effects, which include dizziness, nausea, and weakness.

BLOG 3: THE CONTAGIOUS SELF

I've carried two items with me for a very long time now, believing they belong to-gether as pieces in the puzzle of guru democracy. The first is a 1931 recording made by Gandhi (hereafter MKG) for the Columbia Gramophone Company while he was in London for the disappointing Second Round Table Conference on Indian consti-tutional reform.[139] Wryly claiming low expertise on political matters, he offers his thoughts on religion instead. In the course of a meditation upon existential intercon-nectedness, he endorses the "marvelous researches" of the physicist-turned-botanist J. C. Bose for giving evidence of a shared life-energy even among the most apparently inanimate substances. It is not surprising that MKG cites Bose (also much admired by Romain Rolland), who was an ardent follower of Swami Vivekananda and new Indian mysticism, and internationally famous in early twentieth-century science circles for his public demonstrations of acute affective sensitivity in tin foils, metal plates, mimosa plants, and palm trees. Seeking to prove there was unity rather hierarchy in nature (no higher/lower forms, just shared livingness), Bose frequently records the vertiginous sensation of symbiosis as he conducts experiments during which he finds himself catching the mood of the recording machine or influencing, by his own psychic state, the disposition of the plant (or other substance) under observation.[140]

At about the same time as Bose's researches, MKG had also commenced similar politico-spiritual experiments of his own to test whether work on the self had a com-munal effect—not by way of influence and example so much as by a spectral circuit: for example, did fasting not just symbolically but alchemically expiate the violence of others? Was there a sympathetic magic whereby acts of personal expropriation or self-reduction actually conjured gifts for the dispossessed? Did the giving up of one's own right to existence yield collateral for life itself? In other words, was the self of *sadhana* contagious? Could you catch the self-work of those around you and, likewise, virally communicate yours across short and long distances? Here are various comments from MKG: "How that chain can be established I do not know as yet. But I'm striving after it." "Individuality is and is not even as every drop in the ocean is and is not. It is not because apart from the ocean it has no existence." "I am an irrepressible optimist. My optimism rests on my belief in the infinite possibilities of the individual to develop non-violence. The more you develop it in your own being, the more infectious it becomes till it overwhelms your surroundings and by and by might oversweep the whole world."[141]

Now for the second piece of the puzzle, which comes with something of a story attached to it. It's the catalogue of an exhibit by Henri Cartier-Bresson (henceforth HCB) at the Museum of Modern Art in New York, published "posthumously" after HCB was assumed dead following his three-year incarceration after being captured as a POW by the Germans during the Second World War, while serving on a film unit for the French army.[142] HCB joined the French resistance upon his release, taking pictures that combined a profound antifascism with acute distaste for the German-baiting that followed the end of the war. Fans of the photographer will recall the morally discomfiting still from his film *Le Retour*, which shows a Gestapo stool pigeon being exposed at a displaced persons camp in Dessau, Germany, by a woman with bared teeth and a hand preparing to strike. In this period, along with his commitments to anti-imperialism and the third-world revolutions sweeping across the world, HCB became increasingly interested in the gurus—partly on account of their growing popularity in the West. Sri Ramakrishna and MKG aside, Sri Aurobindo and Sri Ramana had each been written up in popular US magazines such as *Holiday* and *Life*. Sri Ramana, especially, had shot into fame following W. S. Maugham's fictional rendition of his encounter with the elusive guru in *The Razor's Edge* (he later elaborated this meeting in an essay called "The Saint," for which he got a lot of help from Christopher Isherwood).

To resume my main interest, the copy of the exhibition catalogue is dated New Delhi, 30 January 1948, on the upper right corner, and it's personally inscribed by the author to MKG in words of loving reverence: "To our beloved Bapu, with deepest respect, Henri Cartier-Bresson." In India for the first time, HCB had cycled that very day for a photo shoot with MKG to Birla House, Delhi, in the midst of the great partition carnage sweeping through postindependence South Asia. Leafing, after a longish interview, through the catalogue that HCB brought as a gift, MKG inquired with particular interest about a photo that shows the verse-dramatist, Paul Claudel, on a street in Brangues, France, looking casually upon a stationary hearse beside him. Pausing over the image for a while, MKG spoke three words, possibly his penultimate that day, "Death, death, death."[143] An hour later, as he crossed the garden for a prayer meeting, he would be assassinated by three shots at close range, receiving which he would speak three more words, his last ever: "Ram, Ram, Ram."

Two years later, on a second trip to India in mid-April 1950, HCB found himself in Tiruvannamalai, taking, once again unbeknown to himself, the last photographs of Sri Ramana Maharshi, whose passing on April 14 coincided exactly with a meteor that the former observed, with numerous others, streaking across the night sky: "Hundreds of thousands of people . . . were witness to the meteor of light that streaked across the sky as Ramana Maharshi breathed his last. Chandralekha gasped: 'Look, look, look!' Poet Harindranath Chattopadhyaya shouted: 'Mark the time, mark the time!' Henri Cartier-Bresson bellowed: 'Thirteen (minutes) to nine!'"[144] Only a few days later, HCB traveled to Pondicherry—the first photographer in thirty years allowed to capture images of the gurus there and also the last to photograph Sri Aurobindo before his passing that year on December 5, 1950. From this final photo session, he recalls the extraordinary stillness of his subject, as though competing with the steadfast camera itself—the recorded recording the technology of recordation in a way that makes these stunning pictures the *mise en abyme* of two collaborating mirrors or lenses, standing between which we can sometimes catch our own infinite regression/infinite multiplication (depending on how good or bad we're feeling about ourselves and the world): "Sri Aurobindo did not wink an eye during the entire ten minutes I was watching him."[145] Why HCB? Why was it HCB who recorded, in the end, the passion of the gurus of modern India?

I don't know much about the history of photography, but it seems to me this is one place where we might come closer to understanding the matter of HCB's appropriateness as the last chronicler of the anti-narcissistic (or self-image-dissolving) iconicity of the gurus. I've always been moved by accounts of the subtle and not very long-lived split during the early years of European photography between English amateur artiness and French commercial populism, centered it seems to me on the status of portraiture and the aesthetics of likeness, respectively. The English group (e.g., H. P. Robinson, Julia Margaret Cameron, Octavius Hill) eschews verisimilitude, à la Walter Benjamin, for its association with mass taste. They strive instead to achieve the rare, the unique, or the exceptional in their combined and stylized art. In contrast, by embracing brazenly the art of likeness, the portraiture favored by the French group (Félix Nadar and André-Adolphe-Eugène Disdéri, in particular) is already synecdochally in place of the crowd, the populace, and the multitude.[146] Sometimes this is literally so, as in the case of early studio photographers, whose poor technology resulted in indistinguishable portraits in which everybody simply looks alike, and the subject may as well be anybody at all. But the more conscientious realists in this set actually confronted the democratic possibilities of likeness, thus conceived, and used all available technologies to disperse the main subject or to reveal a multiplicity—always more than one—in any single portrait. Some examples are the accentuated doublings of the *vues stéréo* format and the estranging, cartoonish iterations of the *carte-de-visite* contact sheet. More innovative strategies come from Nadar's amazing photosculptures and autoportraits. Here the subject is placed on a raised platform surrounded by twenty-four cameras operating simultaneously to record as many angular views in a single moment of exposure surely intended to provoke the expostulations, "How are there so many of me in a single instant?" "Can I be so many and still remain identical with myself"? "If I am not where I am, perhaps I am where you are"? "Where I am most, I become the deluge."

We can track the paths of this inheritance in HCB's non-guru portraits. The subjects here are never monumentalized over, above, and against the shifting background of common existence so much as marked, through the 35 mm Leica's art of the candid instant, by their shared, quotidian temporality with the rest: the fatal stretch that exposes the elegant Rossellini's greater girth; the sudden shadow of deep fatigue beneath Nehru's eyes; Susan Sontag in a nanosecond of complete communion with her cigarette. Even more directly democratizing is the point made by those of HCB's countless photos that catch the leader/individual's subject-effect in the manifold of the actual crowd itself, so that you start to feel that perhaps the idea of the crowd is always the perfect verisimilitude of any given subject. Consider, from among HCB's canvasses, for example, the restless and edgy audience that exposes the nerves of the stoic champion wrestlers in Ulaanbaatar, Mongolia; the unimpressed and recoiling old ladies at Aubenas manifesting perfectly the offensiveness of De Gaulle; the barely conscious audiences at Trafalgar Square copying the mind-numbing tedium of George VI's coronation. Or these: the reeling crowd hanging off the train carrying MKG's ashes, and the unmoving devotees at the last rites of Sri Ramana Maharshi, each palpably absorbing and reflecting their gurus. This, then, is portraiture as the photography of contagion. These images are not at all interested in discrete entities or, indeed, in particularity ("That photo is *so* Sri Aurobindo"). Instead their secret interest is in grasping and capturing the subtle thread of common life that runs between us all—in the guise of the shadowy circuitry connecting all elements in J. C. Bose's laboratory, and as the microscopic *asketic* infection so devoutly sought by MKG in his lonely experiments with truth. So we learn, by degrees, that the gurus are all of us: they are our aspirations, our longings, and our likeness. By the same logic (and this may well be the *consolatio* secreted in HCB's serendipitous "last photographs" in India), we are all gurus.

THREE

Elementary Virtues: The Great War and the Crisis of European Man

This chapter deals with the enduring impact of the First World War on transnational democratic ethics. As such, it is braided with an inquiry into matters of method and perspective with respect to this study at large. We will turn to these more substantively in the epilogue. Our present concern is the relation between academic postcolonialism and the forms of ethical anticolonialism that we have been following thus far. Are there any meaningful material and discursive continuities between the disruptive self-work of imperfectionism and the theoretical-reflective mode of current postcolonial analyses? Some answers emerge from intellectual histories of the convergence between postcolonial and critical theory across diverse global locations. In a contentious account, the cultural historian Ian Hunter has argued that the so-called moment of theory was not determined by the appearance of a new or singular object of inquiry or for that matter by the emergence of a common idiom across the disciplines.[1] Rather, theory signifies the surfacing of a particular kind of intellectual or theorist marked by distaste for positivism and the belief that cultivated antipositivism yields a better world than is at hand. Best explained as an *asketic* project with epistemological consequences, then, theory's striking elicitation of metaphysical speculation testifies *pace* Hunter to the formative influence of Husserlian transcendental phenomenology. As such, the moment of theory also coincides with the much-touted ethical turn in present-day humanities and social sciences. Let me clarify how these themes play out.

In the general sense proposed by Hunter, the present discussion concedes that academic work conducted in the name of postcolonialism, from the late 1970s onward, inevitably participated in the moment of theory, thereby gaining access to various conflicting transmissions of Husserlian phenomenology. In non-Western locutions of postcolonial thought—specifically, those movements for the methodological and curricular reform of history and English literature that overtook the South Asian academy (among others) through the 1980s—a phenomenological residue obtains from continental Marxism (Sartre, Althusser, modified or indigenized Gramsci). In Western locutions of the same, phenomenological imperatives appear most vividly under the aegis of French postmodern philosophy—precisely, in the uneven line of alterity-based ethics that runs from Emanuel Levinas to Jacques Derrida and beyond to Judith Butler. These curricular developments, however, are of secondary concern to us and are not pursued in any detail here. Instead, I argue that academic postcolonialism is susceptible to the peculiar *asketic* invitations of post-Husserlian theory for reason of its true archive, namely, the dissonant ethical style of anticolonial politics. To shed more light on these overlapping genealogies, subsequent sections trace the coappearance and mutation of two moral virtues across the colonial divide and in the period between the First World War and mid-twentieth-century decolonization. These virtues, I argue, of "sacrifice" in the colonized non-West, and of "generosity" in the colonizing West, are in some strict sense elementary (both rudimentary and fundamental) with respect to the ethics we have been tracking of the common cause, an other life, *une vie autre*. Taken together, they aspire toward a seemingly impossible form of anticolonial community based on an appeal to exacting reciprocity between historical antagonists. A concluding section reviews the convergence of anticolonial ethics and postcolonial theory (thus, the transmutation of ethical into academic disciplines) under the sign of Husserlian phenomenology.

Segue: Whose War?

On August 5, 1914, following Britain's entry into the First World War, a special *Gazette of India Extraordinary* declared India an officially belligerent country engaged in armed conflict with Germany and her allies. In these incipient days of anticolonial nationalism, this pronouncement was met with enthusiastic affirmations of solidarity with Britain and loyalty to the empire from a range of Indian groups and factions. Overzealous Indian princes preemptively placed the entire resources of their states at the disposal of the king-emperor, and various ordinarily sedentary organizations, such as the chambers of commerce, the bar associations, and several municipal bodies, declared their eagerness to form volunteer corps and otherwise risk life and limb in defense of the empire. The Muslim League and the Indian National Congress, no less, observed in the outbreak of war a welcome opportunity for equality in collaboration with Britain and a chance to present before the world the spectacle of united empire.[2] Endorsing these sentiments, M. K. Gandhi, that curiously postpacifist votary of nonviolence and veteran of the Boer and Zulu wars, reiterated "ungrudging and unequivocal support to the Empire with which we aspire in the near future to be partners in the same sense as the Dominion Overseas."[3] Acting in part out of decorous fidelity to existing bonds of union between Britain and India and upon the belief that initiation into the true *abhaya*, or fearlessness, of not killing could only be undertaken by those with the courage to face death, Gandhi devoted considerable energy over the following years to the recruitment of Indian soldiers for the war effort.[4]

How unintelligible such details are in view of the provincialism of the allied Great War imaginary, with its texts of heroism squeamishly demarcating Britain from the rest of Europe, let alone registering the presence of non-Europeans at the front. All wars tend to be backward-looking, the historian Paul Fussell has argued, but perhaps none more so than the Great War. Even the copious literature of complaint provoked by this war is generally insular. In Fussell's words, "The act of fighting . . . becomes something like an unwitting act of conservative memory, and even of elegy. The soldier dwells . . . on the now idyllic period before the present war as well."[5] Thus war is but an occasion to elegize Edwardian life and times in Siegfried Sassoon's *Memoirs of a Fox-Hunting Man* (1928)—the claustrophobic domestic world of village cricket, groom-gardeners, kennels, and a harmonious pecking order. A few voices in the genre of Great War memoir, however, are strikingly antinostalgic and antiparochial.

The title of Robert Graves's autobiography, *Goodbye to All That* (1929), for instance, coined, as he puts it, a "catch-word" for a dissident subculture for which the war forged welcome paths of escape into the non-Western worlds to which Europe had become inured through imperial self-enclosure.[6] Graves's own war was marked by antiheroic episodes of mutiny and desertion from the senseless fighting and no less from Englishness itself. Left with an aesthetic allergy precisely to the retroactive monumentalization of English culture in vogue at the time, *Goodbye* evinces strong objections to the rise of patriotic English literary studies at Oxford and Cambridge upon the conclusion of the war. But it was at the former university—where Graves belatedly arrived in 1919 as a youthful war veteran—that he unexpectedly ran into kindred spirits. These included the legendary T. E. Lawrence, usually remembered as the crusading war hero who fomented a campaign of internal insurgency against the Ottoman Empire by co-opting the Arabs into an allied push for Damascus. In fact Lawrence eschewed all medals and public plaudits for this war activity, also shying away from the honorific title Lawrence of Arabia. Though acting under the orders of the British Army in Cairo, his war was waged on behalf of Arab independence. As he makes quite clear in his *Seven Pillars of Wisdom* (1926), this was "an Arab war waged and led by Arabs for an Arab aim in Arabia."[7] Faithful to his extranational allegiances, in 1919 Lawrence traveled with the Arab delegation to the Paris Peace Conference as Prince Feisal's translator, only to be bitterly disappointed by the Western handover of Syria to France—one act in the systematic vivisection of the Middle East consequent upon the war. He remained a staunch Arab nationalist to the end, not looking back at the delicate English past so much as ahead toward "the new Asia which time was inexorably bringing upon us. Mecca was to lead to Damascus; Damascus to Anatolia, and afterwards to Bagdad; and then there was Yemen. Fantasies, these will seem, to such as are able to call my beginning an ordinary effort."[8] The war provoked a related shift in the cartographic imaginary of the British writer E. M. Forster. His service on the Red Cross in Alexandria through these troubled years provoked an enduring anticolonialism and a new appreciation for cultural pluralism. Forster's two tributes to the great city are a case in point. *Pharos and Pharillon* (1923), celebrates Alexandria as the melting pot of Mediterranean antiquity, and an earlier book, *Alexandria: A History and a Guide* (1915), extols it as a rare "city of friends" in the midst of wartime.[9]

Graves, Forster, Lawrence, and their ilk were not the only ones to seize upon the transnationalism of the Great War. As attested by the enthusiastic Indian support for the war effort, with which we began this section, this war was genuinely global. Fought in Europe, Asia, the Middle East, and Central and East Asia, it enlisted colonial conscripts from India, Australia, New Zealand, South Africa, and Canada, as well as from West Africa, Madagascar, Indochina, Algeria, Tunisia, and Morocco.[10] The military cosmopolitanism of the Great War is an inaugural context for our discussion. A minor literature of recovered diaries and letters from peasant soldiers at the front is especially germane to the analysis. Read closely, this shows up the vexed migration of soldiers from colonial outposts to the battlefields of Europe and back again as the prompt for an inter-civilizational ethics devoted to rescuing the endangered spirit of Europe from the clutches of imperial-fascism, at the cost of immediate, anticolonial nationalist aims. Secreted within these discontinuous texts, we find an illicit desire to salvage the very best of Europe and an account of how profoundly this effort was appreciated and endorsed by many Europeans at the time. What did such collaborative and reciprocal understanding actually achieve? And what does the best of Europe look like after its non-Western rehabilitation? We must begin with some scenes of death.

Tableau 1: An Anticolonial *Minima Moralia*

On October 21, 1914, the first of two ill-prepared and ill-equipped brigades of the Lahore Division arrived in Marseilles. By the time of the Armistice, India had supplied more than 1.27 million men as cannon fodder to the empire; roughly one in every ten "British" combatants in the war came from the subcontinent. At least forty-nine thousand of these never returned home. Drawn principally from the ranks of the peasantry of northern and western India, the Indians who fought in the Great War were largely illiterate men. They often hailed from landless families, for whom the salary of 11–15 rupees a month given to a sepoy would have constituted a crucial supplementary source of income. Potentially mercenary in composition, and without any real access to the sophisticated rhetoric of the native elite, many of these soldiers nonetheless evolved their own discourse of subtle solidarities with the empire.

Responding to the unexpected suspension of racial and colonial division in war-torn Europe, and the experience of reciprocity and hospitality, especially in France, letters from Indian sepoys convey a sense of perverse proximity between colonizers and colonized at the battlefront. For most of the subaltern Baluchis, Punjabis, Marathas, and Rajputs, not to mention locals at Marseilles, Ypres, Givenchy, and Festubert, among other places, the Great War brought with it a formative encounter with cultural difference. Albeit in onerous circumstances, it enabled "native" soldiers to encounter the world beyond their villages for the first time. Many among these registered the war as an experience of travel and exposure to the novelty of Europe, Europeans, and other native troops from further afield.[11] In addition, participants from colonial outposts and the imperial periphery alike found themselves observing the unexpected conformity of different bodies in matters of life and especially in death. In *Across the Black Water* (1939), possibly the first Indo-Anglian novel set against the backdrop of the Great War, the writer Mulk Raj Anand (whose father fought in the war with the 2/17th Dogras) communicates something of this euphoric sense of collectivity at the front—a redistribution of friends and enemies temporarily liberating colonial inferiors into the *mythos* of equality in heroism: "As the troops turned left and marched up the hill along the Canbiere, the throngs multiplied on the broad pavements . . . and . . . threw flowers at the sepoys while they cried: 'Vievongleshindoos! Vivangleterre! Vievelesallies!' . . . The general of the Lahore Division trotted his horse up to the head of the forces, adjusted a megaphone to his mouth, and shouted in . . . Hindustani . . . : 'Heroes of India. After the splendid reception you have been given by the people of France . . . I have no doubt that you will fulfill your duties with the bravery for which you are famous.'"[12]

The simple, reciprocal camaraderie that Indian sepoys experienced with their Western counterparts was the affective springboard for more profound expressions of collaboration with the British Government. This was in face of what is iteratively foretold as a crisis of metaphysical proportions from which Europe had to be saved for the sake of the larger world. In particular, soldiers' letters written during 1915, in the wake of a bitter and demoralizing winter the year before, report the war as an apocalypse from which no one would be spared but for decisive acts of interracial fearlessness on the Western front. Testifying to the cosmic significance of the calamity facing Europe, Muslim sepoys consistently describe the scene of combat as Karbala itself, the epic site where the army dispatched by the Umayyad Caliph Yazid I defeated and murdered Husayn Ibn Ali, grandson of the Prophet. In a similar vein, Hindu soldiers compare the fighting in France to the carnage of Kurukshetra, the epic battlefield of the *Mahabharata* upon which the war between the Pandavas and Kauravas all but resulted in the end of the world. "I cannot write about the fighting," insists Allah Ditta of the 129th Baluchi regiment, in a letter to his father, "because it is very grievous. But it is not ordinary fighting, it is Karbala. This fighting is the task of those Kings."[13] And this from a wounded Punjabi Rajput, recovering in England: "Do not think that this is a war. This is not a war. It is the ending of the world. This is just such a war as was related in the *Mahabharata* about our forefathers."[14]

While giving evidence of the shared significance of the war and its cultural translatability for Indian participants, the epistolary literature under consideration remains adamant that Europeans and non-Europeans (civilian or combatant) experienced the war in discrete though complementary ethical registers. The crisis tempered distinctive cultural and civilizational virtues in each group. The erratic elaboration of this theme yields a subgenre of encomium in which praise of Westerners and non-Westerners occurs within separate catalogues commending the former under the heading of generosity and the latter under the heading of sacrifice. To these headings we must attend closely, for they supply the pivotal tropes for the ensuing discussion.

Observed through the lens of an enthusiastic Occidentalism, the goodness of Europe is registered first and foremost as the fact of its wealth; especially to the trained eye of the peasant soldier, the land itself exemplifies the dazzling prosperity of the culture. The fields of France, writes Saif Khan of the Fortieth Pathans to a comrade in Persia, "are full"; every man's land "yields him thousands of *maunds* of wheat"; gardens grow "anywhere"; the fruit of a single tree could feed "several regiments"; "each house is a sample of paradise," each Frenchman "well-to-do," each Frenchwoman "rosy [of] cheeks and dainty [of] ringlets."[15] Much like the reflective landscape, human nature too displays the edifying symptoms of opulence; the "well-being" of the nation, Saif Khan observes, produces a "well-mannered" people, their inner qualities shaped by their fortunate material circumstances.[16] In these terms, the exemplary nature of European generosity is explained as the moral effect of plenitude: a virtue appropriate to affluence.

Experienced by Indian soldiers either as the hospitality of the local French population or in the care available to wounded soldiers in English military hospitals, "white" generosity manifests itself under the sign of excess. Letters from convalescent soldiers hyperbolically recount the surpassing of duty apparently common among wartime English nurses: "ladies" who, "without any further motive" than the comfort of their patients, "pour milk into our mouths"; hospitals where "men . . . are tended like flowers."[17] In these cases care achieves the status of a gift on the strength of a humanizing superfluity. So too, in a different setting, the basic protocols of refuge and shelter attain to hospitality on the strength of an ennobling surplus; whether this be the substitution of apple cider for water in common French homes or the yielding by local hosts of favored fireside places to freezing Indian soldiers. We might further observe that, in its very singularity (as that which is structurally unpredictable, unforeseen, and surprising), the event of a surplus at any given scene of hospitality/generosity registers the particularity of each encounter (that is, its difference) within the *genera* of cross-cultural encounter. To such excessive moments of regard for the peculiarities of their foreign-ness, Indian sepoys are especially attentive. Consider the amazement of Mahomed Zabu Shah of the Sixth Cavalry, who finds his eager local hosts in France have overnight taken to preparing *halal* meat on learning of his religious prohibitions. As he reports in a letter of late November 1916 to a male relative in Farrukhabad District, Uttar Pradesh, "The old people in the house are full of kindness. They wash my clothes and take even better care of me than you when I am on leave. One day they cooked a hare for supper, and they were very much excited when I would not eat it. They asked the reason and I told them. The next day I found a fowl hung up with its throat cut and they said, 'Now you will have to eat this fowl.'"[18]

If generosity is a virtue peculiar to the prerogatives of European plenitude, an antonymous corollary shows a uniquely Indian virtue of sacrifice emerging from uniquely Indian conditions of scarcity. Recognizably traditional or received in its disposition, this wisdom was put to the test in the circumstances under consideration as letters from India to enlisted sepoys brought regular news, especially over the summer of 1915, of famine, drought, increased poverty, and plague in the Punjab, which was the recruiting ground for the majority of Indian soldiers. Here is a typical account from August 1915 of hardship on the land, sent to Sowar Amir Ali Khan of the Thirty-sixth Jacob's Horse by his mother:

I must inform you that in the first instance there was much foot and mouth disease here, through which your father has got into debt, and all our jewellery was pawned. . . . And although indeed there was an abundance of grain this year, we have had to sell a portion of the grain to pay for the redemption of the jewellery, and now the cattle disease has begun again. Much millet and corn was sown, but God knows whether a famine is not coming. Grain has been growing dearer daily, and wheat is five rupees eight annas a *maund*, and barley three rupees eight annas. If you had sent money to your father why should he have to sell the grain? . . . Without fail send money to your revered parent. I implore you urgently to do so; . . . your father is ashamed to write himself.[19]

Amidst such demands for money and expressions of acute concern, each exchange on these matters is inter alia a catechism of austerity. Seeking consolation for the additional sacrifice of sons and husbands, those sending reports of starvation from India proudly display a moral training in self-denial. Letters from sepoys enumerate familiar continuities between hardship and military stoicism, insisting—in an aphorism put to instrumental use in the neo-colonial wars of the last few decades—that it is the poorest men who make the best soldiers. "I have been starving for food. Money has become scarce and foodstuffs are very dear," writes a Tamil woman to her husband in late-February 1915, "Show a brave spirit in the midst of this war of machines. Fight with all your might."[20] In a similar vein, a wounded Garhwali soldier declares it "a noble fate for us to be allowed to sacrifice our bodies."[21]

In such examples lack is disclosed as the condition of possibility for those habits of nonattachment that sacrifice in its turn exemplifies. It is on the heels of this thought that the rhetoric of scarcity (about the lack, that is, of material goods) gives voice to a demand for compensatory spiritual goods, presenting penury as preparation for a desirable dematerialization of existence. In other words, here we have a didactic schema (quite literally making a virtue out of necessity) that reveals impoverishment as the path, for a chosen few, to an enlightened nihilism. "Material existence," Sonu Gaekwar of the 107th Pioneers observes from his deathbed in Kitchener's Indian Hospital at Brighton, "is merely an illusion."[22] And, we might add, what remains of the material world after such austerities quickly becomes a hindrance from which death alone can offer, especially to the sepoy, the most welcome liberation. As letter after letter rehearses upon this logic a desire for death as reward rather than as punishment, as indulgence rather than sentence, there suddenly comes into view a new reading of sacrifice. No longer mere shorthand for the renunciatory capacity unique to those who live (or who have chosen to live) a life of poverty, sacrifice also translates into a state of accelerated commerce between gods and men (advisedly). Such is the consolation that Abdul Ghani of the 125th Napier's Rifles offers to his brother by drawing upon a text that speaks potently to our themes:

When the Almighty by way of trial ordered Abraham (on whom be peace!) to sacrifice his son Ishmael he was pleased and said 'Amen: for thou O God gavest him to me, and he is thy property." And when Abraham took his son, his beloved son, into the wilderness to sacrifice him, he said to him, "My son! I am about to sacrifice you in the name of God." Then Ishmael also was pleased and said, "Oh my father! Bind my hand and feet with your cords; that way, when you slay my body, neither my hands nor my feet shall be in your way; for my will is His will." My brother . . . give thanks to God . . . for my time is come to be sacrificed.[23]

Let me bring the story I have been telling into more obvious alignment with the disciplinary intent of this discussion. Between 1914 and 1918, we have conjectured, a traumatic encounter between North Indian peasant soldiers, rural, elderly French couples, and devout English nurses augmented in popular consciousness a possibly unprecedented sense of collaboration between colonizer and colonized against a common crisis. Many participants at these scenes came to believe that the protection and defense of an admittedly partisan Europe was instrumental for the salvation of the wider world. They also believed themselves equipped for this task by the complementary virtues of generosity and sacrifice that were clarified on the common ground between colonizer and colonized but also borne of demographically discrete backgrounds of plenitude and scarcity. Appearing together and codependent, furthermore, the virtues proper to plenitude and scarcity ultimately conform to contradictory etymologies: the former committing the hospitable (and reluctant) colonizer to an apologetic idiolect of regard and relationality; the latter permitting the (equally reluctant) colonized to speak a language of disregard and invulnerability. Here, then, even in its rudimentary form, we can observe a moral partnership between congenial antagonists: a type of "intimate enmity," á la Ashis Nandy, or "implacable dependence," á la Albert Memmi, straining in perpetual dialectic between the colonizer's moral obligation to extend precisely those invitations that the colonized revolutionary would, in time, be morally obliged to refuse.[24] A congenial dialectic between the mutating forms of generosity and sacrifice by no means exhausts the ethics specific to transnational and collaborative anti- or postcolonial endeavors. Yet it has a crucial place in its genealogy. Two further intervals illustrate the transmission of the schema we have been reviewing. One, to be considered directly below, concerns the ethos of mid-twentieth-century decolonization. A composite intertext of imaginative and juridical documents from this scene enforces a strict existential division between European and non-European critics of empire, whereof, once again, the ethical objections of each group are forced into two discrete but coappearing catalogues, amenable to the devolutions of plenitude and scarcity. Another interval, roughly between 1934 and 1939, belongs to the laborious elaboration of Edmund Husserl's later phenomenology as a response to the ethical crisis facing European "man" and the European "sciences." Marking the crucial philosophical synapse between anticolonial thought and the disciplinary forms of postcolonial theory, Husserlian phenomenology conveys its insights through two practices or methods: "reduction," or the ethical subject's austere supersession of the empirical world, and "intentionality," or the ethical subject's effort to reconstitute itself through a relational engagement with various terminal others. In their postcolonial adaptation, discussed below, reduction and intention are made to provide discursive quarters for the ethics of sacrifice and generosity, respectively.

Taken together, our combined archive, framed as it is by conditions of historical crisis, constitutes a minor/lesser ethics, or *minima moralia*: a concept famously developed in Theodor Adorno's 1951 book by that name, written during an American exile wrought by the events of fascism. Adorno's interest is in identifying an ethics that implicitly contradicts the *Magna Moralia*, sometimes attributed to Aristotle, and positing a normative or universalizable science of excellence/goodness for individuals seeking success in the public domain.[25] But what, Adorno asks, is the use of this upbeat Greek science of public achievement, given the impossibility of a good life (especially a good political/common life) in the inhuman twentieth century? In the wake of Europe's multiple catastrophes, all that remains is damaged life and the courage of fidelity to the crisis at hand in its shattered variety.[26] "The splinter in your eye," as Adorno famously observes in a gloss upon these procedures, "is the best magnifying glass."[27] This adage certainly holds true for the elementary virtues born of colonial encounter in the theaters of twentieth-century world war. Additionally, narrating the truth of any *minima moralia*—that is, showcasing it for what it is—involves its own formal *askesis* and distorted vision. The virtues of lesser ethics inhere in the inmost recesses of individual lives and cannot—indeed, must not—be rendered with any reliable objectivity, let alone turned into moral law. In Adorno's words: "The specific approach of *Minima Moralia*, the attempt to present aspects of our shared philosophy from the standpoint of subjective experience necessitates that the parts do not altogether satisfy the demands of the philosophy of which they are nevertheless a part. The disconnected and non-binding nature of the form, the renunciation of explicit theoretical cohesion, are meant as one expression of this."[28] Such constraints apply to our study as well: no strict law of historical causality, staunch archival trail, or philological necessity enforces the connections we are after or distils core principles for their future application. But a certain imaginative labor imputes common cause to the febrile letters of subaltern colonial conscripts and the dense philosophical exegeses of transcendental phenomenologists. Might we allow ourselves to wish that participants from these disparate discursive environments had responded alike to their own victimization by Europe by seeking to reform Europe? Could we fabricate a Europe that took heart precisely from the individuals, groups, and cultures it had tried so hard to extricate from its civilizational fabric? The postcolonial ethics we are after certainly inheres in elusive and micrological data. It also obtains from our own retroactive aspirations.

Segue: Whose Human?

The solidarities between Indian sepoys and their European counterparts during the Great War were by no means unassailable. Military loyalties to the empire were put under particular strain by policies of forced recruitment introduced into the Punjab by late 1916 in response to the demand for an urgent expansion of the Indian army. Acting on the authority of Michael O'Dwyer, the repressive Governor of Punjab, recruitment of-

ficers resorted to forms of abduction and torture in the rural country-
side, humiliating reluctant conscripts before their families and allegedly
kidnapping "womenfolk."[29] The war thus hardened habits of colonial
enforcement, which fed into subsequent regimes of martial law in the
region. Coercive recruitment also stimulated answering habits of resistance to imperial policing, which found expression in a series of violent
revolts. Such antagonisms resulted in the violent colonial conflicts of
Amritsar in 1919. On April 13, a company of British forces comprising
twenty-five rifles of the Ninth Gurkhas, twenty-five rifles from detach-
ments of the Fifty-fourth and Fifty-ninth Sikhs F. F. (accompanied by
forty Gurkhas carrying *kukris*, or small curved machetes, for good measure) were ordered by the infamous General Dyer to fire into a crowd of
their own people, some twenty thousand of whom had gathered for a
peaceful protest in the city's enclosed Jallianwala Bagh. Hundreds were
killed immediately, and thousands critically wounded. Declaring Europe
a "satanic civilization," Gandhi launched the Non-Cooperation Movement the very next year with the single aim of obtaining immediate self-
rule for India.[30]

The very conditions of war, then, generated the anti-imperial momen-
tum that led inexorably to the demand for decolonization or total liberation from Europe. And it was war, again, that yielded the first transnational
movement for solidarity among colonized subjects at large. In November
1914, Turkey, home of the Khalifa claiming spiritual leadership of Muslims
the world over, joined forces with Germany. Soon after, the war was pro-
nounced a *jihad*, summoning all Muslims into action against the Allies in
the cause of their faith. Turkey's new alliances were generally explained
away by the Allied faction as part of a feeble German plot to bring down
the British Empire by harnessing the ever-explosive and ever-ready forces
of militant Islam.[31] Yet, albeit under the partisan banner of pan-Islamism,
these alliances clearly formalized the terms of civilizational contestation
between Europe and non-Europe, giving breath to a far-reaching discourse
of anti-Western polemic.

On the battlefront there were mutinies by at least three South Asian
Muslim units, the 130th Baluchis, the Fifth Light Infantry, and the Fif-
teenth Lancers, each of which refused to enter into armed conflict with
coreligionists. Progressively there were numerous desertions from Pathan
units until enlistment from among this group altogether ceased by mid-
1915. A few years later, the brothers Muhammed and Shaukat Ali launched
the Khilafat movement from Aligarh in British India with the aim of compelling the British government to restore the Turkish sultan to his former
sovereignty. Though widely perceived as an Islamic movement, Khilafat

soon became one of the cornerstones of Indian independence. By 1920 Gandhi had committed Hindu India to the Khilafat cause in the name of an inclusive and ecumenical anticolonialism. "I say that if Hindus and Muslims are brothers, it is their duty to share one another's sorrow," he publicly declared during a Khilafat Conference at Delhi. "We must not say that the question of Khilafat is exclusively for the Moslems to grieve over. No, it belongs to all Indians."[32]

Many historians and cultural commentators hold that the prickly new coalitions of the First World War bestowed an irreparable (and retrograde) Manichean logic upon anticolonial thought. The resulting impasse of colonizer/colonized, paired in a reified structure of domination and sub-ordination, bears little resemblance to the hybridistic thinking favored by contemporary academic postcolonialism. Thus postcolonial discourse is said to displace (and possibly improve upon) its anticolonial precursor. If anticolonialism became mired in the exclusivities of cultural national-ism, or so the argument goes, postcolonialism emerged out of a distinctly Western critique of nationalism per se, born of the desire to make Euro-American, liberal-capitalist democracies all the more inclusive and mul-ticultural and then export this vision to the less-developed world.[33] The putative breach between these two discourses (anticolonialism/postcolo-nialism) is strongly affirmed in a strain of Western apologia for human rights that is relevant to our materials.

In a typical argument, the historian Samuel Moyn claims that the evo-lution of human rights thinking in the post–Cold War era comprised a key shift of emphasis from the themes of non-Western politics toward some-thing like post-anticolonial ethics as the proper bearer of global justice. By his account, early human rights were derailed and hijacked by the decolo-nization movements of the 1940s and 50s—and it is, indeed, insufficiently acknowledged that several representatives from the colonized world were appointed to serve among the original eighteen member nations of the Human Rights Commission. A proportion of this group (including rep-resentatives from China and Lebanon) were charged with joint respon-sibility for drafting an international bill of human rights: the Universal Declaration of Human Rights (UDHR), adopted by the United Nations General Assembly on December 10, 1948. The content and history of this document testify to its diverse authorship. Anticolonial sentiments were registered in extensive debates over Article 2 of the declaration, concern-ing the universal applicability of the human rights covenant without dis-crimination "on the basis of the political, jurisdictional or international status of the country or territory to which a person belongs, whether it be independent, trust, non-self-governing or under any other limitation of sovereignty."³⁴ In due course the UDHR was established as a common standard of achievement for all peoples and all nations.³⁵ The independent constitutions of several former French colonies (Algeria, Niger, Cameroon, Chad, the Ivory Coast, Senegal) invoked the UDHR, often in lieu of the canonical Declaration of the Rights of Man and the Citizen, as a founding or source document that had paved the way to the recognition of national self-determination as the basis of fundamental human rights.³⁶ Yet, thinkers like Moyn argue, this early emphasis on the nation-state as the crux of human rights was justly targeted by the enlightened antipolitics of a 1970s generation that believed (one wonders why?) colonialism to be at an end and the world itself officially postcolonial. This generation had allegedly not only lost faith in third-world developmentalism but also in the ameliorative capacity of politics itself, as a result of the Vietnamese disaster and a growing public desire to reconceive transnational identity outside Cold War terms.³⁷ One result of this state of mind and heart, Moyn contends, approvingly, was the emergence of a new, Western philosophical landscape marked by a distinctly ethical cast of mind and heart, and focused on the vulnerability of individuals within the nation-state and other such collectivities. As he writes, "The ideological climate was ripe for claims to make a difference not only through political vision but by transcending politics. Morality, global in its potential scope, could become the aspiration of humankind."³⁸ So it is that an ethics apposite to metropolitan postcolonial theory rises, phoenix-like, from the ashes of political claims on behalf of anticolonial nationalism.

This overly tidy rupture (between provincial anticolonial politics and global postcolonial ethics) runs against the very grain of the genealogical continuities that concern us. Following postcolonial thinker Dipesh Chakrabarty, it is our claim that these continuities endured in the form of a minor and intransigent dialogism in spite of—and sometimes, as we will see, because of—the harsh Manichaeism of decolonization proper.³⁹ Postwar anticolonialism certainly resulted in projects of national liberation myopically caught up with the pragmatics of territoriality, security, and development. But these projects were, first and foremost, revolutionary. The spokespersons for most new nationalisms, which were conceived as a reaction against the desperate inhumanity of imperial fascism, refused to push aside human rights, thereby defending new citizens from emergent governments.⁴⁰ Moreover, these projects gave life to the conviction that everybody was somehow jointly responsible for the conscience, if we can call it that, of an incipient global democracy to come, however much the paths to its preservation might vary. As such, they did not transcend the political so much as reinvest it with quarrelsome ethical idealism.

Tableau 2: Uses of Ethical Agonism

From 1919 onward, we have been arguing, as a result of conditions created by the Great War, Indian nationalism increasingly expressed itself
in a mix of anti-Western polemic and anticolonial unity. The mood substantially compromised subaltern allegiance to imperial design, and by
late April 1955, it had entirely colored the charter for the twenty-nine de-
colonized nations represented at the Bandung Conference in Indonesia to
promote Afro-Asian cooperation and oppose Cold War neo-colonialisms
in a joint front. By the time we find ourselves at this conference, much
has changed in relation to our sanguine picture of interracial collaboration at the Western front. The tenuous solidarities between colonizer and
colonized have given way to a scene of militant cosmopolitanism among
those whom Frantz Fanon describes as "the wretched of the earth." Furthermore, where the transnational compact of the Great War was founded
on moral and military opposition to a crisis for Europe, now the name of
the crisis is Europe, and its resolution can only proceed along the lines
of rigorous de-occidentalization. Declaring their convocation a response
to an ethical emergency, the leaders find their themes deepened as Dr.
Mohammmed Fadhil al-Jamali of Iraq begins to speak, with lowered eyes:
"It is our sincere hope that this conference will prove in a very modest
way to be a great moral force of ideological disarmament and moral re-
armament."[41] The April gathering includes those, President Soekarno has
already announced, who are well qualified for such a war of principles
by training in sacrifice: "I recognise that we are gathered here today as a
result of sacrifices. Sacrifices made by our forefathers and by the people of
our own and younger generations."[42] A reparative ethos demands of such
heirs the cultivation now of permanent relinquishment—a refusal of the
temptations of Europe on the strength of what Soekarno calls "moral violence."[43] And yet, as the African-American author and intellectual Richard
Wright tells us in his sensitive report on the Bandung Conference, even in
its most punitive forfeiture of the West, this anticolonial project of exclusion instantiates collaboration. Poised, despite itself, as a "final call . . . to
the moral conscience of the West," the conference is an appeal, he insists,
to Western "generosity": "It was my belief that the delegates at Bandung,
for the most part, though bitter, looked and hoped toward the West. . . .
The West, in my opinion, must be big enough, generous enough, to accept
and understand that bitterness."[44]

In the international literature of anticolonial polemic that emerged after or around the time of the Bandung Conference—specifically, spread-

ing outward from the scene of French colonialism—we can observe some subtle but significant variations on our themes. Both Western and non-Western interlocutors writing within this tradition are distinguished by a harsh diagnostic idiom wherein the insistent identification of postimperial Europe as a disease releases a register of attending therapeutics into the field of anti-imperial moral thought. We can classify them under the two tentative headings of countercontagion (to be against contamination), and con-contagion (to keep company with contamination), variously.

In the countercontagion texts representing the colonized, a poignant realism can only speak the experience of disease, as it were, calamitously. Here, always imagined in conditions of overcrowding and scarcity with uncertain access to cure, the illness that is Europe is deemed fatal, as well as invasive and infectious. Typically, in Albert Memmi's *Portrait du colonisé, précédé du portrait du colonisateur* (1957), it is described as an incurable "cancer" that "wants only to spread"—usually from the site of colonial avarice to "fascist temptation."[45] Writing in a similar vein of Hitler as the proper name for colonialism, Aimé Césaire turns the text of his *Discours sur le colonialisme* (1955) into an almanac of the "European disorder." Colonialism, he reasons, becomes the harbinger of civilizational death both for perpetrators and victims, and with every act of imperial self-indulgence, "a gangrene sets in, a centre of infection begins to spread."[46] Thus, the colonized must enclose themselves against Europe. This is easier said than done. If as yet unharmed by the malaise of Europe, the colonized is ever susceptible to colonial contagion on the basis of her "want." Memmi makes the case strongly: "Everything in the colonized is deficient and everything contributes to this deficiency—even his body, which is poorly fed, puny and sick. . . . Being a creature of oppression, he is bound to be a creature of want."[47]

Memmi's subject clearly understands her sense of psychic endangerment before the contagion of Europe as a susceptibility to the perils of revenge and counteroppression, in other words, as the temptation of mastery. To gain immunity she must follow the allopathic law of a demanding quarantine for which she is trained through habits of scarcity and to which she will submit, once again, sacrificially. An unforgiving puritanism, as we now know to our cost, inhabits the heart of this pious posture of refusal and expresses itself too often as a form of moral hygienicism. We can hear it even in Memmi: "He does without tobacco if it bears the colonialist's stamp! These are pressure methods and economic sanctions, but they are, equally, sacrificial rites of colonization. . . . He will . . . choose the greatest of difficulties. He will go so far as to prohibit any additional conveniences of the colonizer's tongue. . . . To go all the way with his revolt, it seems necessary for him to accept those inhibitions and amputations."[48] We do have access, let us note at this juncture, to another anticolonial taxonomy in which these punitive gestures of quarantine and refusal attain their true ethical import as the preliminary to that vast project of self-mastery that Gandhi summoned, well before the days of Bandung, under the sign of *swaraj*. As the indigenous slogan for self-rule, *swaraj* demands that India must first "drive out Western civilisation," abandoning its railways, doctors, lawyers, and machinery.[49] But because it can also be read as the cultivated practice of inwardness (rather than one of amputation and inhibition alone), Gandhian *swaraj* promises access to the best resources of the self—that is, to a region of exemption from provocation and of concentrated compassion. The proper name for this project is, of course, *ahimsa*, or nonviolence.

The con-contagion texts representing the colonizer adopt a very different approach to the disease of modern Europe. As we learn from Sartre in the course of his Europeanist, anticolonial polemic, self-enclosure is already the colonizer's malady rather than his cure. France, he polemicizes in his preface to Fanon's *Les damnés de la terre* (1961), is "the name of a nervous disease."[50] This condition symptomatically demands confinement to airless, darkened rooms sealed off from the clamorous sounds of freedom emerging from the colonial world. European man, we might recall from Sartre's first novel, is further afflicted by a similar state of "nausea," wherein a chronic revulsion against the empirical world severs the subject from the redemptive pleasures of relationality as well. Sartre eloquently recasts this physical horror of the objective world, undergone by the antihero Antoine Roquentin, in *La Nausée* (1938), in his preface to Memmi's manifesto as the existential crisis of "alienation," or that calcification of personality that falls within the oppressor's part. In his words, "No one can treat a man like a dog without first regarding him a man. The impossible dehumanization of the oppressed, on the other side of the coin, becomes the alienation of the oppressor. It is the oppressor himself who restores, with his slightest gesture, the humanity he seeks to destroy; and since he denies humanity in others, he regards it everywhere as his enemy."[51]

In Sartre's writing, the exemplary European engages in a therapeutic disregard for her own sanitized subjectivity by exposing herself to the world anew. In *Les chiens de garde* (1932), Sartre's peer and friend, the anticolonial novelist Paul Nizan, underscores the message through a homeopathic *pharmakeia* that encourages modern intellectuals to heal themselves by following a self-endangering itinerary through the infectious zone of humanity and human relationships: "Thus, on the one hand, we have the idealistic philosophers who promulgate truths concerning

Man; and, on the other hand, we have a map showing the incidence of tuberculosis in Paris, a map which tells us how men are dying."[52] The reformist (and therefore true) philosophers disregard the barriers between these two terrains, thus also submitting to the existential contamination of mere academic expertise. These themes are subtly recalibrated in the discourse on hospitality, and then emerge within contemporary French philosophy. In his writings on the sterility of knowledge systems that are divorced from bodily or empirical experience, the philosopher of science Michel Serres, for instance, suggests that the disposition that produces an openness toward aliens and others is ethically and structurally the same as the hardy disposition that produces a willingness to cohabit with infection. The result is a mode of thought that protests all forms of quarantine. As he writes,

What is cancer?—a growing collection of malignant cells that we must at all costs expel, excise, reject? Or something likes a parasite, with which we must negotiate a contact of symbiosis? I lean toward the second solution, as life does, . . . why? Because, objectively, we have to continue living with cancers, with germs, and with evil and even violence. . . . If we were to implacably clean up all the germs, as Puritanism would have us do, they would soon become resistant to our techniques of elimination and require new armaments. Instead, why not culture them in curdled milk, which sometimes results in delicious cheeses?[53]

The only prophylaxis entertained within this thinking (so much heir to the anticolonial radicalism of a prior generation) is against the self-protective subject of European colonial history. For Europe to reconvene itself as a culture fundamentally responsible to others, it must remain open to the visitation even of those guests who could jeopardize the founding principles—the very hospitality—of the culture that admits of them so impartially. Such commitments require what the thinker Jacques Derrida has called "the logic of auto-immunity": a practice of altruistic care liberated by apparent carelessness toward the prerogatives of self. In his words, this entails "that strange behaviour where a living being in quasi-suicidal fashion, 'itself' works to destroy its own protection, to immunize itself against its own immunity."[54]

These multiple, generic, ethical dispositions (born of counter- and con-contagion) further elaborate the reparative agonism characteristic of colonial encounter to which we have given the founding place names *sacrifice* and *generosity*. They also feed into the disciplinary development of postcolonial theory and supply significant raw materials for its yet to be articulated futures. That they do so through the route of transcendental phenomenology is no surprise, if only for the reason that Husserl also sources Western philosophy with the wherewithal for a uniquely agonistic ethics: specifically, harmonizing the apparent antithesis of reduction/intention as but two sides of the same convertible currency.

Tableau 3: Phenomenology and the Moment of Theory

Quite apart from Husserl's availability to postcolonialism at the scene of critical theory, there is an additional case to be made for the unique amenability of transcendental phenomenology to the enduring inheritance of anticolonial ethics. This becomes visible by degrees. If, as suggested earlier, the phenomenological method supplies ready accommodation for the complementary moral antinomies we are tracking, it is also integrally congenial to the ethical itself. Marking a historic shift from epistemology toward a new ontology, phenomenology's concern for "being" very quickly became an effort to distil an unbiased view of life itself, and nowhere more sharply than in the work produced by Husserl toward the end of his life, between 1934 and 1937, which includes a lecture entitled "Philosophy and the Crisis of European Man," delivered to the *Wiener Kulturbund* in Vienna, in May 1935, and a series of talks offered later that year in Prague that were subsequently gathered into his final work under the title *The Crisis of the European Sciences and Transcendental Phenomenology*. These years refine the strictly reparative modalities of the phenomenological process. The works that belong to this period were composed at a time when, under suspicion for reasons of his Judaism by the prevailing Nazi orthodoxy, the ageing Husserl had been forbidden to publish or speak publicly in his native Germany. Their iterative theme of crisis announces a diagnosis and urgent cure for the disease of Europe. And already, we could say, transcendental phenomenology has entered the discursive field of anticolonial moral polemic.

"How is it," Husserl asks his mid-war May gathering at the Vienna Kulturbund, "that . . . there has never arisen a medical science concerned with nations and with international communities? The European nations are sick; Europe itself, they say, is in a critical condition."[55] Attributing the malaise of Europe to the loss of "a purely theoretical attitude," Husserl embarks, here and in successive writing, upon a critique of Western materialism (we have encountered an earlier instance of this theme in a previous chapter). The ascendancy through the nineteenth century of positive, naturalist, and instrumental sciences, he argues in *The Crisis of European Sciences*, has led to a divided and disenchanted world, whose very uninhabitability is the precondition for a culture of profit in which the needs of humanity are always superseded by those of prosperity.[56] In response, phenomenology offers therapeutic methods for the recuperation of pure "theory," represented here as a region of radical immunity; its fantastical immaculacy is a function of its originality as "a science of true beginnings . . . of *rhizomata panton.*"[57] But—and this is where Husserl begins to speak directly to ethics—this recuperation of theory will not be axiomatic and universal. Indeed, it will barely be epistemological, involving, rather, the embodied practices of "lived actualization" undertaken by each individual theorist on behalf of humankind.[58] "In our philosophizing then," Husserl proclaims, "we are functionaries of mankind, . . . our inner personal vocation bears within itself at the same time the responsibility for the true being of mankind."[59] And here, qua vocation, the phenomenological method splits into two separate yet concerted ethical disciplines: the practice of reduction, which can be utilized, in our retelling of these events, for the procedures of sacrifice and inwardness, and that of intention which can be made to fit the requirements of generosity and relationality.

Briefly, phenomenology begins to oppose the alienating dualism of the postpositivist world through the rigors of the Cartesian *epoché,* wherein all external reality must be progressively reduced to consciousness, and the relentlessly bracketed empirical world rarefied into those forms in which it appears to/as subjectivity. Never a process to be accomplished once and for all, however, reduction is the laborious cultivation of a renunciatory attitude before the ever-recurring charms of ontic positing. Understanding it thus, and variously, as "ascese," "sacrifice," and as "a work of purification," Husserl himself pronounces *epoché* that painful project of self-mastery upon which the freedom of consciousness depends: "Pressing forward through the hell of an unsurpassable, quasi-skeptical *epoché,* . . . I refrain from taking any position on the being or non-being of the world. . . . I deny myself every ontic validity related to the world."[60] A condition of inhibition and amputation (and so, potentially of solipsism and egology), reduction nonetheless finds its consolation in the adjacent discipline of intention. Arguably the concept upon which Husserl's most significant modifications of Cartesian philosophy depend, intentionality disallows *epoché* its punctuation in the arid emptiness of *cogito,* or the subject of thought. Showing reduction to be the ground upon which there occurs the redemptive experience of perfect correlation between the world and world-consciousness, object and subject, phenomenological intention insists also upon a symbiosis between *cogito* and *cogitatum*—that is, between the thinking subject and the empirical objects of its reflection.

The objective world, we now learn, is actually intended by consciousness. But the latter is itself merely an effect of the appearances given unto it, so that, in Levinas's gloss, "the mind, while receiving something foreign, is also the origin of what it receives."[61] This symbiosis between subject and object Husserl magnifies in the fifth of his Cartesian meditations into a text of radical intersubjectivity. For now not only does *cogito* appear with alien *cogitatum* but also, on the strength of the transformative experience of empathy (*Einfühlung*), in mutually constitutive intimacy with radically other selves, so that every ego is, coevally and coefficiently, its alter ego. "In this way," Husserl writes, "transcendental subjectivity is expanded to become intersubjectivity, to become an intersubjective transcendental community."[62] Or, we might add, the frugalities of phenomenological *askesis* are shown to cohabit with a rich ethos of radical relationality, specifically in its occurrence as a hospitable disposition to alterity.

While they come together within an ultimately composite method, the procedures of reduction and intention that we have been canvassing were developed at discrete stages of Husserl's career, thus giving credence to the idea that phenomenology is (albeit most productively) fractured along the axis of a split idiom. So, where reduction and the labor of *epochē* dominate Husserl's earlier writing, from *Logical Investigations* to the *Cartesian Meditations*, the theme of intention is properly developed only in work that belongs to the last ten years of his productive life. Observing this fissure in his work, many of those French postmodern theorists of alterity whose work has supplied crucial nourishment for a Western postcolonial disposition have attempted to draw from Husserl a practice of intention sans reduction. Thus, it is principally the subject-object correlation in phenomenology that concerns Levinas, for whom intentionality becomes the starting point for an ethics of relation with otherness.[63] Likewise, ever wary of the straight and narrow path of *epochē*, Paul Ricouer's substantial work on Husserl has tended to foreground the themes of intersubjectivity, inclusivity, and *Einfühlung*.[64] Derrida, too, approaches his own more palpably anticolonial work on hospitality and cosmopolitanism through a formative consideration of Husserl as the moralist of "opening" and "exposure."[65]

It is possibly only in Sartre—in an oeuvre, as we might recall, that listens so acutely to the manifesto of anticolonial peoples and intellectuals—that the reductive labor of *epochē* is retained in the logic of "willing," "choosing" and "*dépassement*." Here phenomenology is shown to be the morality of freedom; in itself that coefficient of adversity earned through selective acts of withdrawal from, and refusals of, the contaminating world.[66] Mediated by the spectres of Althusserian interpellation and Gramscian hegemony, the modes of *epochē* carefully incubated in Sartre's thought reappear in that work of purification or disciplinary reform so characteristic of non-Western postcolonialism. In the austere renunciation of the categories of history and English, the sacrifice of canonicity, and the rhetoric of suspicion and ideological quarantine so forcefully endorsed by Edward Said, among others, some residue of reduction certainly remains.

Afterword: After Colonialism

Aiming to show that a genealogy of postcolonial theory can only be developed upon a groundwork of anticolonial ethics, we have argued that the conduit of Husserlian phenomenology enables the construction of crucial continuities between certain ethical and academic disciplines. These continuities are, in a strict narrative of transmission, minutely tropological and metaphoric, so that the elementary virtue of colonized sacrifice mutates by degrees into the themes of quarantine, immunity, refusal, reduction, and *epochē*. On the other hand, the elementary virtue of colonizer generosity transmutes, by degrees, into hospitality, relationality, exposure, intention, intersubjectivity, and so on. Emerging from the material and existential particularities of scarcity, on the one hand, and plenitude, on the other, both sets of moral clusters remain, nonetheless, radically complementary and codependent, always speaking in the discordant yet collaborative terms of colonizer and colonized, East and West. What is the promise of this dialogic idiom? To which juncture has it brought us? And where does it tend?

In his famous lectures on the intimate enmity of the master and slave in Hegel's *Phenomenology of Spirit* (delivered just a few years after Husserl's inaugural lectures on phenomenology at the Sorbonne), Alexandre Kojève, concedes moral priority to the latter. The master, unable to recognize any Other and committed only to the cause of his own enjoyment, finds himself at a solipsistic and "idle impasse."[67] In contrast, the slave attains both freedom and consciousness through her commitment to reciprocity and work. Thus, Kojève writes, "laborious slavery . . . is the source of all human, social, historical progress."[68] This too is the simple conclusion implicit in all the texts of implacable dependence that we have been considering, so that we might confidently render all anti/postcolonial ethics into an ethics that tends toward slavery—the colonized finding her ethos among the wretched of the earth, and the colonizer, likewise, becoming hostage to the same.[69] Or perhaps we should wait just a little longer upon that day that Nietzsche has promised us, when both masters and slaves will be surpassed in favor of a more joyful morality: "The day we can say with all our hearts, 'Onwards!' Our old morality too is part of the comedy!"[70] Perhaps the life beyond damaged life can be both ascetic and ludic? Here is a future for postcolonial theory.

FOUR

Inconsequence: Some Little-Known Mutinies Around 1946

Early in 1946 there was an outbreak of mutinies amid Allied troops, especially those stationed in the Levantine and Pacific theatres of the Second World War.[1] Most were explicitly anti-imperial in character. International newspapers report that this year began with increased civilian hostilities toward occupying armies, notably in Egypt and Southeast Asia. Such agitations won the sympathy of colonial regiments recruited for the war effort and for the ongoing domestic management of native populations. Additionally, Western common soldiers, including American GIs and British personnel awaiting disbandment and demobilization orders, joined the protests as well.[2] While subject to the same savage reprisals for insubordination as their Axis counterparts (among whom discipline did not break down in the period), Allied troops publicly combined arms, it sometimes appeared, as though against militarization itself.

Many mutineers attributed their unrest to the lessons of antifascism they had absorbed during the war. So we learn from the following public statement issued by rebellious troops at the Indian naval establishment HMIS *Akbar*: "Toward the end of the war we have been in a few countries which had already been liberated from FASCISTS. We have seen among the people a new life, a new spirit, a new hope for better existence. Thus we learnt what it means to be free."[3] Trusting in the rhetoric of freedom under whose banner they had risked their lives, troops such as these declared their unwillingness to defend any type of authoritarianism, as enshrined in the cultures of war and also at the core of all imperialisms, whether of the Axis or the Allies. But this was easier said than done. As a dissident British serviceman is reported to have told M. K. Gandhi, an imperial soldier's conscientious exit from the armed forces—and from all the authority and privilege attached to that occupation—involves the tougher task of first exiting his or her self-fashioning as a voluntary sentinel of an unjust status quo.[4] Thus, mutiny can be as much internally directed as against objectionable external command. At some level, and for the individual soldier (or sailor), it involves those practices of auto-disassembly so eloquently described by Michel Foucault as an ethics of releasing oneself from oneself (*se dépendre de soi-même*), and of *égarement*, or "straying afield from" or "deserting" oneself.[5] This chapter concerns the buried ethical content, thus conceived, of the transnational, anti-imperial mutinies in and around 1946, with a focus on the centrifugal Royal Indian Navy Mutiny (henceforth RINM). We can begin with a brief overview of this event in its immediate context.

The Royal Indian Navy Mutiny: An Overview

By any standard of revolutionary pitch and moment, the RINM of February 1946 was a spectacular event in the history of mid-twentieth-century decolonization. Its outbreak secured screaming headlines in most leading domestic and international newspapers of the time. "INDIAN RATINGS MUTINY AT TWO CENTRES," the *Hindustan Times* announced on the front page of its February 22 edition, elsewhere emphasizing the anti-imperial flavor of the protests: homemade freedom flags, and prognostications (albeit in barrack-language) about the imminent collapse of the Raj. "You are forgetting that India is free now," some graffiti declared, adding the following instructions: "You try against to this and see the result. But don't blame any body no body will come to save you, Desi your self and make hasry oh, you fool. You baster, don't try to behave improperly. Jai Hind."[6] Even larger fonts narrated the RINM's Hollywood-style termination in pitched battle on Bombay's streets and harborside between British reinforcement troops and common Indian sailors, or "ratings" as they were called. The former comprised a substantial cache of non-native regiments backed by Mosquito fighter-bombers and at least two warships of the Royal Navy speedily dispatched to Bombay following an adjournment motion of the House on "the grave extension of mutiny among a section of the Royal Indian Navy."[7] The latter were made up of some seven thousand ratings armed to the teeth with supplies from raided ammunition depots and manning the portside guns of docked RIN warships. So severe was the escalation of armed conflict and the consequent paralysis of activity in Bombay that by February 23, neither the Provisional Indian Assembly nor the British Parliament could entirely determine "whether there was a state of war."[8] And if there was, what sort of war would this be, and to whom would it belong: civil or imperial or anti-imperial, British or Indian? All this attention notwithstanding, the RINM was officially declared a political flop.

As it happens, by the time of the RINM, there was little ostensible reason to protest the British presence in India. In 1942, following M. K. Gandhi's catchy "Quit India" slogan, the country had erupted into a decisive civil disobedience movement for complete and immediate independence. Faced with an ungovernable and newly hostile subject population, and with strong evidence that South Asia was no longer a reliable commercial asset, the imperial administration was more than ready to act on Gandhi's directive.[9] "Cheer wogs, we are quitting India," was often chalked on the side of railway carriages. The sentiment was repeated in a favorite marching song of the time: "Land of shit and filth and wogs / Gonorrhea, syphilis, clap and pox: / Memsahibs paradise, soldiers' hell. / India fare thee fucking well."[10] Over time, in the way that any sudden desire to leave a place generates instantaneous claustrophobia, these blasé chants soon translated into panic for the hundred thousand or so European civilians sealed off in clement but remote hill stations. Besides stealth operations to evacuate British troops from port cities under cover of darkness each night, the government launched various "Bedlam" and "Scuttle" emergency plans to get European civilians safely out of India in a hurry. On advice from the war office, the cabinet also agreed to secret measures preventing any British women or children from booking a passage to India. E. M. Forster's time was well nigh over.[11]

These quitting operations had been set in motion following the resounding Labor victory over Churchill's government in the July 1945 British polls—thanks, in no small part, to the backlash against the conservatives from numerous burnt-out soldier-voters.[12] C. R. Atlee's new government galvanized all available administrative machinery to facilitate the process of Indian autonomy. So it was that on the very day of the RINM outbreak, Viceroy Lord Wavell announced a Cabinet mission on Indian independence under the stewardship of the secretary of state for India and Burma, Lord Fredrick Pethick-Lawrence, a man with something of a radical-socialist past.[13] Due to arrive in India the following month, the stated and sole intention of the mission was to transfer power from Britain to India.[14]

For these reasons, nationalist leaders argued, the untimely outburst of the RINM caused the same embarrassment as a sociopathic child's "You can go now" to finally departing dinner guests who had not yet relinquished the gifts they had initially been invited to bestow. The RINM had no reasonable cause, and, given that Indian independence was now a foregone conclusion, it could bring about nothing but chaos and anarchy. It was, in a word, inconsequential. Various spokesmen emphasized the need for political decorum now that India's struggle had conclusively entered its "final phase."[15] Iterating this sentiment in a somewhat labored nautical metaphor for his miscreant sailor audience, the Congress Party leader, Vallabhai Patel, urged the following: "India's ship was nearing the shore and had to be piloted as carefully and cautiously as possible out of the shoals that lay ahead."[16] The revolution was over, and it was time to grow up and get real. This theme gathers force in Patel's official verdict on the RINM, read before a mammoth rally of the Bombay Provincial Congress Committee on the evening of February 26. Here are some salient excerpts from the report on Patel's speech, printed in the *Hindu* newspaper on the following day: "'I cannot understand why the people should think of an uprising against the Government when the Congress had not given a call for revolt but was engaged in normal peaceful constructive activities.' The duty of the people was clear. It was not to listen to the advice of such misguided people but to follow the lead of the Congress, which knew when to fight and when to negotiate. . . . He said those who, against the advice of the Congress, had called for a general hartal on Friday to express their sympathy and solidarity with the ratings on strike were living in a fool's paradise. . . . Knowing the real situation, the Congress was handling the question in the most appropriate manner."[17]

It was over the issue of handling the RINM debacle that the anticolonial leadership visibly transformed into a successor government, and full participant in the psychodrama of political heredity and generationality haunting the transfer-of-power proceedings. British officials portrayed their task as the headache of finding suitable heirs for the Raj, rather than bringing an end to imperialism. "The depressing thing," we hear from Wavell, "is that one should have to hand over the control of India to such small men."[18] Elsewhere he bemoans his Indian successors from the leeward point of family romance: "I am left with one rather sickly infant, the Constituent Assembly, and one still-born babe, the Interim Government."[19] For their part, the Indian elite, by now caught up with internecine jostling for rank, chiefly spoke in the language of state-formation rather than that of anticolonialism—that is, with respect to the problem of constituting and not contesting the law. Jawaharlal Nehru, the heir-apparent, favored for his

Harrow and Cambridge credentials, expressed keenness to head "a strong, virile, active and stable Government which knows its mind and has the courage to go ahead, not a weak, disjointed, apologetic government which can be easily bullied or frightened. . . . To give an impression to the country and our people that we are merely a casual and temporary Government . . . is to undermine the prestige and authority of . . . Government."[20]

The dangers of the naval mutiny were crystal clear to all parties with such aspirations. No stable government, indigenous or imperial, could turn a blind eye to the riotous behavior of partisan armed forces. Nor could it entrust national security to men whose discipline was easily swayed by strong public sentiments.[21] To prohibit any further politicization of military misdemeanor, then, RIN protestors were denied access to the indemnities ordinarily available to anticolonial agitators. They were tried, instead, under the sole auspices of British military law pertaining to mutiny and indiscipline in the ranks. So keen was the interim government under Nehru to expunge these events from public political memory that by the following year it issued an effective ban, under the IPC 132 "abatement to mutiny" provisions, on cultural and specifically theatrical representations of the RINM story. The force of the court order endured for decades after.[22] In 1965, the theater impresario Utpal Dutt was imprisoned, under the guise of preventing antigovernment disturbances, for his production of *Kallol*—a dance-drama based on the RINM events, featuring an Indian police commissioner of Bombay as the oppressive villain of the piece.[23] The RINM story was only ever staged without government proscription in a 2005 Calcutta production. On that occasion a giant steamer on the river Hooghly played out its spectacle to two thousand spectators precariously perched on bobbing barges and pontoons to view a play said to commemorate the non-Western "victory over fascism."[24]

There have been a handful of revisionist readings of the RINM by participants or their family and friends, and a few by imperial historians as well. Those seeking to set the record straight and give credit where it is due contend that the mutiny was a catalyst for the transfer of imperial power because it revealed how compromised the military foundations of empire were, nearly a century after the mutiny of 1857.[25] I do not wish to assert such a place for the RINM within nationalist historiography. In fact, quite the contrary, I argue that the official verdict on the RINM was both astute and accurate. In making this claim, our approach follows, with variations, some methodological recommendations made by the South Asian historiographer Ranajit Guha.

When faced with the task of gleaning the fragile truth of subaltern events from the better-preserved records of official or elite discourse, Guha urges caution and strongly advises against the temptation of too much hermeneutic suspicion. The indices of elite/official discourse (which Guha terms "the prose of counter-insurgency") are, as he tells us, always susceptible to ideological inversion precisely because they are so judgmental. In his words, these indices "introduce us to a particular code so constituted that for each of its signs we have an antonym, a counter-message, in another code. To borrow a binary representation made famous by Mao Tsetung, the reading, *'It's terrible!'* for any element in one must show up in the other as *'It's fine!'* for a corresponding element and vice versa."[26] Guha's circumspection about the ultimate evidentiary worth of the derived and inverted countercode of insurgency supplies the cue we need. The antagonism between the series beginning "terrible"/"fine" is, as he puts it, "irreducible and there is nothing in this to leave room for neutrality. Hence these documents make no sense except as a code of pacification."[27] But consider the following alternative procedure. What if we assume the indices of counterinsurgency to be homonymic, as in correctly identifying while contextually and semantically misconstruing an insurgent species-type of "terrible"? Were we to concede this possibility (in the context of our concerns), we would not get very far if we responded to the counterinsurgent condemnation of the RINM with the knee-jerk assertion: This event was consequential rather than inconsequential. An apt rejoinder might be better served by questions such as these: What sort of inconsequential? In which disciplinary and semantic field might the inconsequentiality of the RINM become legible as a motivated practice—that is, as something possessing its own content and intent, rather than as the privation of some other set of normative revolutionary values? And, finally, what kind of consequentialism was it trying to counteract—moreover, what sort of real and imagined, moral and political worth obtains from a principled resistance to the abstract laws of consequence itself?

There is strong material evidence for the motivated nature of the mutiny's inconsequentiality in the papers and reports of the Royal Indian Navy Mutiny Commission, convened in May 1946 to inquire into the causes and effects of the February uprising. These are odd transcripts. Mutineers circumvented all efforts by the defense (and sometimes the prosecution as well) to clarify their revolutionary credentials and significance in traditional terms, such as protesting the intolerability of racism in the British army or establishing the legitimacy of armed struggle as a political practice. Instead, cross-examination records communicate the peculiar message that the overriding concern of the ratings, and one in which they had the full support of collaborating citizens, especially in Bombay, was simply for more tasty and luxurious cuisine than was available in Indian military messes. Believing the demand for very tasty food entirely consistent with anticolonial imperatives, accused rebels submitted various menus rather than charters of demands for official consideration.

When I first started working through the core documents for this chapter in the National Archives in Delhi, I was enormously disappointed by the startling triviality of the testimonies. Yet some intriguing anomalies did not quite add up. Notwithstanding ample evidence for the nationalist dismissal of the mutiny as an event of no consequence, mutineers hinted at the revolutionary worth of their own apparent self-trivialization. The present chapter takes this latter possibility seriously. To this end, while attempting to make historical sense of the naval mutiny in the context of the colonial militarization of South Asia, we will also consider it as an exemplification of a generalizable ethics of inconsequence (that is, of symbolic nonreproduction and anti-generativity). In the following sections we will therefore read the RINM across three registers: first, as the act of an anticolonial counterpublic that willfully harnessed the private-sphere affects deemed impertinent or ungenerative for political life by the prevailing/emergent public mainstream; second, as an instance of non-utilitarian (specifically neo-Kantian) *askesis*, at odds with considerations of causality (otherwise, sequence and effect) in moral procedure. Third, we will access the RINM in terms of its genealogical relation to the mutiny of 1857. From the mid–nineteenth century or so, colonial armed forces in South Asia regularly protested the invidious conversion of colonial worlds into garrison states designed to make the business of empire efficient and internally reproductive. Both through armed resistance against imperial officers and pacifist strategies of self-disarmament, these prior troops endeavored time and time again to undo the perpetuation of empire in themselves. Their refusal to be of any consequence to empire and its heirs was, I submit, inhabited, updated, and also globalized by the RINM and other mutinies in the world around 1946.

An Anticolonial Counterpublic

The RINM was an event of extraordinary scale and scope. Within a few days, every naval establishment across the country and off the coasts of the Arabian Sea, the Indian Ocean, and the Bay of Bengal was in open revolt against imperial military regimen. Ships as far afield as Aden and Bahrain set sail for Bombay to join the insurrection. Sympathizers included other branches of the armed forces, both native and non-native. The testimony of a British soldier, Sergeant A. B. Davis, speaks volumes: "Many of us sympathize with the Indian cause. We Socialists in the Army, and there

are many, are in a difficult position. Let not the people at home, therefore, blame us if 'authority' finds that it has to deal with us, as well as the
Indian people."[28] The revolt also gained mass civilian support across the
country, with scores of workers and students joining in demonstrations
and strikes.[29] Far from being spontaneous, this accelerated constituency
was produced by complex networks of communication and exchange.
Stemming from the RIN signal school HMIS *Talwar*, mutineers made visual
and wireless signal communication a top priority from the outset. Densely
coded semaphore messages transmitted to ships in the breakwater were
passed along to citizens via public address systems hitched to army lorries
cruising the streets.[30] A ratings-group memoir, *The RIN Strike*, showcases
the event as a buzz of conversation across normally antagonistic demogra-
phies (Hindu/Muslim, male/female, civilian/military), regrouping the city
into unlikely clusters of talk: "The whole of Thana was astir as the ratings
entered the town, shouting slogans. . . . The citizens going about their
daily business stopped to look at this strange and welcome sight. Gathered into knots they discussed this new upsurge among servicemen."[31] The
RINM also published itself through the circulation of cyclostyled leaflets
within greater Bombay. The last of these, issued upon surrender by the RIN
Central Strike Committee, represents the mutiny, not for the first time in
these proceedings, as a peculiar and somewhat sensationalist form of civil
society: "Our strike has been a historic event in the life of our nation. For
the first time the blood of men in the services and the men in the streets
flowed together in a common cause."[32]

The RINM premium on discursive interaction is a classic symptom, if
Jürgen Habermas is to be believed, of an emergent public sphere. Yet, pace
Vallabhai Patel's verdict (cited earlier in this discussion), due to its radical
divergence from an already existing oppositional mainstream, the RINM
collectivity is more accurately described as an anticolonial counterpublic. Some clarification of conventional usage is in order. First elaborated in
Habermas's classic work, *The Structural Transformation of the Public Sphere*
(1962), the concept "public sphere" designates an idealized locus of free,
consensus-forming, discussion in civil life: "a sphere of public deliberation
and resolution concerning the direction and administration of every process necessary for the reproduction of society."[33] Its function as the vehicle
of participatory democracy is to mark out an arena of political life not only
distinct from but also directly critical of the sphere of public authority (the
state, the economy, "the fictitious civil society of the legislature").[34] An opti-
mal public sphere attains, in Habermas's words, "the subjection of political
domination, as a domination of human beings over human beings, to reason."[35] Hence we obtain the aphorism, so rarely fulfilled within representa-

tive democracies, that only those governments are legitimate that take the talk of the public sphere as seriously as they do the votes of an electorate.

As various critics tell us, however, notwithstanding their historically critical/oppositional intent, modern publics are scarcely as universal or inclusive as they are taken to be, for at least two reasons. First, even the most open-minded of publics is susceptible to hegemonic saturation, namely, deference to the opinions of a single class or group that deems its own values to be more universal than those of others.[36] Second, the oftentimes prescriptive devolution of deliberative commonality—"there is one way in which we can talk ourselves into agreement"—can make even the most unrestricted of publics into zones of conformity. This happens by degrees. In their structural-democratic need for commensurable interlocutors, publics are said to exact nominal uniformity and neutrality from attending participants. The process requires the provisional erasure—Husserl might call this the *epochē*—of social and personal distinctions, whether of wealth or status. Such admittedly visible prohibitions are no bad thing, of course. In ideal circumstances they facilitate a socially pedagogic theater of equality in which a divergent citizenry practices intersubjective speech, testing out the livability of a world in which the most crucial existential resources (reason, speech, and time, among others) are now shared and held in common.[37] Yet, as we hear from a host of thinkers, the *epochē* of social distinction smuggles in a subsidiary mechanism of censorship. The mandatory impersonality of public spheres involves formal supersession or transcendence of what it marks as the first-order/primal or, strictly speaking, prepolitical realm of private life, with its inessential personal details: star-signs, hobbies, lucky numbers, and, in their wake, also illicit sexuality, mental illness, domestic violence, and other unspeakables.

Such pressures yield counterpublics: reactive formations constituted around the remaindered nuclei of personal life forms and styles.[38] These are reengaged, if only for reasons of chronology, as a type of second-order or postpolitical privacy (that is, a public privacy elicited rather than superseded by the event of politics). Some qualifications pertain. The counterpublic personalization or subjectivization of politics, as Michael Warner (following Hannah Arendt) tells us, instantiates a salutary socialization of private life. In Warner's words, "This entails the working assumption that the conditions of gender and sexuality can be treated not simply as the given necessities of the laboring body but as the occasion for forming publics, elaborating common worlds, making the transposition from shame to honor, from hiddenness to the exchange of viewpoints with generalized others, in such a way that the disclosure of self partakes of freedom."[39] Second-order or postpolitical privacy, thus, does not relinquish publicness so much as posit a corrective and, sometimes, competing public. In so doing, to cite Warner again, it "maintains at some level, conscious or not, an awareness of its subordinate status."[40] In this mood it is capable of harnessing its own secondariness—understood this time in the sense of "inferior," "minor," "lesser"—for the public good. Here the interest is not in the reification or exaltation of the personal to the given standards of political life, but in loving attentiveness precisely to what is uniquely inessential and unimportant about private life; in other words, to the realm of its constitutive inconsequentiality.[41]

To clarify: both publics and counterpublics can be said to reach for competing conditions of universality/inclusivity through competing appeals to self-forgetfulness. The former requires that we rise above our intimate *desiderata* (not to mention unwashed existential laundry) in order to qualify for the work of consensus-formation. The latter asks that we strive to fall short of social inscriptions (soldier, leader, parent, teacher, masculinity, wifeliness) so that civil society remains, to borrow some words from Derrida, "the theme of a non-presentable concept."[42] Let us gloss this a little further. Many theorists draw attention to the performativity of counterpublic political style.[43] By this is meant a politics whose worth is determined solely by the actions that constitute its reality, which we may therefore describe as "world-making"—that is, inventive/ creative rather than mimetic/semblative.[44] But, at its most eccentric, performativity (à la J. L. Austin) is also a studied impatience with antecedent or objective referents, or the view that signs must either stand for something already out there or designate it.[45] When counterpublics exercise performative impatience with already existing referents, they take on an additional task of world-unmaking—that is, of forging an exit or escape from given conditions. In other words, radical counterpublics (of the sort we are tracking and imagining into being) designate procedures of collaborative and communicative erasure. Their premium on cultivated secondariness undoes the multiple ways in which we are formally and institutionally recognizable (by office, role and function)—in the hope that we might together start over, perpetually and as though from an ideational ground zero.

Though generalized, this schema may yet orient our reading of the RINM's motivated inconsequentiality in the face of nationalist opprobrium, subject to a footnote. The properties we have been canvassing above obtain all the more starkly in anticolonial counterpublics and vis-à-vis the unique anomaly of the eternally absent/vanishing public sphere in colonial conditions. What does this mean? Liberal empire, as we learn from the postcolonial critic Homi Bhabha, is always prey to the paradox of

Janus-faced governmentality: the one, at home, born of public opinion—
"the spirited sound of the *vox populii*"—and another, abroad, entirely deaf
to the same.[46] To put this plainly, under empire (as under all totalitarian
conditions) there is no public sphere but only public authority. Paradoxi-
cally, when the imperial administration finally acquires the habit of cor-
recting its "own opinion and collating it with those of others"—as happened with the transfer of power proposals of February 1946—it briefly
conjures a public sphere only to reabsorb it immediately within public
authority, as a successor government.[47] The latter is no less eager to partake
of the shared line of descent, the inheritance on offer, by those degrees of
counterrevolutionary Thermidor so eloquently described by Karl Marx in
The Eighteenth Brumaire of Louis Bonaparte. "An entire people," Marx writes,
"which had imagined that by means of a revolution it had imparted to
itself an accelerated power of motion, suddenly finds itself set back into
a defunct epoch and, in order that no doubt as to the relapse may be possible, the old dates arise again, the old chronology, the old names, the old
edicts, which had long become a subject of antiquarian erudition, and the
old minions of the law, who had seemed long decayed."[48] This, to resume
our narrative, was the situation when the RINM broke out. In other words,
even as the Indian national movement retracted into an Indian national
government and relapsed into the infrastructure of the Raj, the inessential
sloganeering of the RINM (bidding the quitting empire to quit town and
wishing long life to the defunct independence struggle) declared the work
of anticolonialism to be still unfinished. But where were these declarations
situated—outside the new public sphere or inside the vacuum created by
the vanishing revolution? Do they belong to a counterpublic, a public, or
to something in between, dispersing inconsequentialist energy into the
ethical enclaves of an emerging civil society?[49] And what might an ethics
of inconsequence look like?

The RIN mutineers of 1946, we have been arguing, certainly had recourse to the structural opportunities of counterpublic formation in order to make the best of their disqualification in the immediate milieu of
mainstream anticolonial nationalism. The next section considers their
inconsequentiality, in more general terms, not merely as a contingent
discourse but as the locus of positive ethical value reaching for conditions
of unprecedented social inclusivity. The abstract ethical prototype that
we are after, however, is not without philosophical complications. The
political thinker John Rawls alerts us to this in the argument that no ethics
worth its salt can wholly disregard consequences in matters of moral judgment and action. As he puts it, "All ethical doctrines worth our attention
take consequences into account in judging rightness. One which did not

would simply be irrational."[50] Yet Rawls is circumspect about the extremist consequentialism of perfectionist or teleological ethics—utilitarianism is his prime example—for which the good in the sense of the greatest net balance of satisfaction is all that matters. The proper counter to this position, he suggests, resides in deontological intuitionism: an approach that is not exclusively ends-driven and gives equal merit to process and means, allowing questions of rightness, fairness, and distributive justice to intercept the summum bonum in moral calculation. The ethics that I am calling inconsequentialist belongs to intuitionism, though it altogether rejects the principle of moral causality (or causal temporality in moral matters) as too integrally bound to the conditions of an existing world order and subtended, thus, by an invidious logic of symbolic reproduction. In so doing, it appears as strictly ungenerative and as a type of symbolic celibacy. It is clarified, per se, in a significant, queer-theoretical uptake of Kantianism, as the refusal to participate in any perpetuation of the status quo and as a commitment to inconsequentials (or unimportant and inessential things) in social and political life. These emphases are exemplified at the source, in Kant's foundational critique of cause-and-effect reasoning and, more subtly, in the trope of dandyism secreted within his proposals for the categorical imperative. To such ethical modeling of inconsequentialism we can now turn.

Inconsequentialist Ethics and Nonreproductive Thought

Among the politics of nature that Bruno Latour laments in his book by that name, perhaps the most pernicious is the logic of symbolic reproduction as an unchallenged principle of social and political, not to mention, biological life.[51] Reproduction is the technology, Michel Foucault has amply demonstrated, for the regulatory mechanisms of modern bio-power. With time, the family takes over the franchise of the state, populating it and serving as "a privileged instrument for the government of the population."[52] These procedures are haunted by Vico's commendation of the family as the actuating principle of human ascendancy—becoming nation, extending law, acquiring property, "language, land, nuptials, name, arms, government."[53] In the transmission of these Vichean tropes, we can observe the sheer tenacity of reproduction as the metaphor-template not just for regulatory but also revolutionary forms of politics. Vico, for instance, is a key source for Marx's thinking about progressive historical development as a drama of generationality.[54] As we learn from another famous passage in *The Eighteenth Brumaire*, "Men make their own history, but they do not

make it just as they please; they do not make it under circumstances chosen by themselves, but under circumstances directly encountered, given
and transmitted from the past. The tradition of all the dead generations
weighs like a nightmare on the brain of the living."[55] Elsewhere, Marx
emphasizes the procreative modality of the dialectic itself. To say that
one class creates the conditions for its own vanquishment by another is,
eo ipso, to declare that "everything seems pregnant with its contrary."[56]
Through such emphases, intergenerativity has become the global sign of
our common condition and proxy symbol for radical universality.[57]

Yet queer thinkers have long taken the lead in looking outside the biological family for alternative models of social and political life. Michael
Warner's counterpublic is, after all, a model of affective community based
on inventive styles and forms of kinship—both affiliative, as Edward Said
might have it, and, more truculently, antifiliative.[58] In like register, Judith
Butler hails Antigone as an almost-queer heroine whose countermand to
the state derives from her messing up of given familial circuits (she is her
father's half-sister and her brother's aunt).[59] In recent years a telling shift
within this influential critique submits that the sociological problem of
the generative family is as nothing when compared to the naturalized
temporality that it standardizes in its wake. In other words, the difficulty
is not just that the traditional family generalizes as socially good the sole
proprieties of sexual difference. It is rather that it thereto institutionalizes
a purely procreative political futurity, overdetermined by the principles
of sequence and succession—that is, as Lee Edelman protests, by the figure of the child. In Edelman's words, "The image of the Child invariably
shapes the logic within which the political itself must be thought. That
logic compels us, to the extent that we would register as politically responsible, to submit to the framing of political debate—and, indeed, of the
political field—as defined by the terms of . . . reproductive futurism. . . .
What, in that case, would it signify *not* to be "fighting for the children"?[60]
If Edelman's polemic calls for the suspension of causative thinking/action,
Heather Love's book, *Feeling Backward*, goes a step further and asks that we
reverse the imaginary of successive time.[61] In so doing, kin theorists argue, we exit the privileges of real and symbolic/social reproduction. More
acutely, we democratize our consciousness by sacrificing our *telos*.[62] Thus,
to be nonsuccessive, as Judith Halberstam contends, augurs voluntary
nonsuccessfulness: a "queer art of failure."[63] Heather Love's backwardness,
likewise, is the stigmata of "disqualified identity": the basis, à la Warner,
for a "common experience of being despised and rejected."[64] Or as Annamarie Jagose suggests in her book, *Inconsequence*, to step out of established
sequence is to draw strength from "irrelevance."[65] This program for un-

generative community is heavily underwritten by the influence of Kantian ethics—also the true source for our speculations.

Many commentators have noted the recursivity of ethics in the last decade or so of Kant's work.[66] Read together, his *Groundwork of the Metaphysics of Morals* (1785) and *Metaphysics of Morals* (1797), especially, refine a model of universalism based on ego-reduction and, thence, a critical offensive against causative temporality. Very often in Kant's ethical writing, self-love is figured as self-perpetuation; a "complete well-being and satisfaction with one's condition," that makes an instrument, or mere end, of other entities.[67] Though there are various spheres for the pursuit of self-perpetuation ("power, riches, honor, even health"), the sexually generative family remains a key material domain and clear example of the moral hazards involved in uncritically reproducing ourselves and our mortal comforts in and through others.[68] Procreating adults, Kant infamously observes, connotatively cannibalize each other: "The woman is consumed with pregnancy and perhaps fatal delivery resulting from it, or the man by exhaustion of his sexual capacity from the woman's frequent demands upon it."[69] They also cannibalize their children, through a strange "right to use them," without so much as a contract, in "the *service* of the family (*famulatus*)."[70] Ethics can arrest the compulsive iterativity of the ego, however, through practices of strict submission to the unconditionality of what Kant calls the categorical imperative. This entails a self-work of symbolic celibacy whereby inconsequence is affirmed as the cornerstone of radical intuitionism.

To recall, the Kantian categorical imperative inhabits the sixth sense that makes us simultaneously the subjects and objects of our free will by compelling us to treat others as we would have them treat us. Replacing the figure of the "dear self" with the figure of "everyone," it tricks us into becoming other-regarding precisely when most self-regarding. Differently, it closes the gap between *freedom* and *goodwill* through fractional reductions that extract an ultimately equivalent value from these inimical terms.[71] By this law, our sovereign spirit becomes the route to radical intersubjectivity, through which we discover "humanity in our person" or "humanity in our subject."[72] To become alert to such intimations of psychic democracy, however, we must routinely disengage from the principles of causality or generative/successive/sequential temporality. Why? Because the categorical imperative is an uncaused causelessness. Lacking both past and future, it is an apodictic principle temporally marked by the character of immediacy.[73] Two rules follow. First, we cannot be coerced under its dictate by any prior law.[74] In other words, there exist no antecedent models or examples for it by which it may be acquired through skills of imitation or through capacities of understanding.[75] Thus, to possess it or know it is, strictly speaking, unremarkable. "Virtue," Kant tells us, "is not to be defined and valued . . . as an aptitude."[76] Second (and with similar conclusions in train), there is no way of establishing successful outcomes for virtue since it is its own end; it lacks measurable effect to the same degree that it lacks an efficient cause. Accordingly, achievement is no measure of moral worth: "If with its greatest efforts it should yet achieve nothing and only the good will were left, . . . then, like a jewel, it would still shine by itself, as something that has full worth in itself. Usefulness or fruitlessness can neither add anything to this worth nor take anything away from it."[77] Furthermore, Kant submits, as a science of "oughts," ethical consciousness is structured by failure; it is an earnest striving for goods that must nevertheless remain unfulfilled: "It is a human being's duty to strive . . . for perfection, but not to reach it."[78] Thus we get the following multivariate linear regression: the critique of self-perpetuation equals a disregard for the principles of causality, which equals a subject markedly shorn of aptitudes, gifts, or inheritances and also lacking in any feats, achievements, legacies, or consequences to write home about.

How does this project compare with actual practices of sexual/biological non-generativity? Out of the wealth of available materials, a quick look at the temporal adjustments of the early Christian celibates, whom Peter Brown has brought so vividly to life in his *The Body and Society* (1988), yields some instructive conundrums.[79] In this prior tradition, Brown suggests, the discourse on celibacy sometimes manifests as but a *de contemptus mundi* type of social critique, offering to protect elect votaries from the contaminants of the contemptible world. The tradition tends in the opposite direction of ameliorative ethics whenever it supplements the desire for moral immaculacy for a chosen few with reversed proposals to protect the world at large from elite self-interest. When figures such as John Chrysostom and Gregory of Nyssa describe celibacy as a disinvestment in material perpetuity, whether of bloodline, wealth, or status, for instance, non-generativity expresses specific disinterest in worldly distinction or in the desire to secure a privileged place in historical time.[80] In these cases, celibacy becomes an art of self-extinction, not unlike the one at the heart of queer Kantianism. While intersecting with such crucial prior sermons on humility, charity, and continence, however, the inconsequentialist ideal and regimen of symbolic celibacy we are tracking possess a signatory comic-bathetic register as well. After all, inconsequence also stands for inessentials, trifles, and superfluities—namely, non-self-serious forms of self-reduction. This more playful mode is surprisingly well substantiated by Kant himself and is accessible by the route of the established consequentialist critique of Kantian ethics, beginning with Hegel and reaching a zenith with nineteenth-century utilitarianism.

The view that actions are right or wrong only in view of their consequences, or what they actually engender in the world, has long defended itself as a credo of "the concrete" pertaining to the necessary needs of robust tangible beings.[81] When applied to the matter of Kantian inconsequentialism, such objections frequently turn personal. The charge that Kant is too anti-empirical to be useful in real-life situations is common among his detractors, and smuggles in contingent distaste for something rather like his unmanly unnaturalness. Hegel famously decries Kantianism as the cringing project of "not wanting to go into the water before we have learnt to swim."[82] Ignoring the training procedures of synchronized swimmers (whose moves are often rehearsed outside the water, and who certainly remain quite immaculate within it), the spirit of Hegel's critique haunts the tired theme of Kant's sexual nonbiography. How frequently we hear the complaint that Kant had no life because he was a confirmed bachelor. Since he neither "married or travelled," writes one editor, his life was "so outwardly quiet and routine as to defy biographical narration."[83] Another commentator puts it more plainly: "Kant lived a life of celibacy, and had none of the joys nor the cares arising out of the married state: hence we have neither courtship, nor marriage, nor births, nor deaths, to relate."[84]

As it happens, we do have access to a well-closeted, queer biography for Kant, wherein his celibacy denotes a wealth of life practices, not all of them (if any) sexual. We learn from Manfred Kuehn, for example, that Kant and his old friend Johann Georg Hamann shared a mutual friend, the son of an old Hansa trading family, who was sent to London to be cured (unsuccessfully), of certain tendencies. Through the latter, Hamann "came into close contact with members of London's homosexual community."[85] The correspondence between Kant and Hamann (some concerning this friend) is no less void of its own passionate remonstrance. In one letter of rivalry over yet another mutual friend, Hamann accuses Kant of wanting to play Socrates to the other's Alcibiades.[86] Surely these were loaded references for a generation already tutored by Johann Joachim Winckelmann's scandalous life and writings, the latter revealing an ancient Greece of erotic male friendship and male beauty at the very font of European culture.[87] Add to this the concatenation of very young men at Kant's lunchtime salons, and we arrive at the possibility that, as Eric Clarke puts it, "Kant, it might seem, was simply an old queen."[88] So what, we might ask? Only that it reveals a particular life where one had so noisily been lacking. In what, then, does this way of life consist, and how does it square up with the more substantive content of this philosopher's ethical program?[89]

Kantian symbolic celibacy, it appears, is not underwritten by its author's tragic failure to marry and be generative. Nor is it animated by artful
homosexual escapades. Instead, we do find detailed material as to Kant's
fastidious dandyism: a single-minded pursuit of inconsequentials in dress,
deportment, and sociability that substitutes recreation for procreation—
namely, taking doing nothing very seriously indeed. These anomalous
fripperies crop up in the dullest accounts of Kant's bachelor existence. The
details in most cases come from a memoir of Kant's late years, written by
Ehregott Andreas Christoph Wasianski, a former student of the philosopher's who had long departed the university system to become an amateur
florist.[90] From Wasianski, and from Thomas De Quincey's English paraphrase and embellishment of the former's text, we learn about the artistry
of Kant's daily lunch parties, which lasted several hours around a table of
never less than two nor more than five young men. Even at five feet nothing or so, it seems that Kant was something of a beau—an elegant *magister*,
inclined to ornamentation and nonfunctionality in costume. He held to
the maxim that the color of dress should follow the flowers. Thus a brown
coat required a yellow vest. This combined with his love for outerwear
with golden borders made him somewhat conspicuous amidst the blacks
and grays of pietistic Königsberg. Understandably keen not to despoil his
clothing, he tried never to perspire, sometimes standing still for ages to
fend off the unwelcome onset of sweat during a walk. Emblematic of this
care for unnecessary detail is the impractical and elaborate garter device
that Kant invented to keep up his exquisite stockings. Here is a description
in De Quincey's words:

In a little pocket, somewhat smaller than a watch-pocket, but occupying pretty nearly
the same situation as a watch-pocket on each thigh, there was placed a small box,
something like a watch-case, but smaller; into this box was introduced a watch spring
in a wheel, round about which wheel was wound an elastic cord, for regulating the
force of which there was a separate contrivance. To the two ends of this cord were
attached hooks, which hooks were carried through a small aperture in the pockets,
and so, passing down the inner and outer side of the thigh, caught hold of two loops
which were fixed on the off-side and the near-side of each stocking.[91]

Among the handful of commentators who enable us to connect Kantian lifestyle to Kantian ethics, Michel Foucault remains exemplary. He
makes no direct reference to the details canvassed above, notwithstanding
his own early work on Kant's *Anthropology*, which explicitly praises fashion as the sphere in which there is "no regard to utility" or to "custom,"
and which, therefore, represents "mutable ways of living."[92] Yet, in his es-

say "What Is Enlightenment," Foucault connects the apparent sobriety of Kantian *Ausgang*—the "way out" or "exit" from received truths recommended by so many enlightenment philosophes—to the subcultural practices of modern *dandysme*. According to Foucault, *Ausgang* and *dandysme* together represent related limit-attitudes designating "a philosophical life in which the critique of what we are is at one and the same time the historical analysis of the limits that are imposed on us and an experiment with the possibility of going beyond them."[93] And one way of going beyond the historical limits imposed on us, as we have been arguing and, perhaps, as Kant hints as well, is by refusing to take them seriously. By stepping out of time (or getting out of sync) with prevailing norms/means of social and biological self-perfection, we may also begin to intuit the sympathetic other-regard enshrined in the categorical imperative.

In summary, a certain problematization of temporality within contemporary queer theory sharpens critical-theoretical distinctions pertinent to this discussion. We learn that much remedial thought divides into competing attitudes of symbolic reproduction and symbolic celibacy. Symbolic reproduction defends consequentialism in ethics and politics. This means valuing actions by virtue of what they actually achieve in the world or in the terrain of empirical existence. It is marked by an aesthetics of generativity, succession and sequence deriving from the romance of the reproductive family and focused on progressive achievement. In contrast, symbolic celibacy takes the form of inconsequentialist ethics. Its program for radical universality is marked by a perverse and implicitly queer critique of causality, which treats virtue as its own end, without care for rewards and commendations that might accrue to the bearer. It also suggests that rich ethical possibilities inhere in a lifestyle of little or no consequence.

Did the RIN mutineers have access to an indigenous ethics of inconsequence in these terms? There are some clues in the genealogical relation between the 1946 mutiny and its 1857 precursor that point to the nonsuccessive and success-averting energies of anticolonial mutinies in general and in relation to the logic of perpetual war. This history, along with the material practices of inconsequentiality subsequently developed by South Asian and other transnational mutineers around 1946—and disconcertingly in evidence at the RINM trials—occupies the remainder of our discussion.

A Genealogy for Anticolonial Mutiny

In *The History of the Indian Mutiny of 1857–58* (1888), Sir John Kaye is at some pains to exonerate the Indian soldiers who broke out in armed rebellion during the great mutiny of 1857, nearly a century before the transnational mutinies of 1946. His view that the events of 1857 constituted a revolt rather than a mutiny of undisciplined troops is born of the conviction that the "black commandant was once a great man," and that "the fidelity of the native army of India was an established article of our faith."[94] Far better, Kaye concedes, to attribute the unrest to political factions still under fealty to the declining Mughal Empire and its degenerate potentates. Though for different reasons, there is a surprising degree of historiographical consensus on the ultimately marginal role played by the *sipahi* (or "sepoy") in the making of the sepoy mutiny. Nationalists such as Jawaharlal Nehru argue that what happened in 1857, "was much more than a military mutiny" for the reason that "it spread rapidly and assumed the character of a popular rebellion and a war of Indian independence."[95] Karl Marx and Frederick Engels also concur in their journalistic dispatches on the event, calling the mutiny "the first Indian war of Independence." While rejoicing in the eruption of social revolution in asiatically despotic India, they register a low opinion of the *sipahi*'s contribution to the cause, and condemn his lamentable fighting spirit. "One grand and unanimous act of bolting," they observe all the way from the British Library in London; "a general helter-skelter to the rear, . . . they fall pell-mell, and without any resistance, under the volleys and bayonets of the advancing British."[96] Yet what would happen if we allowed the sepoy to inhabit the center of this story?

Early in his history of military unrest in the empire, Kaye notes, with some pride, the extraordinary success with which Britain had progressively transformed the Indian subcontinent into a garrison state.[97] He describes the systematic measures whereby, from the late eighteenth century onward, the "handful of blacks" engaged in the Battle of Plassey against French interests in India evolved into a gigantic army of which "a small part only . . . was composed of our countrymen."[98] This disproportionate representation, he insists, was entirely justifiable for the following reasons: "Neither the manhood of England nor the revenues of India could supply the means of defending the country only with British troops. A large majority of our fighting-men were, therefore, natives of India, trained, disciplined, and equipped after the English fashion. We had first learnt from the French the readiness with which the 'Moors' and the 'Goths' could be made to adapt themselves to the habits and forms of European warfare, and, for a hundred years, we had been improving the lesson."[99] Though intended as a standing army, these forces soon proved indispensable to British expansionist efforts and muscle-wielding both within India and beyond its borders, along the Northwest Frontier and as far afield as China and Persia. Native troops were also marked for action in the Crimean war.[100]

Almost every such attempt to engage native troops in the business of European territorialism, however, yielded a minor mutiny—never mind how intently Kaye avoids calling insubordination among native ranks by that unfavorable name. Indian soldiers regularly refused to enter forcibly acquired provinces in the guise of an invading army. They also refused to bear arms and receive remuneration for expansionist activities. Over time, the sepoy, as Kaye reluctantly concedes, "had evinced a disposition . . . rather to injure himself than to injure others."[101] Accordingly, most imperial military strategists of the time were of the view that, though indubitably loyal to his masters and their colors, "the *sipahi* is not the man of consequence he was. He dislikes annexations."[102]

These explanations of mutiny as a product of the *sipahi*'s historic loss of consequence must be taken seriously. They gain substance in the testimony supplied to Kaye by a Brahmin Jemadar, a low-ranking commissioned officer of the Oudh Artillery: "He [said] that he knew that we had plenty of men and money but that Europeans are expensive, and that, therefore, we wished to take Hindus to sea to conquer the world for us. On my remarking that the Sipahi, though a good soldier on shore, is a bad one at sea, by reason of his poor food, 'That is just it,' was his rejoinder. 'You want all of us to eat what you like that we may be stronger, and go everywhere.'"[103] In this account (corroborated by various other participant testimonies), mutiny is finally described as indexical of the growing fear among native soldiers that colonial armed service would transform them, by degrees, into proxy conquerors: a conquering race of conquered men compelled to reproduce empire in themselves through somatic-occult interference in matters of dress and diet. *Sipahis* feared the transforming effect of the leather in their military regalia; they believed that cow-bones had been mixed into the very salt that sealed their loyalty to British regiments. So too, we hear often enough of the religious taboos that provoked the events of 1857: the classic rumor, for instance, that cartridges were being greased with pork and beef tallow, making them unusable both for Hindu and Muslim soldiers. But Kaye's Jemadar glosses the concept of taboo in far richer register. His dietary anxieties do not concern the loss of traditional identity so much as the intolerability of gaining an unwanted identity—in this case, turning imperialist. Thus, we might surmise, the crisis of 1857 was not just caused by men of compromised loyalty caught on the troublesome cusp of an emergent nationalism. It also expressed ethical squeamishness about the shared entitlements of world conquest.

The perception that anticolonial mutiny may be a form of conquest-aversion was certainly registered in the army recruitment reforms brought into effect by the final decades of the nineteenth century. A telling anomaly starts to show up in the official *Recruitment Handbooks* written by India-hand British officers and issued from the 1890s onward by the Government of India. These texts, which guided recruitment strategy until the Second World War, clarify strict protocols for identifying nonmutinous character along with an apparently contradictory premium on so-called martial races.[104] More precisely, recruitment guidelines and statistics iterate as a rule of thumb that tribes or subcastes that remained loyal during the mutiny were also those with three accompanying characteristics: first, highly developed conquering instincts; second, a circumscribed range of emotional sympathies; and, third, a noticeable lack of reflexivity and inwardness. Those of mutinous character, on the other hand, had a low violence threshold, a wide kinship range, and far too much interiority. By the start of the Great War, this tripartite formula was established as foolproof, and the Jemadar's fears were well and truly confirmed.

A theory of martial races had implicitly guided enlistment practices within the British Isles from at least the mid–eighteenth century. Warlike Scottish highlanders and Irishmen were consistently overrepresented in the British Army. It remained an informal discourse, however, until its codification for Indian recruitment purposes clarified the martial race/type paradigm as a taxonomy of aggression. Subsequent recruitment manuals uniformly declare vengefulness, fanaticism, criminality, spleen, and irascibility as desirable traits for a good fighting man and safeguards against mutiny in the ranks. The Alpial, we learn from J. M. Wikely's handbook on Punjabi Muslims, is, "wonderfully quarrelsome."[105] In like vein, Major Holland-Pryor reasons of the otherwise irregulable Moplahs that "the power of their fanaticism was astounding."[106] In general, colonial martial race theorists believed they had discovered the secret factors for governable native blood lust and for identifying fighting men with special immunity against the nationwide temptations of *ahimsa*, or nonviolence. Indian soldiery, we hear from the redoubtable Sir George Macmunn, "have resisted inoculation with the Ghandi [*sic*] poison." Elsewhere he proclaims certain species of bellicose native soldiers to be born of a rare stock, "whom surely Baba Ghandi [*sic*] never fathered."[107]

Though later writers like Macmunn absorbed the martial race theory within the contemporary discourse of racial ethnology (discussed in chapter 2), others insisted on the non-ethnological motivations of their work.[108] The preference for men from endogamous rather than exogamous tribes, we learn, was only secondarily an interest in establishing pure bloodline. Rather, it signaled the military worth of circumscribed affect or emotional provinciality. Endogamous men only married "within the circle of near relations, and marriages between first cousins are common."[109] Such men were also naturally xenophobic. Thus, the legendary Gurkhas, as Major C. J. Morris avers, are appealingly rude to those who do not speak their language and reliably "suspicious of strangers."[110] In direct contrast, exogamous men are unfit for work in an imperial-territorial army for reason of their sweeping sympathies and willingness to forge common cause with aliens in unknown lands. A series comes into view. The bad character of members of the Lilla tribe, who permit widow remarriage and intermarry at random, is of a piece with the low "moral character" of the diasporic Tanaoli who "have taken to seeking work abroad and . . . are not by any means fully recruited."[111] The nomadic Ghilzai are equally suspect: "A large number . . . migrate annually into British India; . . . some even travel as far afield as Australia, and it is not uncommon to hear the greeting 'Morning Boss' in an Australian twang from a shaggy coated Ghilzai on the frontier."[112] It is here that recruitment procedures are very precise. To safeguard against individuals with ambient kinship capacity, they instruct, men must never be enlisted at bazaars and fairgrounds. Most of all, "recruiters should be warned against picking up boys on the road."[113] Thus, recruitment ledgers became tests of eligibility. A candidate was only rendered fit for enlistment if he could be reliably situated within the tightest geographical and psychic radius: "It is imperative to ascertain that the village from which the man comes belongs to the clan the man claims to belong to, and that the man has a hereditary share in his land. . . . His name should appear in the . . . book of hereditary landowners."[114]

Matching this embargo on widened affective circumference was another, albeit harder to track, against reflexivity. Time and time again we encounter the nexus between warlikeness and stupidity as one endorsed by a policy favoring recruitment from regions with the highest illiteracy and lowest exposure, especially, to Western education.[115] Such individuals, cheery like the rural Punjabi, or simple like the hill-dwelling Gurkha, were considered supremely amenable to command. The thinking they could not do for themselves, John Masters recalls, "we were there for."[116] Detested, in contrast, were individuals with hidden depth or zones of interiority inaccessible to external interference. Shia sects for instance, were rarely recruited for reason of their alleged ability to conceal their inmost faith from view, "by a sort of religious compromise called 'zakia' (guarding oneself)."[117] This figurative space of zakia, to recall our discussion of Kant in the previous section, is not dissimilar from the autonomous terrain of the self-regulatory categorical imperative. A safeguard against external command (military discipline, political power, and religious authority), it also threatened to transform "the guardians of empire," as Indian soldiers were so often called, into subjects potentially resistant to the temptations of imperialism.

If the army reforms of the 1890s conceived of nonmutinous character as the capacity to reproduce empire without troublesome ethical reflux, then, how far did subsequent mutinies reverse or stall this programming? Is there anything in RINM procedures that shares the spirit of Kaye's Jemadar, phobically refusing to advance the business of world conquest in himself, even at the risk of appearing inconsequential? Indeed, does inconsequentialism become recognizable as a critique of conquest and advancement and as a badge of postcolonial democracy in the time lag between the Jemadar and the rating? Though we can certainly engage such questions through the evidence of the RINM trial proceedings, these material coordinates do not strictly exemplify our conceptual paradigms. This archive, as with any other, merely helps us to place the realm of happening in tentative dialogue with the realm of possibility.

Food for Thought

The RIN mutineers were tried in camera in the summer of 1946 by a Commission of Enquiry. Along with other sources, the testimonies gathered by commissioners confirm that, much like their 1857 precursors, these mutineers sought to exit the obsolete imperial army to which they were hostage and to exhibit this act as its own revolutionary end. With near equal fervor, however, they wished to apprise the international public of their commitment to good food. Unlikely though it may seem, the twin procedures of exiting the army and being fastidious about food are ethically of a piece.

The RINM began as a symbolic exit from the barracks, announced with the slogan, *"bahar chalo!"*—literally, "Come outside." Newspaper reports point to the subsequent craze for civilian clothing among conscripted men and note their conspicuous reentry into the common crowd; marching in demonstrations with the denizens of Bombay and mingling with commuters on the city's many suburban trains and buses. Civilians joined in the enterprise and urged naval officers to discard military insignia. Officers who obliged voluntarily, through public acts of disinvestiture, were commemorated enthusiastically, as this example from RINM mythology tells us: "Suddenly an Indian officer, a Lieutenant, entered the room. There was a suspicious silence. Everyone looked at him, hostility in his eyes. . . . But the Lieutenant paused only a few seconds to look at the astounded groups of ratings and promptly began to address them. 'I have come to join you,' he said. . . . Dramatically he tore off his badges of rank. Spontaneously the ratings cheered."[118] Such rituals are clarified in mutineer testimonies as a therapeutic theater of self-reduction, born of the diagnosis that military service invaded the soldier-host's temperament as an accretive habit of hierarchy. "We the Indian defense forces were fighting to keep down our brother nations[s] and keep them down under subjugation," we hear from a rating who was enlisted for the suppression of anticolonial nationalisms in Southeast Asia.[119] "Servicemen were the stooges of British imperialism," another protests, bemoaning the inherited nature of totalitarian consciousness: "Servicemen too behaved in the railway trains and other places as if they were the '*herrenvolk*.' They never shirked to boss over their people."[120]

Though witnesses highlighted the inwardly directed nature of their struggle, they refused to accrue moral credit for their convictions. Available transcripts show defense and prosecution attorneys alike pressing the accused to communicate the exceptionality of the outbreak: "What were the immediate causes, . . . any kind of cause? . . . Would it cause a mutiny if a rating was arrested for doing any error or default or for misconduct? Why should it cause a mutiny?"[121] Answers invariably reverted to the problem of food in imperial military messes for native soldiers/sailors. For example, A. K. Mitra (a writer in HMIS *Feroze*) said, "Because first and foremost the food was bad,"[122] and P. M. Thomas, the wireless and telegraph operator in HMIS *Nasik*, said, "Because we were getting bad food always."[123] Such explanations were severely contested during cross-examinations and, at the outset of the proceedings, declared inadmissible for their triviality. The complaint would not hold, an Indian officer reasons, within a functioning household, far less in a military mess: "I consider it frivolous that if I had the same *chappati* at home, I would kick up a fuss and row with my mother."[124] Others are bewildered that so minor a grievance should "end up in a conflagration of this nature,"[125] especially when the grievance appears as a self-directed *ad hominem* attack, and the participants minimize the heroics of their cause by deriding their personal exemplification of it. The evidence that the ratings' lowering discourse on food was in fact fabricated and put into circulation only after the outbreak of mutiny further complicates the case. In the transcripts, Mr. Justice Iyenger asks, "So you say till February 19th when the mutiny broke out you never had any complaint about food, verbal or written from the ratings?" An Indian officer from the HMIS *Castle Barracks*, H. Arjun Singh, replies, "After the mutiny we got many complaints. I did not receive any complaints before then."[126]

Outraged by the willful lack of gravity among witnesses, the officials, as well as some ratings, struggled to establish the political *bona fides* of the unrest. "You joined this mutiny for the freedom of your country . . .? And not for food?" a defense attorney asks encouragingly of a witness.[127] A sailor capitulates before such cross-examination: "Our cry was 'Jai Hind,'

'Quit India,' 'Down with Imperialism,' etc. not 'Bread, butter and jam. . . . To revolt against imperialism, that is the main point of our strike, why to blame *dal*."[128] On occasion officials prompted witnesses to link disaffection among the ranks to racial discrimination in the services. To this end, some pointed to increased naval recruitment, among officer-classes, of former plantation bosses: men weaned on racial hierarchy and bad language. Others hinted at the ratings' additional exposure to racism due to the wartime rerouting of ships through South African ports, already infamous for their bigotry. By another track, and with reference to the directives of the recruiting manuals examined in the previous section, British military witnesses attributed the mutiny to the accelerated naval intake of "educated boys" during the Second World War: "The type of man required to deal with modern developments must be more highly educated than the old-fashioned sailor or the average soldier. Such men recruited from the student class have in all countries shown a dislike for discipline and, particularly in India, an exaggerated sense of their dignity and importance."[129] No less suspect was the contingent cosmopolitanism of naval service. "Navy . . . people," an attorney avers, "go out, mix with peoples of other countries."[130] And literate sailors with extensive seafaring experience, he adds, invariably possess seditious reading matter. A sailor called Solomon, for instance, had a copy of Nehru's *An Autobiography* concealed in his trunk. Material confiscated from the telegraphist B. C. Dutt, of the HMIS *Talwar*, included one revolutionary diary, some of Nehru's selected speeches, a book entitled *Communist Answer to the Congress Charges,* and a well-thumbed if obscure history of the 1857 mutiny.

Frustrated by the poor witness uptake of prompts refuting the political vacuity of their cause, notaries gradually began to engage with the putative issue of food as the trials progressed, though sometimes with misplaced earnestness. The prosecution, for instance, arbitrarily built a case out of the problem of quantity. Individual vital statistics were painstakingly compiled and analyzed in the courtroom so as to offset the potential complaint that ratings were not being fed enough. Most mutineers, we learn, improved their physique sizably on the given naval diet.

Question to A. K. Khan, Telegraphist, HMIS *Talwar*: How much do you weigh now: Do you know?
Answer: No sir. Not exactly.
Question: Do you know that when you went to the HMIS *Bahadur* your weight was only 78 lbs. . . . ? You left *Bahadur* 16 months later, and you had grown an inch and a half and that was at the age of 17. Do you not consider that you put on quite a considerable amount of weight?[131]

In reaction, the defense rebuilt its case upon evidence for the poor quality of military food, often with respect to its alleged inedibility. Baroque descriptions ensued. We hear that the meat served in naval messes was 70 percent bone, the flour full of sand and worms, and that the rice contained some 20 percent of cleverly disguised stones. During these protracted sequences, defense lawyers, especially, capitulated to a food-fastidiousness of their own, their line of questioning dwelling in increased detail on the ideal taste and texture of raw and cooked foods.

> Mr. Tricumdas (to officer in charge of food tasting in one naval establishment): Have you tasted the food quite a number of times . . . ? Is the procedure something like this. I have some experience of how food is tasted in jails. What is done is, the "C" class is brought before the medical officer and he takes a minute particle of the food and says: "*accha le jao*" ("fine, take it away"). I want to know if that is the procedure you adopt on the occasions when you taste this food?
>
> Lieutenant Kohli: I would not say I take a minute particle of food, but a full mouthful is taken.
>
> Mr. Tricumdas: I take it that you come across stones in the rice?
>
> Lieutenant Kohli: Sometimes.
>
> Mr. Tricumdas: Quite a quantity of stones?
>
> Lieutenant Kohli [visibly agitated]: How can you have a quantity of stones in a mouthful?[132]

As it happens, RIN mutineers were relatively unconcerned about the issues of quantity and quality. When questioned along these lines, they insisted that their plainly inessential demand was for exceptionally tasty food, not more food or quality-controlled food. The mutiny, we gather, concerned the palate as much as the stomach. "We do not *like* the cooking," as G. Ramachandra Rao from the HMIS *Feroze* put it starkly. Another gormandizing witnesses complained that too much of the navy *ghee* ration was expended in crude curry (where it could scarcely be detected), when some should have been reserved for use, to more palpable effect, on *paranthas* and toasts. It was especially regrettable, he adds, that ordinary *chappatis* were served more frequently than festive *paranthas*.[133] Elsewhere we hear objections regarding the "improper proportion of *masala*" and poor food presentation, what with "some *dal* and some curry, all in one plate."[134] Rare was the day at the HMIS *Talwar*, apparently, "when the cook somehow manages to stumble in putting the proper-proper proportion of condiments."[135] Thus, while supporters beyond the courtrooms waited patiently for a verdict, litigators and witnesses at the inquiry combined in animated conversation about the culinary arts, sharing regional preferences and swapping recipes. Moved by one mutineer's food fantasy, a presiding judge, Justice Mahajan, as transcripts report, momentarily lost himself in a reverie about the decline of pure cow's milk *ghee* in India: "Do you know that the real *ghee* has vanished from India?"[136]

Not everyone was thus moved, however, least of all Admiral J. H. Godfrey, the flag officer in charge of the Royal Indian Navy who had quelled the RINM with a massive show of British military reinforcements and a decisive ultimatum that ratings prepare to "submit or perish." Godfrey's snide testimony at the witness stand stresses the particular impropriety of the RINM's preoccupation with state-of-the-art cuisine in the context of the dire famine threat that was hanging over the Indian subcontinent in the early months of 1946. At the time of the RINM outbreak in mid-February, the imperial administration had declared the food situation in India to be desperate, perhaps more so than ever before in the twentieth century. This was not a matter of shortage but "of stark complete hunger," potentially devastating to an already undernourished population with few reserves of energy to draw on. Widespread food riots were expected, and an estimated ten million people were declared likely to perish in the imminent famine.[137] In view of the impending catastrophe, the viceroy, Viscount Wavell, issued a severe ration cut throughout India and "asked for sacrifices by rich and poor to avert starvation."[138] Admiral Godfrey righteously summoned such sentiments in answer to the mutineers. "In any other country," he protested, "this demand, raised at a time when famine threatens the whole community, would have put the entire nation against the mutineer, but in this country, where there is no such thing as public opinion, this was not the case, and not one voice has been raised in the press against this demand."[139] It is striking, as Godfrey points out, that public opinion was so overwhelmingly in favor of RINM concerns over food at a time of potential mass starvation. The reason, we can only conjecture, may have something to do with the acuity with which mutineers conveyed the global import of their agitation, and the continuum between eating sumptuously and self-disarmament. They did so, let me further suggest, through a subtle variation on the spectral, neo-Malthusian ethics haunting Wavell's and Godfrey's recommendations of austerity as the only attitude proper to famished populations. In a previous chapter we have observed the voluntary recourse to this catechism of sacrifice among native soldiers in the Great War. But none were willing to have it enforced upon a subject population by imperial conscience-keepers in the context under review here. Why not?

As is well known, the Malthusian ratio whereby population growth is always greater than food supply is often accompanied by the adage that famine is nature's restraint on the impoverished multitude and inducement for their self-restraint in matters of consumption. In these cases the recommendation is not merely that the poor should reproduce infrequently but, as we learn from the neo-Malthusian James Bonar, that they must acclimatize to necessity. In other words eating/having less is the stark neo-Malthusian corollary to breeding less. As Bonar puts it, "So far as legal relief goes, Malthus would recommend . . . martial severity, and try and put men on their guard against poverty by making them bear the discipline of its consequences."[140] More succinctly, to cite Bonar again, "It was the poor man's interest to be thrifty and sober."[141] In this authoritarian moral system, moreover, the selective prophylaxis on the very life of the poor is pari passu with arguments defending the protected symbolic perpetuation of those believed to count for more, in civilizational terms, and so forth. By this route, colonial neo-Malthusianism, especially, becomes a discourse of entitlement. This the view taken by the economist-philosopher Amartya Sen, who points to the comparative rarity of famines in democratic regimes, where the law encourages a greater measure of resource sharing and intrahuman commensurability. By Sen's account, starvation is rarely, if ever, an effect of food shortage per se; it is rather an effect of the decline in the exchange entitlements of a given group or individual that affects the bundle of material and immaterial worth that they embody or command.[142] These themes are prescient in respect of the historical moment that concerns our discussion.

It is clearer now than ever before that the new imperialisms of the twentieth century were implicated in a ruthless struggle for food hierarchy provoked by the rising living standards and increased consumption of their respective urban-industrialized populations. In the resulting conflicts to secure and monopolize food supply, especially through the Second World War, an estimated twenty million people—variously considered to be superfluous eaters by policymakers—died from starvation, malnutrition, and associated diseases. Though Germany and Japan were unmatched in the exploitation of imperial resources, Allied forces were also culpable of mismanagement and neglect. In Africa Britain interfered disastrously in traditional crop production and in agrarian life by diverting native workers to mines and subsidized "white-farms."[143] In India, during the long lead up to the events surrounding the RINM, Viceroy Wavell had overseen the exacerbation of famine conditions through the implementation of Winston Churchill's wartime scorched-earth policy. This involved the destruction of territories (and contingent food sources) potentially vulnerable to enemy access. From 1941 onward, the administration guarded itself against the threat of Japanese invasion through the preemptive destruction and wasting of the food supply across Burma and coastal Bengal. In the face of the consequent Bengal famine of 1943, which claimed an estimated three million lives, remaining food resources were stockpiled in rations for postwar Europe, ignoring the need for emergency relief in India.[144] Churchill reportedly claimed that Indians "had brought these problems on themselves by breeding like rabbits and must pay the price of their own improvidence."[145] Now another such famine was on the way, and the imperial administration was urging yet more frugality from the native population in an impossible twist on the neo-Malthusianism canvassed above. The updated adage was clear to all and quite bereft of moral argument: famine is but the price that some must pay for the wars that ultimately concern the worth/meaningful futurity of others; that is, unless some soldiers simultaneously refused both war and starvation.[146]

Suffice it to say that the RINM performative obsession with food is resonant in the context of the duplicitous official discourse on the ethics of native starvation. By its very excess—and apparent disconnection from the crisis at hand—it insinuates what Jean François Lyotard would have called a *differend* into the litigation, divesting the plaintiff administration of its very idiom and means of accusation/complaint.[147] The legend of the ghee-soaked *parantha* altogether voids the reasoning that some must starve so that others may secure themselves. In this vein, throughout the RINM trials, mutineers refuse an *askesis* of compulsory frugality for the poor. As we learn from the testimony of Mr. Ahmed, "They became angry with the words—'Beggars are not choosers.'"[148] Read through this lens, the RINM's self-reducing legend regarding its own lunchtime can be claimed as an effort to democratize entitlements to life itself, so that all may be nourished, safe, and free. Apparently, upon surrender, the accused ratings presented Admiral Godfrey, in lieu of a charter of demands, with a menu detailing the nutritional needs of each and every Indian.

A. K. Roy, Telegraphist under detention at RIN Camp: In this 20th century when people of the world talk about "equal right of living," we found ourselves mere slaves.[149]

O. B. Sigamany, HMIS *Godavari*: A balanced diet must be provided. It would consist of 15 percent calories made up of protein foods such as meat, eggs, fish, etc.; 35 percent calories made up of fats such as cream, butter and nuts; 50 percent calories from carbohydrates such as bread, potatoes, and sugar. Decent food like eggs, butter, jam, cheese, fruits should supplement the present diet.[150]

On the eve of famine, soon after the public announcement of Wavell's new public rations measures, the streets of mutineer-civilian Bombay resembled a feast day. Sources recount that the final days of the mutiny were marked by a defiant exchange of food packages among participants and their sympathizers. Restaurants declared open-house conditions, and there were many public discussions regarding the cuisine appropriate for revolutionary circumstances. In 1946, when these events occurred, the techniques of the political fast were, of course, well known and well practiced in anticolonial South Asia, thanks to Mahatma Gandhi. If less familiar as a political strategy, the RINM political feast followed similar core principles—namely, the belief that one must and can repair collective injustice in one's own person. And sometimes this involves overeating: "It was a colorful sight. Everywhere from all sides they came with baskets of food in their hands. There was everything one could ask for—fruits, milk, bread, vegetables, and what not. They were the rations of the poor workers, the struggling lower middle class families, even of well-to-do Indians. . . . Yes, food was not a problem."[151] There are also some reports of beggars carrying food packets to the mutineers.[152]

To conclude, reading the RINM as an anticolonial counterpublic at the outset of our discussion, we considered some structural opportunities for inconsequence arising from the disqualification of the mutiny by official anticolonial interests. We built on the suggestion that counterpublic players sometimes act out their imputed irrelevance in order to widen the available sphere and content of politics proper. To derive a positive rather than merely conditional model for the uses of nonsuccessiveness and nonsuccessfulness, we turned to Kantian ethics, both at the source and in some recent queer iterations. These materials yielded the complementary perspective that inconsequentialism concerns the renunciation of symbolic and social self-perpetuation. As such, it is a moral stance that defies unendurable historical limits and expresses the desire to exceed them for the sake of greater universalism and inclusivity. These conceptual paradigms do not (and need not) strictly apply to the historical events and genealogies of concern to us. Yet they supply a cue for assessing the RINM as a protest against the potential foreclosure of democracy—understood as an open or hospitable public sphere—upon the threshold of Indian independence. In the case at hand, this work on civil society notably took the form of an anticolonial mutiny among what were imperial native military forces. Thus, it summoned the anti-generativity evinced by earlier colonial troops in the face of imperial expansionism and global militarization, and dispersed it in two directions: first, against an emerging global order entirely lacking in the intrahuman commensurabilities that comprise just democracy and, second, against a successor government on the verge of imperial conversion.

Across all these diverse conceptual and historical registers, ethical/political inconsequentialism and its correlatives can be summarized as a force of interruption in the worldly drama of repetition, reproduction, and duplication, so that newness might reenter the world. In an influential essay on postcolonial time, the theorist Homi Bhabha offers some apposite reflections on the subject of the new with which to close our discussion. The desire for newness, he proposes, does not directly address the remediation of the present. Notwithstanding its semantic association with the news (as in current affairs), that which is radically new is not necessarily a thing pressingly pertinent or, indeed, useful to the moment in any straightforward way. Rather, newness achieves its temporal significance as an event or modality that renders the future "once again an open question," liberated from causativity as also from utopian overdetermination.[153] Thus conceived, minimally, as a procedure that enforces hospitality upon the future (or as one that reopens the future), newness certainly prevents the foreclosure of our best dreams, but it provides no guarantee of respite from our worst nightmares in times to come. It merely makes available, in Bhabha's words, "an agency of initiation that enables one to possess again and anew . . . the signs of survival."[154] This does not intrinsically result in the clarification of modular or axiomatic technologies, manifestos, programs, and sciences of change so much as the abandonment of all that is given, fixed, held, inherited, known, capitalized, consolidated, and calculable in the realms of subjectivity and sociality. In Bhabha's terms, the first symptoms of newness (within an individual life, or an age, or epoch) are, accordingly, more apparently dissolutive than plainly creative, "inscribed in the 'in-between,'" the "temporal break-up," "the disintegrative moment," the "sudden disjunction of the present."[155] The reopening of the future, in other words, is contingent upon the reopening of the present; a painful replacement of the habits of being for the muddle of becoming, which proceeds as the work of unworking, or as a direction liberated through primary disorientation.

Coda: Operation Bow-Wow

As mentioned at the outset of this chapter, the Royal Indian Navy Mutiny catalyzed numerous sympathetic mutinies among other branches of the Indian armed forces. It was also part and parcel of a wider world situation of mutiny between January and March 1946 among Allied troops at large. The Western media duly noted the anticolonial bent of protests by non-Western combatants as a "revolt of the colored peoples" or a "revolt of the subject races," variously. In one such editorial, entitled "Revolt in the East," the *New York Times* concluded, somewhat ruefully, that "the imperialism of the white race over the colored is passing."[156] Whereas mutinies among native troops could be explained away in terms of a simplified racial schema, those among non-native troops were harder to grasp. Yet, many British soldiers and American GIs, especially, joined in protest against the postwar slowdown in demobilization following a subtle policy shift in favor of occupation.[157] The earliest of these protests, dubbed "Negro mutinies," arose among African-American GIs stationed in Le Havre, France, and in Manila. White troops (American and others) quickly joined the agitations and exempted themselves from the afterlife of empire. Acting in sympathy with Javanese rebels, British occupation forces in Indonesia prevented Netherlands marines from landing in Java. Australian dockside workers, likewise, did what they could to foil the loading of munitions supplies on ships bound for Indonesia.[158]

Some American GIs combined their protests against ongoing occupation with a scathing indictment of militarization itself, which they declared un-American and undemocratic. Speaking in these terms, a senior US military spokesman accused the American army of being, "class conscious, ultra-conservative, absolutist," and an "excellent breeding ground for totalitarianism."[159] In this antimilitary (if not quite pacifist) spirit, American GIs protested in various European theaters of war. Some five hundred convened in Trocadero, Paris, to publicize an enlisted man's Magna Carta, with a core demand that the army abolish its entrenched systems of rank and priority.[160] Such protestors were prosecuted for undermining the civilizational work of perpetual empire. As an editorial from the *New York Times* put it, "In countries where hate still runs strong for the American conqueror, no one will argue that an Army whose troops are picketing the commanding generals is much of an example for the conquered."[161] Thus, servicemen who had reverted without warrant to the base condition of civilian life were canned as irrelevant to the great historical opportunities liberated by war.[162] Calling American mutineers "boy scouts," the provost marshal of the United States Army in Yokohama, Japan, allegedly roared invective at his mutinous command. "If you want lace panties," he expostulated, "I'll get them for you."[163]

If not through the medium of lacy lingerie, many protesting GIs upheld inconsequentiality as the standard for their desired retraction from noisome conquest. If "staying abroad" signified occupation, their counterpolemic expressed itself in the public baby talk of a "we wanna go home" movement (also the key slogan of the 1946 GI mutinies). Participants clamored in earnest for inessentials, such as the right of asylum for the stray animals that they had domesticated during wartime. When conceded, the procedure to honor these requests was given the name Operation Bow-Wow. A report from the *New York Times* describes the situation in detail: "A thousand dogs have been shipped here from Europe since the beginning of the year for soldiers who obtained them overseas and wanted to keep them as pets. The process of shipping them, known unofficially as 'Operation Bow-Wow' . . . was a joint venture by the Army and shipping and custom-house brokerage concerns here. . . . A custom broker here said almost every known breed of dog had been represented in the groups that have arrived."[164]

How tempting it is to claim the passage of these ships of pets across the war zones of the mid–twentieth century as a fitting emblem for an ethics of inconsequence—and no less to position the globalization of mutiny in 1946 as the world-historical apotheosis of our materials. But to do so would impute consequence to inconsequence, *telos* to deontology, and public authority to counterpublic affect. This happens. So let us consider some other names for Operation Bow-Wow: extravagance, luxury, indulgence, superfluity, and profligacy certainly lurk in the shadows of inconsequence. Try as we might, we cannot be rid of these.

Paths of Ahimsaic Historiography

In the composition of this book I have been keenly engaged by questions of methodology: how best to glean and represent the elusive arts of imperfection? More pressingly, does the ethics of imperfection require an imperfectionist style of narration and of thought? In this concluding meta-reflection, I would like to shift the scene of analysis directly to questions of disciplinary or academic *askesis*: a topic already anticipated in chapter 3, which reviewed the convergence of anticolonial ethics and postcolonial theory and, in that regard, the transmutation of ethical into academic disciplines under the auspices of Husserlian phenomenology. My conclusions in this epilogue as to questions of critical form are directly provoked by my own dilemmas, of course, but they gain their charge from the genealogy of twentieth-century imperfectionism, in and as a manifesto for *ahimsaic* historiography. In what follows I propose a two-part analysis, first, generalizing some themes from the material we have already canvassed and, second, turning summary attention to an additional archive drawn from postwar ordinary-language philosophy. This body of thought, more strictly theoretical and intellectualist, may seem abstracted in relation to what has preceded it in this book—practices and modes of thought that are situated in relation to complex material and political conditions. Yet it shares a thick historical milieu with these conditions and adds a postscript to the previous century's transnational ethics of radical democracy. It is one way, albeit tentative, of schematizing the principles of an *ahimsaic* historiography for further accrual.

Common Knowledge: The Path to *Ahimsaic* Historiography

The Common Cause has presented a transnational ethical history of democracy in the first half of the twentieth century. Looking anew at some
of the most familiar political forces and events of this era, we reconsidered
democracy as a disposition to be refined through various *askeses*, namely,
exercises, practices, and regimens of self. During this inquiry, the topic
of ethics also underwent significant semantic variation. To recall, in the
early twentieth century the concept of ethics achieved a peculiar ubiquity
and dissentient elaboration. It no longer described the things we commonly understand as the proper subject of moral philosophy: how to distinguish right from wrong, what are good and bad behaviors, and so on.
Rather, in certain enclaves it came to designate all projects of disciplined
self-fashioning: good, bad, and ugly. These could tend either toward exclu-
sivity and hierarchy or toward a more inclusive universalism, depending
on the players. Such ethical conceptions, secreted alongside, or prior to,
or supplementary to formal politics, point to the emergence of shared perfectionist values—a moral *perfectionism*—at the heart of the most patently
totalitarian tendencies of the time, including fascism and New Imperialism. Even the more progressive coeval ideologies (e.g., New Liberalism),
came into unexpected contiguity with totalitarianism through this perfectionist ethos of self-elevation and cultivation, bent on excluding (though
along variant paths) the unexceptional, the ordinary, and the unremarkable. Invidious and pernicious though this ethos was, it subtends the alternative ethical practices—on the other side of perfection—at the crux
of this investigation. The first half of the twentieth century was rife with
occulted anti-imperial and antifascist practices of moral *imperfectionism*
that emerged in hidden transnational pockets, events, and encounters.
These supply the ethical conditions for a global democracy, oppositional
in its own context, and still awaiting elaboration.

    Besides the orienting claims of the introduction, which placed New
Imperialism and New Liberalism center-stage as unlikely allies in the amplification of ultimately totalitarian values, we reviewed related forms
of exclusionary perfectionism in the period 1900–1955. These include
the *phusikaphobic* antimaterialists encountered in chapter 1, repulsed by
the physical world and the spectacle of the consuming poor, and thus the
bearers of an austere asceticism for poverty and against the poor. The racial
ethnologists of chapter 2, a direct source for twentieth-century fascism,
provided a different context in their defense of a nature-liberty politics—
strictly opposed to the obedience-equality matrix of democratic thought

and realized as an art of ascent concatenated around the racialized project of "becoming-Aryan." Remaining chapters canvassed the collaborative and totalizing enterprise of anticolonial state formations and postwar neo-imperialisms.

Our main interest, however, has been in the dissident offshoots of ethical imperfectionism, singular in regimen and ascetic idiom if united in an ethos of self-reduction or being less rather than more. We observed hedonistic, antimaterialist workers refining a *phusikaphilic* love for the alienated objects of possession—the women of Bermondsey marching in their Sunday best at the height of summer on behalf of disenfranchised comrades. We also met antinomian mystics in the midst of experiments with a *sadhana* of descent based on interrupting (or skillfully botching) the self-liberation or salvation at the core of orthodox spiritual endeavor. In the hands of scattered disciples and interlocutors, this *sadhana* underwent further mutation. Transplanted in diverse political ecologies, it took the form, variously, of *cosmophilia*: the cultivation of enfeebling attachments to the world; neutrality: the refusal to take sides in violent conflict, always against the temptation of heroism yet with total disregard for personal safety; and, finally, contagious subjectivity: the transformation of the self into a laboratory in which to work upon the world. The colonial soldiers of chapter 3 manifested a more evidently robust ethic of sacrifice born of the desire to rescue an endangered Europe from imperial-fascism even at the cost of immediate nationalist aims, thus intimating the possibility of interracial harmony, perhaps a democracy to come, between colonizer and colonized. Their descendants, the global mutineers of chapter 4, harnessed a contrasting ethics of inconsequentiality. Their seemingly trivial grievances about the unsavory food on ships and in the mess halls marked a refusal to participate in the militaristic reproduction of empire. The forms of behavior that disqualified mutineers from representation in the political mainstream were also constitutive of an anticolonial counterpublic—a site of performative world-making in an age of war and violence.

These analyses have gained much from Michel Foucault's last lectures describing Greek Cynicism as an ethics of non-sovereignty and non-value. Our framing dialectic of ethical perfectionism/ethical imperfectionism is, likewise, clarified by Foucault's suggestion that ancient Cynicism protested another, more normative moral law and custom, or *nomos*, that was premised on the values of excellence and mastery both over the self and (more problematically) over others.[1] The transnational projects of self-ruination and radical relationality that came to view in the twentieth century extend this genealogy and radicalize its political effects upon democracy. Their adherents contend that true democratic existence is not merely the condition of passively inhabiting or even participating in/with the culture of a given mass or collectivity. It is, rather, an acutely individuated dedication to becoming common—the effect of an idiosyncratic disregard for the self by the self for the cause of inclusive sociality.

The stakes of this project and its organizational structure are clearer upon its conclusion than they were in the execution. It has been challenging to access, document, and integrate the archives of minor, largely non-Western traditions. The texts and traces of all subordinate traditions tend to be fragmentary and fugitive, yet Western subcultures are comparably better documented than those of the colonized. So much of Sri Ramana's crucial early teaching, for instance, was noted on erasable slates and on the shifting sand of ashram grounds, in aide-mémoire merely. In other cases, conventional resources for research were hard to find. Consider the problem of the tenuous evidentiary nature of reported and heavily mediated subaltern agencies—namely, the crowds, demonstrators, armies, and anonymous strikers whom we have been following with intent. More than all these issues, however, the main complexity has been with respect to presenting a history of inner or ethical lives and times, especially such as eschew exemplarity. Inmost narrative threads rarely consist of things that happened; they most often consist of ethical aspirations that might have happened or ought to happen. The interpretive reconstruction of such content calls for imaginative guesswork auguring scholarly uncertainty in its wake.

Even when identified and placed in comprehensible interrelation (as a democratizing ethics of imperfection), my materials yielded ongoing disciplinary conundrums. I did not want to lose the fugitive and tremulous quality of the archives I was dealing with after all—subaltern soldiers' letters from the front, spiritual diaries, courtroom testimonies, eyewitness and journalistic accounts. How to develop forms of academic writing and communication to reproduce the immediate and personalized nature of the archive while remaining faithful to the obligations of objective scholarship? Also, besides gleaning cultural history from the material at hand, the project called for its enlistment in a dialogue with the better-known genealogies of modern philosophy, twentieth-century thought, and postcolonialism. In the chapter on military cosmopolitanism, for example, it was certainly important to highlight the surprising material presence of colonized Indian soldiers in the trenches of the Western front and to plainly register the South Asian chapter of the First World War. Yet it was only by deciphering in these semiliterate soldiers' letters an intuitive grasp of the crisis of European man, akin to that of the philosopher and phenomenologist Edmund Husserl, that their fragmentary resources could also be registered as a meaningful rejoinder to the conceptual register of twentieth-century totalitarianism. A similar effort to parse the triviality of 1946 mutineers as ethical or as a type of moral philosophy provoked the decision to intersperse my reading of the RIN trials with a consideration of Kantian inconsequentialism. But as Kant settled into mutually interruptive conversation with mutineer testimonies, he was estranged from the history of Western academic philosophy.

I foreground these anxieties of scholarly endeavor for reasons pertinent to an as yet buried theme in *The Common Cause*. The more I struggled against the vertiginous effects of extradisciplinary analysis, the more I realized that there were guidelines to be mined from the very materials and themes of this book. The moral imperfectionisms of interest to this inquiry are themselves premised on antidisciplinary ethical disciplines and conscious cultures of nonexpertise—in this case truly exacting and purposive. What lessons can we find here?

The subjects of *philophusikia* break from established styles of antimaterialism in order to achieve an affective reorientation toward the object-world. The art of descent is a rigorous *askesis*, yet it eschews legibility within the established canons of spiritual behavior. The ethic of inconsequence comprises a conscious effort to fall short of given moral and political standards so as to usher in a new world from the resources of existential disorientation. These are lived and everyday practices, on the ground. But even the least apparently tactual and canonical thinkers we have encountered tend toward conscientious nonexpertise. Husserl makes philosophy reparative by reducing it to the first principles not of ontology but of lived actualization, a labor to be undertaken by each individual philosopher on behalf of humankind. Bergson's "An Introduction to Metaphysics," (1903) offers up the most foundational themes of Western philosophy as a science for beginners and amateur metaphysicians—namely, as something to be done more than thought. Theodor Adorno shatters all method—indeed, form itself—in a bid to grasp the problem of cohabitation with catastrophe. The paradigmatic Cynic philosophies we discussed in the introduction communicate their heterodox content through artful unsystematicity. Much of the force in the putative teachings of Diogenes consists in the unexpected manner of their rendition. We know that the Cynics were therefore often berated for lacking coherent dogmas.

The focus of these philosophical interlocutors—harder to grasp—is simultaneously interpretive and performative. It helps substantiate the smallest of ethical gestures and teaches us to recognize them in the midst of grand historical noise. More excessively, the reflective antiexperts embedded in the present study demonstrate how forfeiting disciplinary ambitions equips us to enter into direct partnership with occluded objects of analysis, the better to amplify their inchoate meanings and best possibilities. This pathological over-identification of scholarly subject/minor object is the kernel of what we might term *ahimsaic*, or nonviolent, historiography. Devolving from Gandhian semantics, the threshold concept of violence, or *himsa*, at play here is already hyperbolic, implying not only a willingness to harm but also, and even more, the failure of exorbitant care. Nonviolence, or *ahimsa*, in context, must recover and reestablish such frustrated exorbitance. The popular Bollywood hit movie *Lage Raho Munna Bhai* (Keep at it Munna Bhai) gets at the project keenly in its tale of a Bombay mobster who develops a streetwise version of Gandhism: an oppressed underclass (comprising workers, women, lovers, and the elderly) is encouraged to deal with corrupt or bullying government officials/patriarchs by sending them flowers and "Get Well Soon" greeting cards. Consider Gandhi's own advice, in *Hind Swaraj*, that a nonviolent attitude toward thieves and robbers must combine disregard for personal property with strong regard for the ethical well-being even of perpetrators. In Gandhi's words,

You set this armed robber down as an ignorant brother; you intend to reason with him at a suitable opportunity; you argue that he is, after all, a fellow-man; you do not know what prompted him to steal. You, therefore decide that, when you can, you will destroy the man's motive for stealing. Whilst you are thus reasoning with yourself, the man comes in again to steal. Instead of being angry with him, you take pity on him. You think that this stealing habit must be a disease with him. Henceforth, you, therefore, keep your doors and windows open; you change your sleeping-place, and you keep your things in a manner most accessible to him.[2]

Translated into a heuristic (or a way of reading the world, *tout court*), the *ahimsaic* attitude entails a similar relation of radical accord—in this case, with the intractable and fallen object of analysis—by positioning oneself at its level, in the hope of channeling its potentiality.

Such recommendations are corroborated by the thinkers who figure in this book in assorted iterations. By exiting the consolations of disciplinarity, Husserl, Bergson, and others instantiate a nonviolent and democratic epistemology: not anti-intellectualist but seeking equipotential with the object being studied. This is at the nub of the Bergsonian desire to enter into fellowship with things or of Adorno's quest for a scholarly style at the level of damaged life. There's another surprise here. Hard though this task is, it is consistently accompanied by imaginative recompense and creative joy: variant forms, we could say, of cynic laughter. Bergson promises that luminosity and inventiveness will fill in for academic certainty in his practices. Husserl guarantees that the gifted practitioner of his embodied, philosophy will experience a cinematic dissolving of the frame of scepticism into another fleeting but epiphanic shot of pure relationality, unadulterated by the violence of history. In his words,

We perform the epochē—we who are philosophizing in a new way—as a transformation of the attitude which precedes it. . . . It is through this abstention that the gaze of the philosopher in truth first becomes fully free: above all, free of the strongest and most universal, and at the same time most hidden, internal bond, namely, of the pregivenness of the world. Given in and through this liberation is the discovery of the . . . conscious life of the subjectivity which effects the validity of the world . . . and continues actively to shape it anew."[3]

It is in a riff on the conceit of innovation and play secreted within communizing knowledge that the Weberian intellectual's self-attrition also delivers a brand-new bagatelle: the perfectly miniaturized sublime.

The signatory inventiveness of democratizing scholarship is all the more vivid in the oeuvre of the gurus we met in chapter 2, wherein ethics and epistemology are perfectly harmonized. Sri Aurobindo consistently urged even the most serious of his disciples to try their hands at poetic composition. A classicist and firm believer in the merits of quantitative meter, the guru was, nonetheless, disinterested in promoting creative writing as yet another supplementary skill for ashramites.[4] Rather, it is as a practice of descent—a way of being extracurricular in the midst of *sadhana*—that Aurobindonian poetics points the way toward a progressive disaggregation of self whereby we must teach ourselves to hear through our eyes, to love from the regions above the head, to speak without language, to separate sound from sense, and so on. This wishful poetic rupture (from the strictures of normative judgment and cognitive protocol) liberates an unexpected critical faculty that allows us to discern, Sri Aurobindo argues, "the Beauty that is everywhere. . . . One must or may discover and reveal beauty in a pig or its poke or in a parish pump or an advertisement of somebody's pills. . . . By extension one should be able to extract beauty equally well out of morality or social reform or a political caucus."[5] There are no personal rewards or accolades for this worldview, though these will seem ultimately superfluous in the measure. At the acme of quite literally envisioning "a devastating catholicity," the personality of the poet-seer, "disappears"—not into the void of mere anonymity but, more bracingly, "into sight; the personality of the seer is lost in the . . . vision."[6]

Such is certainly the effect, to return to the complicated reasoning of *Hind Swaraj*, of reading the world with an eye (not to mention a conscience, too) for *ahimsa*. This manifesto is rife with the critique of expertise and recommendations to break free of conventional or received forms of disciplinary behavior, albeit with the utmost self-control (homeschooling, home spinning, home remedies, and home rule are salient examples). Among the professional lawyers, doctors, and politicians whom Gandhi condemns for their deadening rote effect upon the spontaneous homework of democratic sociality, he reserves special spleen for disciplinary history—needless to say, in an offbeat pitch. Protesting the impossibility of "historical evidence as to the success of . . . soul-force or truth-force," Gandhi avers that history proper does not appreciate the transformative conditions of cooperative coexistence because these seem so ordinary to the expert/s eye.[7] The realm of happening—or "it so happened," as Gandhi calls it—deals exclusively with "the doings of kings and emperors [and] the wars of the world."[8] On the other hand, "Hundreds of nations live in peace. History does not, and cannot, take note of this fact. . . . Two brothers quarrel; one of them repents and reawakens the love that was lying dormant in him; the two again begin to live in peace; nobody takes note of this. But, if the two brothers . . . take up arms, . . . their doings would be immediately noticed in the press, they would be the talk of their neighbors, and would probably go down in history. . . . Soul-force . . . is not noted in history."[9] The point is not only that history, à la Gandhi, is inattentive to small details but that it censors the creative leap of faith required to apprehend the extraordinary in the ordinary: "Thousands, indeed tens of thousands, depend for their existence on a very active working of this force. Little quarrels of millions of families in their daily lives disappear before the exercise of this force."[10] We can only grasp the mundane making up of quarrelsome siblings (or their putative "soul force") by simultaneously making up, or fictionalizing, its significance in a recklessly counterfactual or subjunctive appraisal. This requires attentiveness to events, figures, ideas, and moments that deliberately swerve us away from the given—or the "it so happened" of upper-case History—either by withholding their own purpose or by interrupting coeval projects of too-hasty realization. The business of inclusivity/democracy/the commons is thus perhaps better served by an antipositivist art of the possible—namely, the "what if," "would that," "if only," or "let us suppose that" available to elaboration in any set of circumstances. The practice entails perspectives that lack eventful objective referents while hinting, nonetheless, at an alteration of existing forces.[11] Even if nothing summoned by the *ahimsaic* mode can be observed directly, let alone realized concretely, it can and must be imagined. There are moments in political life (and in scholarly-critical life) when it is solely through imaginative dictate that we are able to shrug off the prevailing ideological limit.

Succinctly, then, *ahimsaic* historiography may be clarified as a hermeneutics borne of moral imperfectionism. It combines three elements: first, nonexpertise, or the willing sacrifice of credited disciplinary proficiency in exchange for the knowledge of unimportant/insignificant/minor things; second, accord, or an affiliative relationship with the objects of analysis so as to liberate their best meanings and aspirational content; third, counterfactuality, or a nonveridical critical idealism that concedes that the object's unexpressed content may well call for imaginative analysis (as joyful for the critic-reader as beneficial to the object-text).

Pandemic among the thinkers and scenes of preceding chapters, these elements combine seamlessly and are clarified at the scene of postwar ordinary-language philosophy (henceforth OLP). OLP was in its time a reaction to the pervasive milieu of perfectionism that had spread into the world of the academe as an antidemocratic reorganization of the disciplines at large and of the humanities in particular. Michel de Certeau puts it well in his homage to this body of work as a philosophical politics of culture predicated upon a "radical critique of the Expert."[12] In the context of twentieth-century totalitarianism, the "critical return of the ordinary," he observes, aimed to destroy all "varieties of rhetorical brilliance associated with powers that hierarchize and with nonsense that enjoys authority."[13] In a sympathetic though less historically alert reading, Pierre Hadot argues that the ethical secret of OLP is concealed in its determinedly poor academic form. It is through the carefully crafted disorder of personal notes, the esotericism of the aphorism, and the instability of the dialogue form that such philosophy retracts from the business of information into the far more important labor of re-forming life itself. The best philosophers, Hadot observes somewhat contentiously, choose to "write badly." They deliberately hamper mere intellectual understanding with ideas lacking in "coherence and connection," the better to engage and act upon "our spirit."[14]

In the remainder of this discussion I propose, likewise, that the OLP corpus brings the nonexpert sharply into view as a close companion to the self-reducing mystics, workers, and soldiers of earlier chapters and as the envoy of an ingenious common knowledge apposite to common causes. With this emphasis, however, the vast, conventional, intellectual terrain for OLP becomes proportionally foreign in the context of analytic philosophy alone. But this, Certeau maintains, was an aim for the philosophers of ordinary language. In his words, "Unlike the Expert's discourse, Wittgenstein's does not profit from knowledge by exchanging it against the right to speak in its name; he retains its exactingness but not its mastery."[15]

Ordinary Language: A Path from *Ahimsaic* Historiography

So canonical a field as OLP obtains from complex disciplinary histories. To situate it within the frame of twentieth-century radical ethics, however, we need to desuture it from these more established genealogies and relocate it at the scene of a little-known internecine rivalry between inter- and post-war Oxford philosophy (so-called) and Cambridge English Studies.[16] Both traditions were concerned, albeit in dramatically opposed ways, with the historical consequences of humanistic endeavor. Cambridge English— which now stands roundly critiqued for a discriminatory credo of aesthetic as opposed to pragmatic value—participated in the rise of English as a patriotic and parochial discipline following the First World War and the publication, in 1921, of the government-sponsored Newbolt Report, which supported claims for the spread of English as the world language.[17] Defenders of English literature engaged in such appeals were strong believers in the transformative effects of imaginative writing. But this was transformation very narrowly conceived as elevation above the common lot. As is well known, the field of English studies was forcefully organized around these lines by the maverick Cambridge lecturer F. R. Leavis and his elitist (though demographically quite diverse) circle of close readers. In Leavisite hands, the discipline was fashioned as a bastion against cultural democracy, or, as Leavis himself preferred to call it, "the egalitarian tidal wave."[18]

Curiously, Leavis saw a great threat to this project, besides "telly and pin-table-addicted non-students," in the roughly coeval enterprise of English linguistic philosophy.[19] In books such as *The Living Principle* and the essays gathered into *The Critic as Anti-Philosopher*, he rails at large against these philosophers, reserving particular spleen for Wittgenstein. His essay "Memories of Wittgenstein" is a masterpiece on the uniquely fraught nature of collegiality, with its intimate anti-intimacies and transactive trespasses.[20] Elsewhere he begs that students of English be protected from seminars on OLP.[21] Why such animosity?

Organized most visibly around the later work of the Cambridge philosopher, Ludwig Wittgenstein, specifically his *Philosophical Investigations*, OLP was largely and independently developed in Oxford by figures such as Gilbert Ryle and J. L. Austin. G. E. M. Anscombe, also the translator and editor of *Philosophical Investigations*, was an important conduit for the Oxford-wise transmission of Wittgenstein. Second-generation thinkers, and beneficiaries of her efforts (a high and rare proportion of women philosophers among them), include P. F. Strawson, Michael Dummett, Philippa Foot, and Iris Murdoch, with Stanley Cavell and John McDowell as noteworthy transatlantic interlocutors. Some, though not all, of these figures had their tertiary education interrupted by the event of the Second World War and turned, belatedly, to academic philosophy as alienated veterans, seeking not refuge from the world so much as a path of return to it—"a clear view," as Strawson put it, "of our concepts and their place in our lives."[22]

Very unlike their colleagues in English studies, these thinkers were strikingly cosmopolitan. Even as Cambridge new critics labored to purge British scholarship of the influence of German philology and other European habits of mind and style, ordinary-language philosophers rejected the distinctions between analytic and continental philosophy. Some of the main tenets of the school were formalized at a bilingual, Anglo-French conference at Royaumont in the 1950s.[23] J. L. Austin was among the key speakers at this event and also the first of his peers to bring OLP to America. His impact on the American philosopher-critic Stanley Cavell is well documented by the latter, in particular, as instruction against the temptations of national philosophy.[24] Notably, the second-wave ordinary-language philosopher Michael Dummett achieved prominence as a campaigner for the fair treatment of immigrants and refugees in Britain and Europe. His contemporary, Peter Strawson, counted many South and East Asian philosophers among his students and interlocutors at a time when even the best of British thought was strikingly hostile to non-Western foreigners and foreign influences.[25]

The cultural inclusivity of this cohort was matched, as Leavis decried, by their strongly democratic outlook. Ryle gained particular notoriety in this regard, along with Wittgenstein, for seeking explicit "democratization of the offices of the old elite," beginning with the treatment of intellectual activity "merely as special occupations on all fours with such occupations as tying knots, following tunes or playing hide-and-seek."[26] Ironically enough, Leavis was possibly less offended than he ought to have been by the program for OLP. Presuming that the new philosophy of ordinary language was, prima facie, a movement against literary or subtle language, in favor of plain speaking and plain dealing, he failed to recognize its powerful if labyrinthine antipositivism. It is on the strength of this cached persuasion that OLP effectively counters the worst habits of Cambridge English elitism.

More precisely, OLP thinkers merit renewed interest for their collective attention, in the name of "ordinary language," to a radically subjunctive perspective. This they formulate as the signatory idiom of collective, communicative coexistence. An abbreviated (and admittedly partisan) schema of the OLP testament concerns the following four propositions: (1) We are most meaningful when we speak in ordinary language. (2) Such language is necessarily shared, common, and communicative. (3) Its meanings are antimetaphysical and cannot be known in advance. But they are also antipositivist and cannot be verified once and for all. (4) Ordinary language may be described as an art of the possible. I venture these propositions provisionally as one declension of *ahimsaic* historiography.

1. We are most meaningful when we speak in ordinary language or when, in fact, we are most ordinary (in the sense of nonexpert, nonspecialized, and quotidian).

With this emphasis, OLP displaces the exalted figure of the human (within the humanities) with everyman, thereby making the business of thinking more tacitly democratic than existential or ontological. A new onus on concepts such as ubiquity or the everyday invests the most unremarkable aspects of our shared lives with new philosophical intensity. We can take a definition directly from Gilbert Ryle, once the Waynflete Professor of Metaphysical Philosophy at Oxford, following some war years in intelligence activities of a different kind. "The word 'ordinary,'" Ryle writes, "is in implicit or explicit contrast with 'out of the way,' 'esoteric,' 'technical,' 'poetical,' 'notational,' or sometimes 'archaic.' 'Ordinary' means 'common,' 'current,' 'colloquial,' 'vernacular,' 'natural,' 'prosaic,' 'nonnotational,' 'on the tongue of Everyman,' and is generally used in contrast with dictions which only a few people know to use, such as the technical terms or artificial symbolisms of lawyers, theologians, economists, philosophers, cartographers, mathematicians, symbolic logicians and players of Royal tennis."[27]

Such reduction of the classic figures and conceits of philosophy has inevitable consequences for the discipline that appear, under OLP auspices, to solicit its own collateral dethronement. "Philosophy is a pretty fair mess," J. L. Austin is recorded as announcing at a Royaumont roundtable on the difference between performative and constative utterances. "It's the dumping ground," he insists, "for all the leftovers from the other sciences, where everything turns up which we don't know how to take. . . . The field is wide open to anyone who chooses to enter it; first come, first served, and good luck to anyone who is the first to hit on anything worthwhile."[28] All this encourages unsystematic thought, perhaps to a fault.[29] On the upside, it makes the philosopher's task "homelier," and nowhere more so than in Wittgenstein's later oeuvre, with its emphasis on looking rather than thinking, and on the density of humble words, objects, and folk.[30] The examples pile up here, as in "Back to the rough ground"; "What we do is bring words back from their metaphysical to their everyday use," or, "Is this language somehow too coarse and material for what we want to say?"[31]

It is noteworthy that Pierre Hadot's influential case for Wittgenstein's philosophy as a modern way of life is based on a particular reading of the *Tractatus Logico-Philosophicus*. Hadot argues that the *Tractatus* betrays its appeal to spirit rather than reason alone by its intractability to interpretation.[32] Its ascetic subtext, in other words, is secreted precisely in its esotericism/abstruseness of style. Yet it is only later, in the *Philosophical Investigations*, that we begin to see exactly how complicated Wittgenstein's *askesis* really is. It wrecks philosophy, of course, but also ethics as we know it by demanding that we return not so much to living well (the good life) as to those mundane forms of life wherein we lose all our distinction(s)—the common life. Phillipa Foot advances these themes in her delicate banalization of virtue in *Virtues and Vices*. Moral capacity, she suggests, is the measure of plain common sense, as in the reasoning that it is good simply to live with-and-as others. Nothing more, nothing less. "I was sure," she says, "that it would not do to suppose, that for instance, someone might have a *morality* in whose ultimate principle was [sic] that it was wrong to turn around trees righthanded or to look at hedgehogs in the light of the moon." [33] Foot objects only to esotericism in ethical practice here, not to any inventiveness implied by her colorful examples. This is an important distinction. OLP thinkers would have no problem admitting the ascetic merit, not to mention democratic effects, provoked precisely by creative and unlikely non sequiturs such as moonlit hedgehogs and right-handed woodland circumambulation. The new task of philosophy, Austin demurs, may well consist in recognizing the "extraordinary facts" that imbue "everyday experience."[34]

2. To be ordinary is to derive our meanings from strictly communicative, shared, and common contexts (the situation of the speaker; the occasions of a word; the sudden surprise of intimate understanding).

OLP encourages a shift in linguistic understanding from the semantic to the pragmatic import of words, most famously in Austin's theory of the speech act. This accent on what utterances actually do and how we use them effects a surreptitious secularization of language. There are many accounts of the contingency of speech in the field. Peter Strawson speaks at length about the "contextual requirement" of all expressions, drawing attention to, "the time, the place, the situation, the identity of the speaker, the subjects which form the immediate focus of interest, and the personal histories of both the speaker and those he is addressing."[35] Austin says something identical in his ruminations on the extent to which the occasions of a word help us comprehend the most apparently nonsensical or partial of statements.[36] None of this is a plea for the irreducible objectivity of meanings. Rather, it is an argument for the necessarily exploratory-communicative structure of all speech.

While it is certainly up to us to make language less solipsistic, we learn from OLP, there is actually no way of (or merit in) securing its total transparency once and for all. The point is that most of our meanings are implied rather than spoken explicitly or out loud. We rely constantly on the surprise of intimate understanding to "get" each other. In other words, we do not have to mean what we say—"Do let's spend an extra hour at the gym rather than be happy eating pizza in front of the telly"—in order to communicate our preferred intent. And it is here that OLP achieves its democratic parable. We know how to use language only by participating in it with others, that is, by the conditions of its common use. To speak is to talk together—in effect, to act together.[37] So too, to learn the use of an expression is to achieve knowledge of the way other people speak.[38] This brings with it associated skills of affective insight: guessing at what other people might really have on their minds, not to mention learning how to regard, at least minimally, their disarticulated desires and needs.[39] In this sense we do not speak a private language.

3. The meanings described above cannot be known in advance (that is to say, they are antimetaphysical). Nor can they be fixed once and for all by true-or-false considerations (that is to say, they are also antipositivist, antifactual, and in excess of verification).

Though OLP is commonly subsumed under the generic category of analytic philosophy, it follows an idiosyncratic path of development. It does not descend, as might be expected, uncritically from G. E. Moore and Bertrand Russell, Wittgenstein's early interlocutors at Cambridge. Nor is it fulfilled in the conclusions of Vienna Circle thinkers, such as Otto Neurath and Rudolf Carnap, and later logical positivists like A. J. Ayer: both branches converge in agreement on the physicalist nature of life, and the view that the meaning of a statement derives solely from the criterion of its verifiability.[40] Some alternative histories of analytic philosophy propose for OLP a split inheritance from both Gottlob Frege, the fin de siècle German logician, and his near contemporary, Edmund Husserl; the former supplies materials for disbelief in the a-priori, and the latter for disenchantment with reference as the sole basis for sense.[41] The perverse synthesis of these warring elements is oddly coherent, unified by the assumption that we will never exhaust a certain sort of authoritarian metaphysics unless we also refute the sustaining binary of its equally authoritarian skepticist antithesis.

These ideas are beautifully realized in Gilbert Ryle's *The Concept of Mind*. Ryle rejects simultaneously the post-Cartesian reduction of world to mind and vice versa—that is, the absurd proposition that there can either exist minds or bodies but never both together. So it is that the thinkers under review give the lie both to the "lavishness of the transcendentalist" and "the stinginess of the empiricist."[42] On the strength of these precedents many ordinary-language philosophers believe single-minded assault on the tyranny of the fact to be entirely consistent with the ongoing business of antimetaphysical critique. "Although it will not do to force actual language to accord with some preconceived model," Austin writes, "it equally will not do, having discovered the facts about 'ordinary language,' to rest content with that, as though there were nothing more to be discussed and discovered."[43] Such objections to evidentiary constraints on theories of meaning specifically decry how the fetish of objective referents effectively transforms all words into proper names, which must always stand for or designate something already out there. Yet even the proper name, as Wittgenstein tells us, cannot guarantee the existence of a thing. It is no talisman against perishability. Nor does the absence of a material correlative rob a name of all resonance: "Now suppose that the tool with the name 'N' is broken. Not knowing that, A gives B the sign 'N.' Has this sign meaning now or not?"[44]

By these routes there comes into view a conceptual space for fictionality (very broadly conceived) within OLP procedures. Sophisticated romancing and sophisticated fiction, we hear from Strawson, depend precisely upon statements that might be significant without being true or false.[45] In a similar register, Stanley Cavell's later interpolations within the field seal the case for OLP as a hybrid mode of literary-philosophical criticism. This has various implications for practitioners, such as paying better attention to matters of philosophical style and taking works of fiction seriously as philosophical material. It also requires the cultivation (for the sake of social amelioration) of a critical disposition, which takes on the "cultural responsibility of preserving itself against its own culture, against its own past accomplishment."[46] This last may well entail uncertainty about what one's culture needs, as also about the merit of seeking only to fulfill (or knowing how to fulfill) the needs that are most tangible and immediately at hand.[47]

4. To speak an ordinary language, that is, to be ordinary in the sense of being-in-common or being-with-others (in a word, democratic), is an art of the possible.

"Our investigation," Wittgenstein famously notes in *Philosophical Investigations*, "is directed not toward phenomena, but, as one might say, toward the "possibilities" of phenomena."[48] The clearest tenets for the potentiality of shared meanings, thus conceived, occur in Austin's oeuvre. The performative utterances that he distinguishes as bringing something about rather than referring to something already in place do not themselves need to be sui generis and original.[49] Thus the words that launch a marriage or a ship, or cause an arrest to be made are, indeed, coded, iterable, and therefore citational.[50] So too, their powers of conjuration have a great deal to do with the institutional and modular nature of the things they bring about (marriage, prison, journeys). Nonetheless, performative meanings are always subject to creative deviation, deferral, and/or variation.

A behabitive commendation may fail to make the person being commended feel commended. An apology may take years to have effect, or it may communicate way more or less regret than intended. Likewise, an expositive utterance plainly announcing or explaining what we are about to do may falter mid-route. Famously (and very likely apocryphally), when training as a barrister in London, the young M.K. Gandhi once failed entirely to give birth to the speech he was signaling repeatedly with the words "I conceive—," "I conceive—". It is this type of synapse or interval between utterance and signification—or, indeed, between utterance, signification, and resignification—that Judith Butler so eloquently describes as the "open temporality of the speech act."[51] Performativity, she helps us understand, is not, then, the certainty of effect so much as a "possibility of agency," which need not conform to spatial and temporal specificities, and which, we might add, may also remain unrealized.[52]

To summarize, at the admittedly minor scene (though one embedded in the first half of the twentieth century) of an academic spat between Cambridge English and Oxford ordinary-language philosophy, we find another variant on the binary of perfectionism/imperfectionism. Where Leavisite English studies took up the cause of humanistic elevation against

the threat of egalitarianism, OLP committed to disciplinary dethronement in its name. Both forms proclaimed their own wider application in
the world beyond academe, in different ways. But the special-case, *ahimsaic* path not taken by Cambridge English, and, perhaps, not fully appreciated in the descent of Western philosophy, either, is as yet available for
recuperation. Very clearly, if aphoristically, it reformulates ordinariness
as the basis for a democratic exegetics, which consists in cultivating our
most unremarkable faculties, being suspicious of the facts, and taking
something like mere possibility very seriously as a form of politics and
of knowledge. This sometimes entails giving free play to the fictionality
of any given text situation, by which, in turn, we must mean its socially
critical or reparative-because-unfinished impulse.

There is apt transcription of OLP principles into an ethico-political hermeneutic by William Empson, the antiprovincial critic-poet admired by
Wittgenstein, who spent many years between and after the first two world
wars teaching in China.[53] In terms especially resonant with the "possibility" thematic in OLP, Empson draws attention to the principle of ambiguity encoded within all literary experience. A poem may be fully steeped
in its context—a social work, as it were—yet there will come a point when
its language begins to venture beyond the grammar of its own graspable
world. Add to this the muddy business of reading, and what you often get
besides the inaugural "faint and separate judgments of probability," is the
random surprise of a wildly autonomous final meaning.[54] These ambigui-
ties are a measure of the plurality of likely assumptions secreted within
the work and up for grabs to anybody. In context, the democratic critic's
proper terrain is to exacerbate ambiguity. She must prevent the foreclosure
of collective sense that comes from dealing conclusively or expertly with
the material, or from forcing people to attend to "what is really there" in a
text or situation.[55] Much better, Empson advises, to leave the understanding ultimately unsatisfied and the text or literary experience ongoingly
sociable.

Complex permutations obtain from such recommendations. For instance, we have all encountered textual situations the meanings of which
simply cannot be brought into view no matter how hard we try because
they seem too insignificant or unintelligible in relation to the grammar
and moment of their prevailing circumstances. Yet, à la M. K. Gandhi,
such textual situations can be hypothesized, precisely in their semantic
failure, as aspirational—as bearing the strictly groundless character of a
hoping and wishing that is either at odds with its ambient circumstance or
that seeks to be circumstance-altering: as in, "I wish x could be otherwise,"
or, "I hope against hope that y."[56] Guessing at this aspirational content or,

rather, gleaning insignificance, failure, and unintelligibility as aspirational modes is, thus, an exigent critical task. Similarly, we can also simply refuse to disclose the meanings of a textual situation by pointing to what it actually achieves or references in the world to which it belongs. In other words, we can enforce its failure. When meanings are thus actively retracted from realization, that is, with the disappearance of a fixed or sole referent/object/objective, a galactic if inchoate relational field often comes into view. This comprises the textual situation's "implication threads," "contiguous fields" and "neighboring worlds" (to borrow some themes from Gilbert Ryle); or, à la Wittgenstein, its sympathetic resemblance and kinship to other not even necessarily coeval textual situations.[57] It goes without saying that such close-up readings will be indistinct and blurry.[58] But they may well be proportionally more inclusive, cosmopolitan, and global.

This is but another low-key wager in the spirit of imperfection. In all such cases the risks of self-reduction are finally negligible. If democracy is already here, we win. If it is yet to come, it is still well worth the price. We can gamble thus from a range of venues and in the midst of miscellaneous activities: in Makkali Gosala's cowshed; in Diogenes' bathtub; during a peace protest; as we chat with a friend; in a naval mess hall; during wartime; in the rituals of Kant's complicated couture; even in a library.

Notes

1. We could include here the work of Alain Badiou, Antonio Negri, Michael Hardt, Slavoj Žižek and (to some extent) Étienne Balibar. Although these thinkers do not necessarily conceive of themselves as a cohort, their work is linked by a striking shared revival of certain themes. Salient among these is the case for an urgent rehabilitation of the idea of universalism and, with it, of democracy as the key path to a revaluation of "the common"—a hitherto underworked idea, we are told, in Western political philosophy and social theory. Some among this group of scholars take the view that contemporary postcolonial thought does not qualify as a viable theoretical ally in the task of reengaging democracy because of its investments in difference, multiculturalism, the politics of preference, and philosophical relativism.

2. Subaltern studies scholars have documented important continuities between precolonial popular people's movements and anticolonial national struggles. See Ranajit Guha, "On Some Aspects of the Historiography of Colonial India," *Subaltern Studies 1: Writings on South Asian History and Society*, ed. Ranajit Guha (Delhi: Oxford University Press, 1994), 1–8.

3. See Sunil Khilani, *The Idea of India* (New York: Farrar, Straus and Giroux, 1999); and Ramachandra Guha, *India After Gandhi: The History of the World's Largest Democracy* (New York: HarperCollins, 2007).

4. Amanda Anderson makes an important argument about the collectivist resonance of the arts of living in the context of democracy; see "Argument and Ethos," in *The Way We Argue Now: A Study in the Cultures of Theory* (Princeton, NJ: Princeton University Press, 2006), 134–60.

An additional note about terminology is in order here. The term or concept of *askesis* has attracted a great deal of interpretive attention in recent academic literature. We will canvass many of these characterizations as we go along. My usage abides by the standard definition from the Greek ἄσκησις, *áskēsis*, meaning "exercise" or "training," especially concerning impalpable aspects of the self such as the spirit, temperament, attitudes, affects, and subjectivity itself.

5.   Jacques Ranciere, *Hatred of Democracy*, trans. Steve Corcoran (London: Verso, 2006), 4.

6.   Aimé Césaire, in *Discourse on Colonialism*, trans. Joan Pinkham (New York: Monthly Review Press, 2000), warns the European world at large that colonialism, "works to decivilize the colonizer, to brutalize him in the true sense of the word, to degrade him, to awaken him to buried instincts, to covetousness, violence, race hatred, and moral relativism; and we must show that each time a head is cut off or an eye put out in Vietnam and in France they accept the fact, . . . a universal regression sets in" (35). An earlier cosmopolitan literature of fin de siècle radicalism, to which the materials of this book are heir, routinely makes the case that violence is harmful for perpetrator and victim alike. In his *Animal Rights: Considered in Relation to Social Progress* (New York: Macmillan, 1894), the socialist and anti-vivisectionist Henry Salt argued that enlightened social reform had a twofold task: to seek amnesty for the objects of injustice and also to protect the subjects of injustice from their own worst selves: "It is not only, and not primarily, for the sake of the victims that we plead, but for the sake of mankind itself. Our true civilization, our race-progress, our humanity (in the best sense of the term) are concerned in this development; it is ourselves, our own vital instincts, that we wrong, when we trample on the rights of the fellow-beings, human or animal, over whom we chance to hold jurisdiction. It has been admirably said that, 'terrible as is the lot of the subjects of cruelty and injustice, that of the perpetrators is even worse, by reason of the debasement and degradation of character implied and incurred'" (35). Salt is citing an undated address to the Humanitarian League by Edward Maitland, a leading fin de siècle theosophist, humanitarian, and pro-suffrage activist.

7.   Frantz Fanon, *The Wretched of the Earth*, trans. Constance Farrington (Harmondsworth, UK: Penguin Books, 1990), 255.

8.   Postcolonial scholars typically favor the nineteenth century as the paradigmatic scene of European imperialism. The few studies that emphasize the crucial typological break between nineteenth- and twentieth-century imperialism include Robert Owen and Bob Sutcliffe, eds., *Studies in the Theories of Imperialism* (London: Longman, 1972); Michael Barret Brown, *The Economics of Imperialism* (Harmondsworth, UK: Penguin, 1972); Giovanni Arrighi, *The Geometry of Imperialism: The Limits of Hobson's Paradigm*, trans. Patrick Camiller (London: Verso, 1983); and Harrison M. Wright, ed., *The "New Imperialism": Analysis of Late Nineteenth-Century Expansion* (Lexington, MA: D. C. Heath, 1961).

9. J. A. Hobson, *Imperialism: A Study* (Ann Arbor: University of Michigan Press, 1965), 15–27.
10. Hannah Arendt, *The Origins of Totalitarianism* (London: Harcourt, 1976).
11. Hannah Arendt, "Imperialism, Nationalism, Chauvinism," *Review of Politics* 7, no. 4 (1945), 457.
12. Arendt, *Origins of Totalitarianism*, 123. She issues a similar though more muted warning toward the end of "Imperialism, Nationalism, Chauvinism" (462–63).
13. The Denshawai episode generated considerable unease among British socialist radicals about the hardening of imperial attitudes. The Irish dramatist and Fabian socialist Bernard Shaw wrote a stern diatribe against New Imperialism along Hobsonian lines that was published as "Preface for Politicians" with a 1907 edition of his play, *John Bull's Other Island*: "I have . . . to enforce my warning to England that if her Empire means ruling the world as Denshawai has been ruled in 1906—and that I am afraid is what the Empire does mean to the main body of our . . . Jingo plutocrats—then there can be no more sacred and urgent political duty on earth than the disruption, defeat and suppression of the Empire" ("Preface to Politicians," in *John Bull's Other Island* [New York: Brentano's, 1912], lix).
14. Flavus, "Imperialism and Indian Patriotism," *New Age* 5, no. 17 (1909): 313.
15. Joseph Schumpeter, *Imperialism and Social Classes: Two Essays*, trans. Heinz Norden (Cleveland, OH: Meridian Books, 1966), 6, 64.
16. Schumpeter, *Imperialism and Social Classes*, 6.
17. Ibid., 64, 72.
18. Ibid., 68, 70.
19. On the New Liberalism, see especially, C. F. G. Masterman, *The New Liberalism* (London: Leonard Parsons, 1920); Ramsay Muir, *The New Liberalism* (London: The Daily News, 1924); S. Collini, *Liberalism and Sociology: L. T. Hobhouse and Political Argument in England, 1880–1915* (Cambridge: Cambridge University Press, 1979); Michael Freedan, *The New Liberalism: An Ideology of Social Reform* (Cambridge: Cambridge University Press, 1978); P. Weiler, *The New Liberalism: Liberal Social Theory in Great Britain* (New York: Garland, 1982); Colin Cross, *The Liberals in Power, 1905–14* (London: Barrie and Rockcliff, 1963).
20. C. P. Scott, *C. P. Scott, 1846–1932: The Making of the Manchester Guardian* (London: Fredrick Muller, 1946), 85.
21. Percy Alden, *Democratic England* (New York: Macmillan, 1912), 6.
22. John Morley, *Fortnightly Review* 1 (1864): 491–92; also cited in Peter Clarke, *Liberals and Social Democrats* (Cambridge: Cambridge University Press, 1978), 6.
23. Ibid.
24. For a substantial discussion of the Rainbow Circle, see Clarke, *Liberals and Social Democrats*, 54–61. The concerns of the group are amply chronicled in their monthly publication, *The Progressive Review*, which was launched in 1896.

25. See Alden, *Democratic England*: "Few countries can claim to be wholly democratic in their form of government, but Great Britain has for a generation at least, been regarded as an essentially democratic state" (1).
26. C. F. G. Masterman, *How England Is Governed* (London: Selwyn and Blount, 1921), 262.
27. Élie Halévy, *The Rule of Democracy: 1905–1914*, trans. E. J. Watkin, vol. 6 of *A History of the English People in the Nineteenth Century* (London: Ernest Benn, 1952), 442–43.
28. Prospectus for the *Progressive Review*, August 1896, Papers of Herbert Louis Samuel A/10/5; House of Lords Records Office, London.
29. L. T. Hobhouse, cited in Clarke, *Liberals and Social Democrats*, 68.
30. Francis W. Hirst, Gilbert Murray, and J. L. Hammond, *Liberalism and the Empire: Three Essays* (London: R. Brimley Johnson, 1900), 196.
31. L. T. Hobhouse, *Democracy and Reaction* (London: T. Fisher Unwin, 1904), 22, 48.
32. Winston Churchill, *The People's Rights* (London: Jonathan Cape, 1909), 64.
33. *The First Years of Liberal Government: 1906–1908* (London: Liberal Publications Department, 1908), n.p.
34. Herbert Samuel, Minutes of the Rainbow Circle, 6 November 1895; cited in Clarke, *Liberals and Social Democrats*, 58.
35. Hobson, *Imperialism* and Hirst et al., *Liberalism and the Empire* were by far the most influential works on the New Liberal colonial critique; they were widely cited and debated by allies and detractors. L. T. Hobhouse, *Democracy and Reaction* is another important text. For secondary literature on the relevant debates, see, John Strachey, *The End of Empire* (London: Random House, 1960); Élie Halévy, *Imperialism and the Rise of Labor*, vol. 5 of *A History of the English People in the Nineteenth-Century* (London: Ernest Benn, 1951); Stephen Koss, ed., *The Pro-Boers: The Anatomy of an Anti-War Movement*, Studies in Imperialism, vol. 1 (Chicago: University of Chicago Press, 1973); Richard Price, *An Imperial War and the British Working Class* (London: Routledge and Kegan Paul, 1972); and Bernard Semmel, *Imperialism and Social Reform: English Social-Imperial Thought, 1895–1914* (Cambridge, MA: Harvard University Press, 1960).
36. Hirst et al., *Liberalism and the Empire*, 173.
37. Ibid., 171.
38. Ibid., 173; Hobson, *Imperialism*, 173.
39. Hobson, *Imperialism*, 172.
40. Ibid., 176, 178, 180, 174.
41. Ibid., 184, 172.
42. Ibid., 180.
43. Ibid., 172.
44. Churchill, *People's Rights*, 153.
45. Liberal Song Sheet (London: Liberal Publications Department, 1903), n.p.
46. Churchill, *People's Rights*, 9.
47. See *First Two Years of Liberal Government: 1906–1908* (London: Liberal Publications Department, 1908), n.p.

48. *The Triumphs of Liberalism* (London: Liberal Publications Department, 1908), 10; *The Truth about Tariff Reform* (London: Liberal Publications Department, 1907), n.p.
49. Hilaire Belloc, John Lawrence Hammond, Francis Wrigley Hirst, Philip James Macdonald, John Swinnerton Phillimore, and John Allsebrook Simon, *Essays in Liberalism by Six Oxford Men* (London: Cassell, 1897), 5.
50. *We Couldn't Care More*, in *Liberal Pamphlets: 1832–1908*, British Library, W. P. 8712, n. p.
51. Masterman, *How England Is Governed*, 262.
52. Churchill, *People's Rights*, 154; John Maccum, *Ethics of Citizenship* (Glasgow: Maclehose, Jackson, 1921), 7.
53. Alden, *Democratic England*, 7.
54. Herbert Samuel, *Liberalism: An attempt to state the principles and proposals of contemporary Liberalism in England; with an introduction by H. H. Asquith* (London: Grant Richards, 1902), 6.
55. David G. Ritchie, *The Principles of State Interference: Four essays on the political economy of Mr. Herbert Spencer, J. S. Mill, and T. H. Green* (London: Swan Sonnenschein, 1891), 169.
56. Gilbert Beith, "Foreword," in Edward Carpenter, *Toward Democracy* (London: GMP Publishers, 1985), 12.
57. Edward Carpenter, *Civilization: Its Cause and Cure* (London: George Allen and Unwin, 1917), 42.
58. See Carpenter, *Civilization: Its Cause and Cure*: "That is to say that during the civilization-period, the body being systematically wrapped in clothes, the *head* alone represents man—the little finnikin, intellectual, self-conscious man in contra-distinction to the cosmical man represented by the entirety of the bodily organs. The body has to be delivered from its swathings in order that the cosmical consciousness may once more reside in the human breast—we have to become 'all face' again—as the savage said of himself" (44).
59. Mary Warnock, in *Ethics Since 1900* (Oxford: Oxford University Press, 1966), gives an instructive account of the hold of idealist ethics in Britain and on the continent at the start of the twentieth century. Works dealing with the influence of T. H. Green and British Idealism upon the New Liberals include A. J. M. Milne, *The Social Philosophy of English Idealism* (London: George Allen and Unwin, 1962); and Andre Vincent and Raymond Plant, *Philosophy, Politics and Citizenship: The Life and Thought of the British Idealists* (Oxford: Basil Blackwell, 1984). See also David O. Brink, *Perfectionism and the Common Good: Themes in the Philosophy of T. H. Green* (New York: Oxford University Press, 2007); and Melvin Richter, *The Politics of Conscience: T. H. Green and His Age* (Cambridge, MA: Harvard University Press, 1964).
60. T. H. Green, *Prolegomena to Ethics*, ed. A. C. Bradley (Oxford: Clarendon University Press, 1899), 239–40.
61. Ibid., 226.
62. Ibid., 203.

63. Ibid., 236.
64. Ibid., 253.
65. Ibid., 246; 206.
66. Ibid., 446–47.
67. Masterman, *How England Is Governed*, viii; Sir Henry Jones, *The Principles of Citizenship* (London: Macmillan, 1919), 176.
68. *Triumphs of Liberalism*, 23; Churchill, *People's Rights*, 53–54.
69. Hobhouse, *Democracy and Reaction*, 221; Bernard Bosanquet, *The Principle of Individuality and Value* (London: Macmillan, 1912), 21; Churchill, *People's Rights*, 53.
70. Michael Hardt and Antonio Negri, *Commonwealth* (Cambridge, MA: Belknap Press, 2009), viii.
71. Discussions concerning the New Liberal common good are strikingly hostile to any assumption of equality imputed by this notion. As John Maccum puts it in his *Ethics of Citizenship*, "There is in truth, no fallacy more dangerous, because there is none more inviting, than that which brings what is complex and obscure under what is simple and familiar. And into this fallacy our grandfathers certainly fell, when, in vehement reaction against inequalities which had come to seem intolerable, they could not rest satisfied with anything short of the affirmation of the equality of men. It was more than fallacy. It was bad policy" (2). The New Liberal propaganda pamphlet *The Triumphs of Liberalism* nervously iterates the lesson that liberal democracy is not a doctrine of parity and equality: "That all men are equal in ability, in character, or in energy, and that all therefore are equally entitled to share in the world's gifts, is what no one will seriously contend" (23).
72. See Mrs. Bernard Bosanquet, *The Standard of Life and Other Studies* (London: Macmillan, 1898).
73. Bernard Bosanquet, "Charity Organization and the Majority Report," *International Journal of Ethics* 20 (July 1910): 398.
74. Stanley Cavell, *Cities of Words: Pedagogical Letters on a Register of the Moral Life* (Cambridge, MA: Belknap Press, 2004), 188–89. See also his "Declining Decline" and "Moral Perfectionism," in Stephen Mulhall, ed., *The Cavell Reader* (Oxford: Blackwell, 1996), 321–52, 353–68.
75. Carl Schmitt, *The Crisis of Parliamentary Democracy*, trans. Ellen Kennedy (Cambridge, MA: MIT Press, 1988), 17, 28, 32.
76. John Rawls, *A Theory of Justice*, rev. ed. (Cambridge, MA: Belknap Press, 1999), 19–24, 285–92.
77. Gandhi retained his accent on the ethicization or spiritualization of politics throughout his life. He makes the case vehemently in a 1920 essay entitled "Neither a Saint nor a Politician," in M. K. Gandhi, *Non-Violent Resistance* (New York: Schocken Books, 1961): "The politician in me has never dominated a single decision of mine, and if I seem to take part in politics it is only because politics encircle us today like the coil of a snake from which one cannot get out, no matter how much one tries. I wish therefore to wrestle

with the snake, as I have been doing with more or less success since 1894. . . . I have been experimenting with myself as my friends by introducing religion into politics. Let me explain what I mean by religion. It is not the Hindu religion . . . but the religion that transcends Hinduism, which changes one's very nature, which binds one indissolubly to the truth within and which ever purifies" (111). The essay attracted a great deal of attention in its time, notably from the Jewish philosopher Martin Buber. Though Buber was skeptical about Gandhi's intractable defense of nonviolence for all peoples and in every cir-cumstance, he greatly admired the view that the "transformation of institu-tions" should be built upon "a transformation of men also" (Martin Buber, "Gandhi, Politics and Us," in his, *Pointing the Way: Collected Essays by Martin Buber*, ed. and trans. M. F. Friedman [Schocken Books: New York, 1974], 138).

Like many recent interlocutors, Buber was justly nervous about the pos-sible complications attaching to Gandhi's usage of the term *religion*. Gandhi offers a more amenable gloss in a 1907 translated paraphrase of the pamphlet *Ethical Religion*, written by the American anarcho-socialist and civil rights activist William MacIntyre Salter, who was a brother-in-law of the pragma-tist philosopher William James and the founder of a Chicago chapter of the Society for Ethical Culture. Praising Salter for salvaging the purely ethical (that is to say, inner yet situated) component of religious life, Gandhi writes, "A Society has been founded which has shown, after an investigation of all religions, that not only do all of them teach morality but they are based for the most part on ethical principles; that it is one's duty to obey the laws of ethics whether or not one professes a religion; and that men who would not obey them could do no good either to themselves or to others, in this world or the next" (M. K. Gandhi, *Collected Works of Mohandas Karamchand Gandhi*, 100 vols. (Delhi: Publications Division, Ministry of Information and Broadcasting, 1960–1994), 6:212. All subsequent citations of this text are abbreviated as *CWMG*).

78. See Ritu Birla and Faisal Devji, eds., "Hind Swaraj," special issue, *Public Cul-ture* 23, no. 2 (2011); Ajay Skaria, "'Only One Word, Properly Altered': Gandhi and the Question of the Prostitute," *Postcolonial Studies* 10 (June 2007): 219–37; and Isabel Hofmeyr, *Gandhi's Printing Press: Experiments in Slow Read-ing* (Cambridge, MA: Harvard University Press, 2013).

79. M. K. Gandhi, *Hind Swaraj and Other Writings*, ed. Anthony J. Parel (Cam-bridge: Cambridge University Press, 1997), 116. I have written at greater length about Gandhi's transnational fin de siècle sources in my *Affective Communities: Anticolonial Thought, Fin de Siècle Radicalism, and the Politics of Friendship* (Durham, NC: Duke University Press, 2006). An earlier reading of *Hind Swaraj* has appeared in Mark Strand, ed., *City Secrets: Books, the Essential Insider's Guide*, (New York: Fang Duff Kahn, 2009), 156–61.

80. M. K. Gandhi, *CWMG*, 32:489.

81. These details are available in any biography of M. K. Gandhi, though few foreground the importance of Gandhi's encounter with the New Liberals

per se. For the precise details of this encounter, see James D. Hunt, *Gandhi in London* (Delhi: Promilla, 1993), 55–147.

82. M. K. Gandhi, *CWMG*, 6:274. For more on the New Liberal Ethical Societies, see G. Spillar, *The Ethical Movement in Great Britain* (London: Farleigh Press, 1934).

83. Gandhi, *CWMG*, 9: 516.

84. Ibid., 471.

85. Gandhi, *Hind Swaraj*, 32.

86. Gandhi, *Hind Swaraj*, 30.

87. Gandhi, *Hind Swaraj*, 67, 94.

88. Gandhi, *Hind Swaraj*, 73.

89. Gandhi, *Hind Swaraj*, 68.

90. Gandhi, *Hind Swaraj*, 68, 69, 97.

91. Gandhi, *Hind Swaraj*, 91.

92. Gandhi, *Hind Swaraj*, 69.

93. Ibid.

94. See *The Aryan Path*, 9, no. 9 (1938): 421–56.

95. Foucault's last work on cynicism coincided with the publication and runaway success of Peter Sloterdijk's *Critique of Cynical Reason*, trans. Michael Eldred (Minneapolis: University of Minnesota Press, 1987). In this lengthy and polemical essay, Sloterdijk also makes the case for a modern cynicism, though one that he posits as debased in comparison to an ancient Greek *kynicism.* In his argument the ancient variant promulgates a good realism committed to conscious living through forms of material embodiment that speak the truth of all that lies below in the hierarchy of the normative moral subject: "tongue-stuck out," "breasts," "fart," "refuse," and "pissing" (to cite some leading subheadings). By contrast, modern cynicism is a type of bad realism born of mindful false consciousness. It manifests, variously, as the political apathy, disregard for history, and mistrust for plans that characterize the dominant culture of the contemporary world at large. Both in its origins in the Weimer Republic and subsequent transmission through the century, this negative cynicism combines with a will for self-preservation and self-assertion, namely, the desire to get on in the world at any cost whatsoever. Bound as it is to a distinctly European cartography, Sloterdijk's ethical cartography is not always habitable, though its concession to cynicism's genealogical continuity is pertinent to our analysis. The modern cynicisms that we are tracking run exactly against the grain of the aggressive survivalism and self-elevation that Sloterdijk finds instantiated as fascism and imperialism within the culture of the Weimar Republic.

I am grateful to Tamara Chin for alerting me to the rich resources of ancient Cynicism for postcolonial considerations of radical democracy and ethical politics. In her forthcoming essay, "*Kosmopolitēs/ politēs tou kosmou/ civis mundi*: Preliminary Notes on the First Cosmopolitans," Chin argues that Diogenes' conception of cosmopolitanism asserted a novel ethical approach to politics that was antagonistic to empire and emperors.

96. Michel Foucault, *The Courage of Truth*, vol. 2 of *The Government of Self and Others, Lectures at the Collège de France, 1983–1984*, ed., Fredric Gros, trans. Graham Burchell (Basingstoke, UK: Palgrave Macmillan, 2011), 170. There are accounts of cynicism as a popular movement in R. Bracht Branham and Marie-Odile Goulet Cazé, eds., *The Cynics: The Cynic Movement in Antiquity and Its Legacy* (Berkeley and Los Angeles: University of California Press, 1996), 16; and Farrand Sayre, *The Greek Cynics* (Baltimore, MD: J. H. Furst, 1948), 25.
97. Michel Foucault, *Courage of Truth*, 227. See also Michel Foucault, *Discourse and Truth: The Problematization of Parrhesia*, six lectures given by Michel Foucault at the University of California at Berkley, October–November, 1983; available online at http://foucault.info/documents/parrhesia/.
98. Diogenes Laertius, *Lives of Eminent Philosophers*, vol. 2, trans. R. D. Hicks, Loeb Classical Library, No. 185 (Cambridge, MA: Harvard University Press, 2005), 73.
99. Ibid., 2:41. For more such examples of Diogenes' mockery of kings and kingship, see Dio Chrysostom, *Discourses* 1–11, vol. 1, trans. J. W. Cohoon Loeb Classical Library, No. 257 (Cambridge, MA: Harvard University Press, 2002), 269–81.
100. Foucault, *Courage of Truth*, 287, 244.
101. Diogenes Laertius, *Lives of Eminent Philosophers*, 2:51.
102. Dio Chrysostom, *Discourses*, 1:282–83.
103. Diogenes Laertius, *Lives of Eminent Philosophers*, 2:75.
104. Ibid., 2:55.
105. Foucault, *Courage of Truth*, 188.
106. Diogenes Laertius, *Lives of Eminent Philosophers*, 2:31.
107. Ibid., 2:33.
108. Michel Foucault points to this possibility in his 1983 Berkeley lectures, *Discourse and Truth*: "A historical problem concerning the origin of Cynicism is this. Most of the Cynics from the First Century B.C. and thereafter refer to either Diogenes or Antisthenes as the founder of the Cynic philosophy, and through these founders of Cynicism, they relate themselves back to the teachings of Socrates. According to Farrand Sayre, however, the Cynic Sect appeared only in the Second Century B.C., or two centuries after Socrates' death. We might be a bit skeptical about a traditional explanation given for the rise of the Cynic Sects—an explanation which has been given so often to account for so many other phenomena; but it is that Cynicism is a negative form of aggressive individualism which arose with the collapse of the political structures of the ancient world. A more interesting account is given by Sayre, who explains the appearance of the Cynics on the Greek philosophical scene as a consequence of expanding conquest of the Macedonian Empire. More specifically, he notes that with Alexander's conquests various Indian philosophies—especially the monastic and ascetic teaching of Indian Sects like the Gymnosophists—became more familiar to the Greeks" (n.p.).

109. Plutarch, *The Life of Alexander the Great*, trans. John Dryden (New York: Random House, 2004), 63.
110. Ibid., 63. For more conjectures on the identity of Dandamis, see N. Sen, *Ancient Indian History and Civilisation* (Delhi: New Age International, 1988), 128.
111. Diogenes Laertius, *Lives of Eminent Philosophers*, 2:475–77.
112. Sayre, *Greek Cynics*, 44–46, emphasizes this account.
113. For a succinct delineation of the Brahmana/Sramana divide, see Wendy Doniger, *The Hindus: An Alternative History* (New York: Penguin, 2009), 184–87. There is a rich account of Sramana renunciation and social critique in Freidhelm Hardy, *The Religious Culture of India: Power, Love, Wisdom* (Cambridge: Cambridge University Press, 1994), 168–89. Pivotal to this tradition, Hardy argues, is the rejection of the path of "becoming a *cakravartī*, a universal ruler," in favor of "its alternative, that of the Jina, a spiritual conqueror and victor" (168). This path of spiritual triumph consists in reducing the power to harm others and the temptation to elevate the self. In Hardy's words, "There is general consensus here as to what must be rejected, and what cultivated: total celibacy to overcome sexual passions, total poverty to overcome any clinging to material possessions, total avoidance of doing harm to any living being to get rid of violence, avoidance of alcohol as a prime cause of aggression, lust, and also mental delusion. Truthfulness and not boasting about one's supernatural faculties are further elements here, designed to eliminate more subtle forms of status-seeking and aggression" (176).
114. See Ramkrishna Bhattacharya, *Studies on the Cārvāka/Lokāyata* (London: Anthem Press, 2011); A. L. Basham, *History and Doctrines of the Ajivikas: A Vanished Indian Religion* (Delhi: Motilal Banarasidass, 1981); D. D. Kosambi, *An Introduction to the Study of Ancient Indian History* (Mumbai: Popular Prakashan, 1975), 162–71, and his *The Culture and Civilisation of Ancient India in Historical Outline* (Delhi: Vikas Publishing House, 1994), 96–114. For an imaginative reconstruction of the radical critique of hierarchy and rank among ancient Indian Ajivikas, Charvakas, Buddhists, and Jains, see Ramchandra Gandhi, *Sita's Kitchen: A Testimony of Faith and Inquiry* (New York: State University of New York Press, 1992).
115. Strabo, *Geography*, vol. 7, trans. Horace Leonard Jones, Loeb Classical Library, No. 241 (Cambridge, MA: Harvard University Press, 1995), 99. In his editorial notes Jones transliterates Strabo's "Brachmanes" and "Garmanes" as "Brahmans" and "Sramans," respectively (98, nn. 1, 2).
116. Ibid., 99, 115.
117. Ibid., 105.
118. Ibid., 113.
119. Strabo (after detailing Onescritus's encounter with Dandamis and his fellow naked philosopher "Calanus"), notes that "Nearchus speaks of the sophists as follows: That the Brachmanes engage in affairs of state and attend the kings as counselors; but that the other sophists investigate natural phenomena; and that Calanus is one of these; and that their wives join them in the

study of philosophy" (*Geography* 7:115). Elsewhere he offers this gloss on Megasthenes: "As for the Garmanes, he says that the most honourable of them are named Hylobii and that they live in forests, subsisting on leaves and wild fruits, clothed with the bark of trees, and abstaining from wine and the delights of love" (103).

120. See David M. Robinson, "Ancient Sinope," *American Journal of Philology* 27, no. 2 (1906): 126–334; Owen P. Doonan, *Sinop Landscapes: Exploring Connection in a Black Sea Hinterland* (Philadelphia: University of Pennsylvania Press, 2004); and Sayre, *Greek Cynics*, 40. There is a pertinent discussion of the philosophical exchanges between ancient Greece and India in Thomas McEvilley, *The Shape of Ancient Thought: Comparative Studies in Greek and Indian Philosophies* (New York: Allworth Press, 2002).

121. *The Greek Alexander Romance*, trans. Richard Stoneman (Harmondsworth, UK: Penguin, 1991), 131. *The Alexander Romance* describes the "gymnosophists" as Brahmanas, following the text of Palladius's, *De gentibus Indiae et de Bragmanibus*. In his introduction to *The Legends of Alexander the Great* (London: I. B. Taurius, 1994), Stoneman queries this description without placing too much value on securing the "real" identity of the gymnosophists: "Alexander's encounter with the naked philosophers of Taxila was a feature of all the historical accounts as well as of the *Alexander Romance*. In the *Romance* they are referred to not only as 'naked philosophers' but as 'the Brahmans or Oxydorkai" (i.e., Oxydracae). In fact they may not have been Brahmans at all but some other kind of ascetic, or perhaps Jains. (The possibility has been raised that they might have been Buddhists, but this seems unlikely). Whoever they were (and it is my belief that the information about them in the *Romance* preserves a kernel of historical truth about their beliefs and practices), they quickly became one of the standard features of any description of the East" (xxv). See also Richard Stoneman, "Who Are the Brahmans? Indian Lore and Cynic Doctrine in Palladius's *De Bragmanibus* and Its Models," *Classical Quarterly*, n.s., 44, no. 2 (1994): 500–510.

122. *Greek Alexander Romances*, 133.

123. See B. R. Ambedkar, *The Annihilation of Caste* (Jalandhar: Bheem Patrika Publications, 1982).

124. The literature in this field is rich and salutary. A canonical starting point is B. R. Ambedkar, *The Essential Writings of B. R. Ambedkar*, ed. Valerian Rodrigues (Delhi: Oxford University Press, 2002). See also, Gopal Guru, *Dalit Cultural Movement and Dialectics of Dalit Politics in Maharashtra* (Mumbai: Vikas Adhyayan Kendra, 1997), and his *Humiliation: Claims and Context* (Delhi: Oxford University Press, 2009); Kancha Ilaiah, *Why I Am Not a Hindu: A Sudra Critique of Hindutva Philosophy, Culture and Political Economy* (Calcutta: Samya, 2007). There are instructive discussions of the term *dalit* in the companion volumes, Manu Bhagvan and Anna Feldhaus, eds. *Claiming Power from Below: Dalits and the Subaltern Question in India* (Delhi: Oxford University Press, 2008), and their *Speaking Truth to Power: Religion, Caste and*

the Subaltern Question in India (Delhi: Oxford University Press, 2010). For a path-breaking analysis of *dalit* realist aesthetics, see, Toral Jatin Gajarwala, *Untouchable Fictions: Literary Realism and the Crisis of Caste* (New York: Fordham University Press, 2013).

125. Gandhi, *Hind Swaraj*, 90.
126. Ibid.

CHAPTER 1

1. Zeev Sternhell, "The 'Anti-Materialist' Revision of Marxism as an Aspect of the Rise of Fascist Ideology," *Journal of Contemporary History* 22, no. 3 (1987): 379. Emmet Larkin makes a similar point, arguing that it was only with the emergence of a potent antimaterialism during the early twentieth-century labor unrest that the long-standing but abstract socialist critique of "property" achieved its true charge: "Socialism had proved a threat to the traditional concept of property and the State since the *Communist Manifesto* and the Revolution of 1848. But it was not until the turn of the century that the threat actually became a menace" (*James Larkin: Irish Labor Leader, 1876–1947* [London: Routledge and Kegan Paul, 1965], xii).
2. Although 1914 is the official date for the English translation of Sorel's text, see George Sorel, *Reflections on Violence*, ed. Jeremy Jennings (Cambridge: Cambridge University Press, 2006), xxxv–xxxviii, for an account of the work's wide circulation in Europe from 1906 onward.
3. For Sorel's antimaterialist response to the "revisionist crisis" see Ernesto Laclau and Chantal Mouffe, *Hegemony and Socialist Strategy: Toward a Radical Democratic Politics* (Verso: New York, 2001), 36–42.
4. George Sorel, *Reflections on Violence*, trans. T. E. Hulme (New York: Peter Smith, 1915), 12. All subsequent references are to this edition.
5. Ibid.
6. "Ought Teachers to Form a Trade Union?" *New Age* 1, no. 23 (1907): 355.
7. *The Industrial Syndicalist* 1, no. 1 (1910): 2–3. Several contemporary and more recent commentators assert the syndicalist flavor of the prewar labor unrest. See, for instance, Arthur Lewis, *Syndicalism and the General Strike* (London: T. F. Unwin, 1912); J. W. Scott, *Syndicalism and Philosophical Realism: A Study in the Conditions of Contemporary Social Tendencies* (London: A. & C. Black, 1919); and George Dangerfield's 1935 *The Strange Death of Liberal England* (Stanford, CA: Stanford University Press, 1997). Although this labor unrest is largely obscured by the events of the First World War, contemporary observers all emphasize its seriousness as a revolution. Ernest Bevin, addressing the Shaw inquiry of 1920, cited in W. G. Runciman, *Relative Deprivation and Social Justice* (Harmondsworth, UK: Penguin, 1972), is representative in this recapitulation: "It was a period which, if the war had not broken out, would have, I believe, seen one of the greatest industrial revolts the world would ever have seen" (67).

8. Sternhell, "Anti-Materialist Revision of Marxism," 382. See also his *The Birth of Fascist Ideology: From Cultural Rebellion to Political Revolution* (Princeton, NJ: Princeton University Press, 1994). The specific link between philosophical and ethical antimaterialism and the rise of the revolutionary right is also traced by Mark Antliff, "The Jew as Anti-Artist: Georges Sorel, Anti-Semitism, and the Aesthetics of Class," *Oxford Art Journal* 20, no. 1 (1997): 50–67. Compare Mark Neocleous's view that "fascism regards Marxism and liberalism as the two sides of materialism" (*Fascism* [Minneapolis: University of Minnesota Press, 1997], 2).

9. The lyrics of this 1965 hit single, composed by John Lennon for the album *Rubber Soul,* are strangely apposite to the theoretical concerns of this discussion. The "nowhere man" they describe (also an everyman who is "a little bit like you and me") has no distinguishing plans, ambitions, "point of view," traits or, indeed, any recognizable cultural origin/geographical destination. He seems to prefer this leveling lack of subjective and objective properties over the knowledge that "the world is at your command."

10. The text of Narisinh Mehta's *Vaishnava Jana* can be loosely translated as follows.
    The one with knowledge of the pain of others is the true "Vaishnava."
    He knows no vanity for the happiness he brings (to those who suffer),
    Nor any need for gratitude.

    He worships all,
    Speaks ill of none.
    Blessed is the mother of such a one,
    Whose mind and tongue are reined.

    He sees everything with the eye of equality, and wants for nothing:
    Another's wife is as his mother.
    There is no falsehood (or excess) in his speech.
    He will not touch the possessions of others.

    A true renunciate of earthly goods,
    His real asceticism is self-directed.
    All the holy pilgrimages are embodied in him.

    He is without greed and disingenuousness,
    Without lust and without anger.
    Narsaiyyo sings that the mere sight of such a one
    Liberates seventy-one generations from the cycle of life and death.

11. M. K. Gandhi, *Collected Works of Mohandas Karamchand Gandhi,* 100 vols. (Delhi: Publications Division, Ministry of Information and Broadcasting, 1960–1994), 34:506. All subsequent citations of this text are abbreviated as *CWMG.*

12. Ibid., 44:206, 268.

13. Ibid., 231.

14. Ibid., 48:406.
15. Although R. H. Tawney's association with guild socialism was never as explicit as that of others in the circle around *The New Age*, he did perceive this credo both as a means to overturn the hold that parliamentary laborism had established over British socialism and as an effective counter to the prevailing ethos of increase and consumption with which the unions, to his mind, were becoming complicit. His support for the guild movement is well established in a speech from the early 1920s: "Whether our [economic] reorganisation is an advance or a reaction will depend on the clearness of our analysis of the present situation, and on the programme with which we meet it. Though possibly an unorthodox Gild Socialist, and certainly disagreeing with some of its exponents, I welcome it both for the one and the other. . . . I welcome the gild movement, therefore, in the first place because it brings English socialism out of the back waters and bypaths of government regulation, in which it was boring itself ten years ago, into the mainstream of the Socialist tradition, which has as its object not merely the alleviation of poverty, but an attack on the theory of functionless property" ("Speeches on Various Occasions," Tawney Papers, British Library of Political and Economic Science, London School of Economics; cited in Tawney, *R. H. Tawney's Commonplace Book*, ed. J. M. Winter and D. M. Joslin [Cambridge: Cambridge University Press, 2006], xviii). Tawney proved to be among guild socialism's most innovative and insightful interlocutors. One of his key contributions was to link this movement to the long tradition of indigenous British socialism, which made it much easier for its practitioners to distinguish their credo from coeval developments within continental socialism.
16. Tawney, *Commonplace Book,* 20.
17. Ibid.
18. Ibid., 42.
19. Ibid., 20, 19, 42 (my emphasis).
20. See Stefan Jonsson, *Subject without Nation: Robert Musil and the History of Modern Identity* (Durham, NC: Duke University Press, 2000).
21. Robert Musil, *The Man without Qualities*, trans. Sophie Wilkins and Burton Pike, 2 vols. (New York: Vintage International, 1996), 1:13.
22. Ibid., 1:432. Compare also the following variation on the theme: "It was just such a life that could be compared with a dream in which one finds oneself inside, at the very centre of things, one's ego rarefied, a vacuum through which all the feelings glow like blue neon lights." (1:444).
23. Ibid., 1:11.
24. Thorstein Veblen, *Vested Interests and the Common Man* (New York: B. W. Huebsch, 1919), 161–62.
25. See also Eric Hobsbawm, *The Age of Empire 1875–1914* (London: Weidenfeld and Nicholson, 1995).
26. W. H. Mallock, *Memoirs of Life and Literature* (New York: Harper and Brothers, 1920), 93. For more information on the English chapter of the *belle époque,*

NOTES TO PAGES 36–37

see J. Mordaunt Crook, *The Rise of the Nouveaux Riches Style and Status in Victorian and Edwardian Architecture* (London: John Murray, 1998), and Veblen, *Vested Interests*, 113.

27. There are fuller accounts of European and transatlantic *belle époque* excess and expenditure in Gilbert Guilleminault, *Avant 14: Fin de la belle époque* (Paris: Editions Denoel, 1966), and *Prélude à la Belle Époque* (Paris: Denoel, 1958).

28. Thorstein Veblen, *The Theory of the Leisure Class: An Economic Study in the Evolution of Institutions* (London: Macmillan, 1899), 87.

29. R. H. Tawney, *The Attack and Other Papers* (London: Allen and Unwin, 1953), 170.

30. Cited in Arnold Wright, *Disturbed Dublin: The Story of the Great Strike of 1913–1914, with a Description of the Industries of the Irish Capital* (London: Longmans, Green, 1914), 70. For comparison, see the socialist polemic of George Russell (AE) against plutocratic materialism and soullessness in his "Open Letter to the Dublin Employers," following the Commission of Inquiry into the Dublin Strikes: "Sirs—I address this warning to you, the aristocratic industry in this city, because like all aristocracies, you tend to grow blind in long authority and to be unaware that you and your class and its every action are being considered and judged day by day and those who have the power to shake or overturn the whole social order, and whose restlessness in poverty today is making our industrial civilisation stir like a quaking dog. . . . Your insolence and ignorance of the rights conceded to workers universally in the modern world were incredible, and as great as your inhumanity. If you had between you collectively a portion of human soul as large as a three-penny bit, you would have sat night and day with the representatives of labor, trying this or that solution of the trouble, mindful of the women and children, who were at least innocent of wrong against you. But no! You reminded labor you could always have your three square meals a day while it went hungry. . . . Cry aloud to Heaven for new souls! The souls you have got cast upon the screen of publicity appear like horrid and writhing creatures enlarged from the insect world, and revealed to us by the cinematograph" (*Irish Times*, 7 October 1913, n.p.).

31. Veblen, *Theory of the Leisure Class*, 103.

32. Ibid.

33. The demand for a workers' party unmediated by Liberal intervention or mediation comes from an 1885 speech made by a supporter of Mervyn Hawkes, one of many parliamentary reformers who were attempting to make working-class interests more articulate within the ranks of the Liberal Party: "Is ours a people's Parliament? We are told that Liberals are friends of the people. I don't want friends of the people, I want the people (cheers). Working men manage to create wealth and can therefore manage Parliamentary affairs (Hear, hear, and applause). I hope the necessary educated class will be our own. . . . I don't want 'liberal parties.' I want justice not liberality. I want to manage my own affairs. . . . My party is the people" (*Sheffield Weekly Echo*,

31 November 1885; cited in Sheila Rowbotham and Jeffrey Weeks, *The Personal and Sexual Politics of Edward Carpenter and Havelock Ellis* [London: Pluto Press, 1977], 40). The hint of anti-statism amongst such ardent supporters of a "workers' party" is heir to the anarchism at the heart of fin de siècle socialism. But where the latter simply did not believe in parliamentary laborism, the former inherited a contradictory view of their own enterprise— simultaneously wanting to participate in representative governance, and disenchanted with their own desire for procedural politics and its payoffs.

34. The Trades Disputes Act of 1906 reversed the verdict in the case of *Taff Vale Railway Co. v. Amalgamated Society of Railway Servants* (1901), which declared trade unions liable for any damages incurred in the course of industrial action.

35. For a cogent history of Liberal socialism and wage-reform policies in the period under review, especially in the light of J. A. Hobson's contribution, see Noel Thompson, *Political Economy and the Labor Party* (London: Routledge, 1996).

36. Frank Holmes, "Socialist Imperialism, *New Age* 1, no. 9 (1907): 138.

37. Mary Macarthur, cited in Mary Agnes Hamilton, *Mary Macarthur: A Biographical Sketch* (Westport, CT: Hyperion, 1926), 49.

38. Harry Roberts, *Nation and Athenaeum*, 1 June 1935; cited in Dangerfield, *Strange Death of Liberal England*, 223.

39. Cited in ibid., 240.

40. "Notes of the Week," *New Age* 7, no. 21 (1910): 481–82. There are numerous accounts, in this period, about the corrupting effect of parliamentary culture upon the working-class leader, whose elevation to government allegedly brings him closer to the world of *belle époque* privilege and affluence. The Lib-Lab councilor for Clapham, Fred Henderson (1867–1957), a prolific socialist writer, is especially condemnatory: "As for the . . . Labor Party itself," he writes, "its members, having recovered from their first surprise at finding themselves translated from the workshop and the trade union office to the most comfortable club in London . . . [have] settled down to the club life of the place as to the manner born, . . . purring audibly at every compliment to their political sagacity which they show[ed] by their continued and consistent support of the government in office" (*The Labor Unrest: What It Is and What It Portends* [London: Jarrold and Sons, 1912], 132). From another quarter, as we saw in the introduction, M. K. Gandhi picks up on this particular polemic in the course of his 1909 visit to London, when he singles out Parliament as a crucial locus of Western or modern materialism, in his *Hind Swaraj*: "The Parliament is simply a costly toy of the nation. These views are by no means peculiar to me. Some of the great English thinkers have expressed them. One of the members of the Parliament recently said that a true Christian could not become a member of it. . . . The Prime Minister is more concerned about his power than about the welfare of Parliament. . . . Prime Ministers . . . cannot be considered really patriotic. If they are to be

considered honest because they do not take what is generally known as a bribery, let them be so considered, but they are open to subtler influences. In order to gain their ends, they certainly bribe people with honours. I do not hesitate to say that they have neither honesty nor a living conscience" (M. K. Gandhi, *Hind Swaraj and Other Writings*, ed. Anthony J. Parel [Cambridge: Cambridge University Press, 1997], 31–32.

41. Ramsay MacDonald, *The Social Unrest: Its Cause and Solution* (London: T. N. Foulis, 1913), 96.

42. Fred Crowsley, "Don't Shoot," reprinted in Tom Mann, *Tom Mann's Memoirs* (London: Labor Publishing, 1923), 289–90.

43. Tawney, *Attack and Other Papers*, 163.

44. Dangerfield, *Strange Death of Liberal England*, 213. My description of the strikes draws on the accounts given by George Ranken Askwith, *Industrial Problems and Disputes* (New York: Harcourt Brace and Howe, 1921); Dangerfield, *Strange Death of Liberal England*; Henderson, *Labor Unrest*; Larkin, *James Larkin*; Mann, *Tom Mann's Memoirs*; MacDonald, *Social Unrest*; and Wright, *Disturbed Dublin*.

45. Scott, *Syndicalism and Philosophical Realism*, 13.

46. Philip Mairet, *A. R. Orage: A Memoir* (Hyde Park, NY: University Books, 1966), 67.

47. Wright, *Disturbed Dublin*, 255.

48. James Larkin, cited in Wright, *Disturbed Dublin*, 172.

49. R. M., "The Book of the Week: *Iolus, An Anthology of Friendship*, edited by Edward Carpenter," *New Age* 1, no. 4 (1907): 55; "Guild Socialism," *New Age* 11, no. 24 (1912): 559; R. H. Tawney, *The Sickness of An Acquisitive Society* (London: Fabian Society, 1920), 86. Tawney's classic work first appeared under this title in the English edition of 1920, although it was published as *The Acquisitive Society* in an American edition of the same year, and it is popularly known by this title. In his review of the American edition, Broadus Mitchell, an economist and socialist from Johns Hopkins, notes his strong preference for the moral clarity of the English title: "The book as it first appeared in England had the title, *The Sickness of an Acquisitive Society*, and this caption is more exactly descriptive than used in the American edition. The writer shows how capitalist society is breaking down, is lacking in continuing stamina" ("*The Acquisitive Society*, by R. H. Tawney," *South Atlantic Quarterly* 21, no. [1922]: 87). In recognition of the title by which Tawney's work is best recognized, I often refer to it as *The Acquisitive Society* in the main body of the text. Nonetheless, all subsequent quotations are taken from *The Sickness of an Acquisitive Society*.

50. Hamilton, *Mary Macarthur*, 103.

51. Ibid.

52. See Hamilton, *Mary Macarthur*, 72; Wright, *Disturbed Dublin*, 138–39; Larkin, *James Larkin*, 124; and Mann, *Tom Mann's Memoirs*, 268.

53. Wright, *Disturbed Dublin*, 96.

54. Tawney, *Commonplace Book*, 20.

55. Ibid., 5, 25; Tawney, *Sickness of an Acquisitive Society,* 29.

56. Lewis, *Syndicalism and the General Strike,* 93.

57. For the double meaning of *supplement* as that which adds to something while displacing or supplanting the same thing, see Jacques Derrida, *Of Grammatology,* trans., Gayatri Chakravorty Spivak (Baltimore, MD: Johns Hopkins University Press, 1976), 144–45.

58. Hannah Arendt, *The Human Condition,* 2nd ed. (Chicago: University of Chicago press, 1998), 74.

59. We gain testimony for such a reading when *belle époque* socialist Fred Henderson celebrates the labor unrest as "the entry of the real people of the drama upon the scene again, proclaiming in a manner most jarring to the nerves of political sagacity that they were still there" (*Labor Unrest,* 132–33). In a similar register, and in anticipation of events to come, a dance review of Isadora Duncan's rare music hall performance prior to the unrest reports that all evening "the democracy roared, clapped, stamped and bravoed" (W. R. Titterton, "Isadora Duncan Preaching," *New Age* 3, no. 12 [1908]: 226).

60. Ernest Belfort Bax, *Reminiscences and Reflexions of a Mid and Late Victorian* (London: G. Allen & Unwin, 1918), 46.

61. See Laclau and Mouffe, *Hegemony and Socialist Strategy,* 36–42; and Sorel, *Reflections on Violence,* 141–42. Ernest Belfort Bax was also active in the effort to make Marx metaphysical. Believing that Marx had succumbed to uncritical materialism in *Capital,* Bax advances, in *Outlooks from the New Standpoint* (London: Swan Sonnenchein, 1891), the view that "the dialectic method without metaphysic is a tree cut away from its roots" (187). A critical discussion of Bax's efforts to repair the dialectic in the context of early twentieth-century British and European socialism is available in Mark Bevir, "Marxist, Idealist and Positivist," *Journal of the History of Ideas* 54, no. 1 (1993): 119–35.

62. See Jacques Derrida, *Of Spirit: Heidegger and the Question,* trans. Geoffrey Bennington and Rachel Bowlby (Chicago: University of Chicago Press, 1987) for a critical meditation on the view, announced in Heidegger's corpus, that Western or modern metaphysics insinuates a troubling synonymity between the history of spirit and the history of the subject.

63. Sorel, *Reflections on Violence,* 298. See also Sorel's characteristic fulminations against academic philosophy: "The professors of the *little science* . . . assert very loudly that they will only admit into thought abstractions analogous to those used in the deductive sciences. . . . We do nothing great without the help of warmly-coloured and clearly-defined images, which absorb the whole of our attention; now is it possible to find anything more satisfying from their point of view than the general strike?" (163, 164–65).

64. Ibid., 247.

65. T. E. Hulme, "Searchers After Reality: Philosophy Is a Sign of the Times," *New Age* 6, no. 5 (1909): 108. For Tawney's distinctly Christian exemplifications of "poor philosophy," see his *Attack and Other Papers*: "Obviously religion

is 'a thing of the Spirit.' But the social order is also a thing of the spirit. . . .
The suggestion that a Church which takes such issues seriously must necessarily succumb to a materialist utopianism deserves consideration." "The
view that this world is, of its very nature, a realm of darkness, divided by an
impassable gulf from the Kingdom of the Spirit, and that the Christian is
concerned with the latter alone, has a long history behind it, and does not
lack powerful exponents today. It is a conception, however, which it is somewhat difficult to reconcile either with the facts of experience or with the
doctrine of the Incarnation. Men have always desired to serve two masters"
(173–74, 175).

66. Jerzy Grotowski, *Towards a Poor Theatre*, ed. Eugenio Barba (New York: Routledge, 2002), 16.

67. T. E. Hulme, "Searchers After Reality: Haldane," *New Age* 5, no. 17 (1909): 316.

68. For an account of the syndicalist and Sorelian deployment of the Bergsonian
themes of intuition, vitalism, flux, and the myth, see Sternhell, "Anti-
Materialist Revision of Marxism," 284; Mark Antliff, "The Jew as Anti-Artist";
and Richard Vernon, *Commitment and Change: George Sorel and the Idea of Revolution* (Toronto: University of Toronto Press, 1978). While Sorel directly bor-
rows several terms and phrases from Bergson, he also imitates the latter more
diffusely in matters of method and style. See, for instance, Sorel, *Reflections
on Violence*, 5, 6, 25, 26, 28, 30, 113, 117, 118, 120–22, 133, 134, 237, and *Illusion of Progress*, trans. Charlotte and John Stanley (Berkeley and Los Angeles:
University of California Press, 1969), 1–29. With regard to his transmission
within guild socialist circles, Henri Bergson is first mentioned in *New Age* 5,
no. 10 (1909) in T. E. Hulme's combined review of William James's, *A Pluralist
Universe* (in which the American philosopher is lyrical in his early praise of
Bergsonian metaphysics) and of the 1907 French edition of Bergson's *Creative
Evolution*. Hulme credits James with conveying the French philosopher so effectively across the channel that "now we shall hear of nothing but Bergson"
(198). But a few months later, in "Philosophy Is a Sign of Our Times," Hulme
asserts that, with the ascendancy of Jules de Gaultier, Boutroux, Le Roy, and
Bergson, among others, "the centre of interest in philosophy has shifted
from Germany to France" (107).

69. The curiosity of Bergson's introductory gesture is eloquently clarified by
John Mullarkey, "'The Very Life of Things': Thinking Objects and Reversing
Thought in Bergsonian Metaphysics," in *An Introduction to Metaphysics*, by
Henri Bergson, ed. John Mullarkey and Michael Kolkman (Basingstoke, UK:
Palgrave Macmillan, 2007): "In 1903 Henri Bergson published an essay in
the *Revue de métaphysique et de morale*, a journal that was only ten years in
circulation and yet whose title still dated it as a product of the nineteenth
century. Bergson's essay was 'An Introduction to Metaphysics.' Why did
this metaphysics—a 2,300-year-old discipline—need to be 'introduced'?
This was no student text and there is little mention in it of the rudiments of
traditional metaphysics (the supersensory, the transcendental, deduction,

the *a priori*). So to what was Bergson 'introducing' us, what was he 'leading us into,' in this metaphysics of his? (ix)."

70. In Gilles Deleuze, *Bergsonism*, trans. Hugh Tomlinson and Barbara Habberjam (New York: Zone, 1988), the translators substitute the term *possible* for *potentiality*, although in Deleuze's own readings the possible is identifiably potentiality in the Aristotelian sense. For Deleuze's explanation of Bergson's apparent philosophical preference for virtuality over potentiality or possibility, see chapter 5, "*Élan Vital* as Movement of Differentiation," especially 96–103. Deleuze makes the case that Bergson suppresses the older Aristotelian concept of potentiality in favor of virtuality because the latter concept, which bears no relation of derivation from, or resemblance to, a pregiven actual, is better equipped for the liberation of the themes of novelty, invention, creativity, and difference to which Bergson is profoundly committed. This may well be the case. But the Bergsonians whom I am following in the main discussion distinctly picked up on the ramifications of the concept of potentiality, albeit misguidedly, and my aim is to foreground what they would have regarded as evidence for their claims in Bergson's oeuvre.

71. Henri Bergson, *Creative Evolution* (New York: Cosimo Classics, 2005), 343–44.

72. Ibid., 43.

73. Bergson, *Introduction to Metaphysics*, 6.

74. Bergson, *Creative Evolution*, 8, 9, 16, 18; *Introduction to Metaphysics*, 38.

75. Bergson, *Introduction to Metaphysics*, 128.

76. Ibid.

77. Henri Bergson, *Creative Evolution*, 45.

78. Ibid., 344.

79. Gilles Deleuze, *Bergsonism*, 46–47.

80. Henri Bergson, *Creative Evolution*, 347.

81. Bergson, *Introduction to Metaphysics*, 5, 41; *Creative Evolution*, 107.

82. See Bax, *The Real, the Rational and the Alogical* (London: Grant Richards, 1920).

83. Sorel, *Reflections on Violence*, 94.

84. Eduard Berth, *Les méfaits des intellectuels* (Paris: M. Riviere, 1914), 212; cited in Paul Mazgaj, "The Young Sorelians and Decadence," *Journal of Contemporary History* 17 (January 1982): 182.

85. Mazgaj, "Young Sorelians," 184.

86. Sorel, *Reflections on Violence*, 98.

87. Ibid., 292.

88. Arendt, *Human Condition*, 49.

89. Mazgaj, "Young Sorelians," 185, 186. See George Valois, *L'homme qui vient: Philosophie de l'autorité* (Paris: Nouvelle Librarie Nationale, 1906), and *La révolution nationale: Philosophie de la victoire* (Paris: Nouvelle Librarie Nationale, 1924). See also Peter Dodge, ed. and trans. *A Documentary Study of Henrik de Man, Socialist Critic of Marxism* (Princeton, NJ: Princeton University Press, 1979).

90. Giorgio Agamben, *Homo Sacer: Sovereign Power and Bare Life*, trans. Daniel Heller-Roazen (Stanford, CA: Stanford University Press, 1998): "A principle of potentiality is inherent in every definition of sovereignty. In this sense . . . the sovereign state is founded on an 'ideology of potentiality'" (47n).
91. T. E. Hulme, *Speculations: Essays on Humanism and the Philosophy of Art* (London: Routledge and Kegan Paul, 1924), 48.
92. Hulme, *Speculations*, 63.
93. Tawney, *Sickness of an Acquisitive Society*, 66–67.
94. For an exquisite meditation on modern materialism as a violence that turns human beings into things while they are still alive, see Simone Weil and Rachel Bespaloff, *War and the Iliad*, trans. Mary McCarthy (New York: New York Review of Books, 2005), 5.
95. Tawney, *Attack and Other Papers*, 51.
96. Tawney, *Sickness of an Acquisitive Society*, 67; *Attack and Other Papers*, 188.
97. Hulme, *Speculations*, 116.
98. Ibid., 120.
99. In tracking the philosophical genealogy of this thought, we should note Aristotle's insistence upon both being and nonbeing, the positive and the negative, in fact, as types of *capacities* possessed by all entities: "It is possible that a thing may be capable of being and yet not be, capable of not being and yet be. Similarly in the other categories: that which is capable of walking may not walk, and that which is capable of not walking may walk. A thing is 'capable' of something if there is nothing impossible in its having the actuality of that which it is said to have the potency" (Aristotle, *Metaphysics*, ed. and trans. John Warrington (London: J. M. Dent and Sons, 1956), 227–28.
100. Giorgio Agamben, *Potentialities: Collected Essays in Philosophy*, trans. Daniel Heller-Roazen (Stanford, CA: Stanford University Press, 1999), 181, 182.
101. Tawney, *Commonplace Book*, 17.
102. Arendt, *Human Condition*, 193.

CHAPTER 2

1. The Italian philosopher Gianni Vattimo describes critical interest in spiritually cultivated forms of imperfection, in positive terms, as "weak thinking" or *"pensiero debole."* This gives emphasis "not to the power and glory of God but to God's suffering and love—from the being of God to the story of God's being with the poor, the hungry and the outcast" (Jeffry W. Robbins, "After the Death of God," in *After the Death of God*, ed. John D. Caputo and Gianni Vattimo (New York: Columbia University Press, 2007), 9–10. See also Gianni Vattimo, *The End of Modernity*, trans. Jon R. Snyder (Baltimore, MD: Johns Hopkins Press, 1988); and Santiago Zabala, ed., *Weakening Philosophy: Essays in Honor of Gianni Vattimo* Montreal: McGill-Queen's University Press, 2007). The epilogue to this book takes up the issue of how the analysis of imperfectionist forms of ethical life calls for an imperfectionist critical methodology.

2. William James, *The Varieties of Religious Experience* (New York: Simon and Schuster, 1997), 229, 296.
3. Ibid., 289, 38, 293.
4. Ibid., 295.
5. Pierre Hadot, *Philosophy as a Way of Life: Spiritual Exercises from Socrates to Foucault*, ed. Arnold Davidson, trans. Michael Chase (Oxford: Blackwell, 1995), 88. Peter Sloterdijk also describes ethics as a project of self-immunization in *You Must Change Your Life: On Anthropotechnics*, trans. Wieland Hoban (Cambridge: Polity, 2013). In his words, "The hero of the following account, *Homo immunologicus*, who must give his life, with all its dangers and surfeits, a symbolic framework, is the human that struggles with itself in concern for its form. We will characterize it more closely as the ethical human being" (10). In a curious departure from his arguments elsewhere in favor of a cynic ethics against elevation, Sloterdijk's recent work defends the necessary vertical tensions of immunological practicing life, concluding that this ethical subject must conceive himself in strictly perfectionist terms, as "a being potentially 'superior to himself,'" if not to others (13).
6. Max Müller, *Ramakrishna, His Life and Sayings* (London: Longmans, Green, 1898), 1.
7. Romain Rolland, *The Life of Ramakrishna*, trans. E. F. Malcolm-Smith (Calcutta: Advaita Ashram, 1997), xxi, xviii, 1.
8. Romain Rolland, *The Life of Vivekananda and the Universal Gospel: A Study of Mysticism and Action in Living India*, trans. E. F. Malcolm-Smith (Calcutta: Advaita Ashram, 1995), 20. Vivekananda's mission to the West stands somewhere between the defensiveness of later cultural nationalists and the iconoclasm of earlier Indian reformers, such as Raja Rammohun Roy and Keshub Cunder Sen. In widely publicized British tours, Roy and Sen spoke in favor of the Christianization of Indian life. Jeremy Bentham praised Roy, especially, as an Indian Erasmus and a Bengali Luther. Vivekananda was a more liminal figure, part iconoclast and part nationalist. Like many of the figures with whom this chapter is concerned, his genius lay in celebrating and extending the many traditions of Indian/indigenous self-critique.
9. *The Daily Inter-Ocean*, cited in *The Dawn of Religious Pluralism: Voices from the World's Parliament of Religions*, ed. Richard Hughes Seager (LaSalle, IL: Open Court, 1993), 337.
10. Walter R. Houghton, ed., *Neely's History of the Parliament of Religions and Religious Congresses at the World's Columbian Exposition* (New York: F. Tennyson Neely, 1894), 34.
11. John Henry Barrows, *The Parliament of Religions*, 2 vol. (Chicago, 1893), 1: 18.
12. Alain Badiou, *Saint Paul: The Foundation of Universalism*, trans. Ray Brassier (Stanford, CA: Stanford University Press, 2003), 37, 14.
13. Swami Chidatmananda ed., *Reminiscences of Swami Vivekananda, by His Eastern and Western Admirers* (Calcutta: Advaita Ashram, 1964), 245.

14. Swami Vivekananda, *The Complete Works of Swami Vivekananda*, ed. Swami Mumukshananda, Mayavati Memorial Edition, 9 vols. (Calcutta: Advaita Ashram, 2000), 1:3–4.

15. See Richard King, "Asian Religions and Mysticism: The Legacy of William James in the Study of Religions," in *William James and "The Varieties of Religious Experience": A Centenary Celebration*, ed. Jeremy Carrette (London: Routledge; and New York: Abingdon, 2005), 115; Christopher Isherwood, *The Wishing Tree: Christopher Isherwood on Mystical Religion*, ed. Robert Adjemian (San Francisco: Harper & Row, 1987), 121–22. For a transcript of Vivekananda's address to the Harvard Graduate Philosophical Society, see *Complete Works of Swami Vivekananda*, 1:357–65.

16. Pravrajika Prabuddhaprana, *The Life of Sara Chapman Bull: The American Mother of Swami Vivekananda* (Calcutta: Sri Sarada Math, 2002), 183.

17. There are rich accounts of Vivekananda's successful outreach to the West in Margaret Elizabeth Noble, *The Master as I Saw Him* (London: Longmans, Green, 1910); Swami Bodhasarananda, ed., *The Life of Swami Vivekananda by His Eastern and Western Disciples* (Kolkata: Advaita Ashram, 2008); Eleanor Stark, *The Gift Unopened: A New American Revolution*, 2 vols. (Portsmouth, NH: Peter Randall, 1988); Marie Louise Burke, *Swami Vivekananda in the West: New Discoveries* (Mayavati: Advaita Ashram, 1983); William Radice, ed., *Swami Vivekananda and the Modernization of Hinduism* (New Delhi: Oxford University Press, 1998); Carl T. Jackson, *The Oriental Religions and American Thought: Nineteenth-Century Explorations* (Westport, CT: Greenwood Press, 1981); Carl T. Jackson, *Vedanta for the West: The Ramakrishna Movement in the United States* (Bloomington: Indiana University Press, 1994).

18. M. K. Gandhi, *An Autobiography; or, The Story of Experiments with Truth*, trans. Mahadev Desai (Harmondsworth, UK: Penguin Books, 1982), 14.

19. For Sri Ramana's Western disciples, see A. R. Natarajan, ed., *First Meetings with Ramana Maharshi* (Bangalore: Ramana Maharshi Centre for Learning, 1996), and A. R. Natarajan, ed., *The Inner Circle* (Bangalore: Ramana Maharshi Centre for Leaning, 1996). The best English-language source on Sri Ramakrishna remains Mahendranath Gupta, *The Gospel of Sri Ramakrishna, Originally Recorded in Bengali by M., a Disciple of the Master*, trans. Swami Nikhilananda, 2 vols. (Chennai: Sri Ramakrishna Math, 1942). Peter Heehs, *The Lives of Sri Aurobindo* (New York: Columbia University Press, 2008), is a rich spiritual biography of the yogi. The literature on Gandhi is too voluminous to list here, but Rajmohan Gandhi, *Mohandas: A True Story of a Man, His People, and an Empire* (Delhi: Penguin Books India, 2006) is perhaps the most detailed recent biography, also sensitive to Gandhi's spiritual life.

20. William Barclay Parsons, *Psychoanalysis and Mysticism: The Freud-Rolland Correspondence*, PhD diss., University of Chicago, Divinity School, 2 vols., Chicago, Illinois, March 1993, 2:379, 382, 386. See also his *The Enigma of the Oceanic Feeling: Revisioning the Psychoanalytic Theory of Mysticism* (New York: Oxford University Press, 1999).

21. Parsons, *Psychoanalysis and Mysticism*, 2:384.
22. Romain Rolland, cited in David James Fisher, *Romain Rolland and the Politics of Intellectual Engagement* (Berkeley and Los Angeles: University of California Press, 1988), 48.
23. Parsons, *Psychoanalysis and Mysticism*, 2:377.
24. Geraldine P. Lilla, "Liluli: A Triumph of Disillusion," *North American Review* 213 (May 1921): 676–80; Benjamin de Casseres, "Rolland's Sublime Farce," *New York Times*, 11 July 1920.
25. Hugo of St. Victor, *The Didascalicon of Hugo of St. Victor: A Medieval Guide to the Arts*, trans. Jerome Taylor (New York: Columbia University Press, 1996), 101. Eric Auerbach offers a sympathetic gloss on this passage in, "Philology and *Weltliteratur*," trans. Maire and Edward Said, *Centennial Review* 13 (Winter 1969), 1–17. Though Hugo's dictum, he argues, may help (the philologist especially) to transcend the pitfalls of patriotism, there is equal benefit in resisting its second command to transcend *cosmophilia*: "It is a good way also for one who wishes to earn a proper love for the world" (17).
26. Sigmund Freud, *The Future of an Illusion*, trans. and ed. James Strachey (New York: W. W. Norton, 1989, 41–42.
27. Parsons, *Psychoanalysis and Mysticism*, 2:380.
28. Ibid.
29. Nicolas Berdyaev, *Slavery and Freedom*, trans. R. M. French (London: Centenary Press, 1944), 18.
30. Rolland, *Life of Vivekananda*, 17.
31. Ibid., 21.
32. See Romain Rolland to Sigmund Freud, December 5, 1927, in Parsons, *Psychoanalysis and Mysticism*: "I thank you for being so kind as to send me your lucid and valiant little book. With a calm good sense, and in a moderate tone, it tears away the blindfolding bandage of eternal adolescence, which affects us all, whose amphibian spirit floats between the illusion of yesterday and . . . the illusion of tomorrow.

      "Your analysis of religion is just. But I would like to see you make an analysis of spontaneous religious sentiment, or more exactly, of religious feeling, which is completely different from religions in and of themselves and much more durable.

      "By this I mean: completely independent of all dogma, all credo, all church organization, all Sacred Books, any hope of a personal afterlife etc.—and the simple and direct fact of the 'eternal' (which could well not be eternal but simply without perceptible limits, and in that way oceanic).

      "The feeling is, in truth, of subjective character. But as it is common to thousands (millions) of men recently living with thousands (millions) of individual nuances, it is possible to submit it to analysis with an approximate accuracy.

      "I think you will classify it among the *Zwangsneurosen*. But I have often had the accession to test its rich and beneficial energy, be it in the religious souls of the West, Christian or non-Christian—in the great spirits of Asia, who have become familiar to me—among whom I count many friends . . . and about which I will, in a future book, study two nearly contemporary personalities (the first one belonged to the late nineteenth-century, the second died in the early years of the twentieth) who have manifested a genius of thought and action which has proved to be powerfully regenerative for their country and for the world. [The two personalities are Ramakrishna and Vivekananda, respectively].

"I myself am familiar with this feeling. Throughout my life, it has never failed me; and I have always found in it a source of vital renewal. In this sense, I can say that I am profoundly 'religious'—without this constant state (like an underground sheet of water which I feel flushing under the bark) affecting in any way my critical faculties and my freedom to exercise them—even if that goes against the immediacy of this internal experience. Thus I openly lead, without discomfort and without conflict, a 'religious' life (in the sense of this prolonged feeling) and a life of critical reason (which is without illusion).

"I add that this 'oceanic' feeling has nothing to do with my personal aspirations. Personally I aspire to eternal rest; afterlife by no means attracts me. But the feeling I have thrust upon me is a fact. It is a contact" (2:380–81).

33. Parsons, *Psychoanalysis and Mysticism*, 2: 381.

34. Sigmund Freud, *Civilization and Its Discontents*, trans. James Strachey (New York: W. W. Norton, 1989), 11.

35. See *Civilisation and Its Discontents*: "The idea of men's receiving an intimation of their connection to the world around them through an immediate feeling which is from the outset directed to that purpose sounds so strange and fits in so badly that one is justified in attempting to discover a psycho-analytic—that is, genetic explanation for such a feeling. . . . Toward the outside, . . . the ego seems to maintain clear and sharp lines of demarcation. There is only one state—admittedly an unusual state, but not one that can be stigmatized as pathological—in which it does not do this. At the height of being in love the boundary between ego and object threatens to melt away" (12–13).

36. Ibid., 11–12.

37. See Susan Bayly, "Caste and 'Race' in the Colonial Ethnography of India," in *The Concept of Race in South Asia*, ed. Peter Robb (Delhi: Oxford University Press, 1995), 176–214.

38. Robert Knox, "Race in Legislation and Political Economy," *Anthropological Review* 4, no. 13 (1866): 116.

39. Ibid.

40. Ibid., 115.

41. The rupture between eighteenth-century anti-imperial radicalism and nineteenth-century liberal imperialism is clarified in Tzvetan Todorov, *On Human Dignity: Nationalism, Racism, and Exoticism in French Thought*, trans.

Catherine Porter (Cambridge, MA: Harvard University Press, 1993); Jennifer Pitts, *A Turn to Empire: The Rise of Imperial Liberalism in Britain and France* (Princeton, NJ: Princeton University Press, 2005); and Shankar Muthu, *Enlightenment against Empire* (Princeton, NJ: Princeton University Press, 2003).

42. Étienne Balibar, *Politics and the Other Scene*, trans. Christine Jones, James Swenson, and Chris Turner (London: Verso, 2002), 165. Compare Rousseau's argument that decent communal life calls for a social or civic adjustment to natural or individual goods: "The fundamental compact . . . substitutes a moral and legitimate equality for whatever physical inequality nature may have been able to impose on men, and that, however unequal in force or intelligence they may be, men all become equal by convention and by right" (Jean-Jacques Rousseau, *On the Social Contract*, trans. David A. Cress [Indianapolis, IN: Hackett, 1987], 29). David Hume, the great spokesman of the human passions, also posits politics as a homogenizing artfulness of the state that is crucial for good sociality yet by no means natural to the mind of man. See David Hume, *A Treatise of Human Nature*, ed. David Fate Norton and Mary J. Norton (Oxford: Oxford University Press, 2003), 307–66.

43. J. S. Mill, *On Liberty*, ed. Elizabeth Rapaport (Indianapolis, IN: Hackett, 1978), 57.

44. Ibid., 58.

45. Alexis de Tocqueville, *Democracy in America and Two Essays on America*, trans. Gerald E. Bevan (Harmondsworth, UK: Penguin, 2003), 527; Mill, *On Liberty*, 63.

46. Knox, "Race in Legislation," 120. A similar point is made by James Hunt, in his capacity as president of the Anthropological Society of London: "It has been said that the present slave-owners of America, no more think of insurrection amongst their full-blooded slaves than they do of rebellion amongst their cows and horses" (James Hunt, "The Negro's Place in Nature," in *Memoirs Read Before the Anthropological Society of London*, vol. 1 (London: Trübner, 1863–64), 28.

47. William Jones, "Discourse the Ninth, On the Origin and Families of Nations," *Asiatick Researches; or Transactions of the Society Instituted in Bengal, for Inquiring into the History and Antiquities, the Arts, Sciences, and Literature of Asia*, vol. 3 (London: T. Malden, 1807), 481; Max Müller, *Lectures on the Science of Language, Delivered at the Royal Institution of Great Britain in April, May, and June 1961*, second series (New York: Scribner, Armstrong, 1862), 169, 170.

48. This case is made plainly in H. H. Risley, "The Study of Ethnology in India," *Journal of the Anthropological Institute of Great Britain and Ireland* 20 (1891): "The Indian caste-system is a highly developed expression of the primitive principle of a *taboo* which came into play when the Aryans first came into contact . . . with the Dravidians. This principle derived its initial force from the sense of difference of race as indicated by difference of color" (260).

49. So we learn from John Nesfield, *Brief View of the Caste System of the North-Western Provinces and Oudh, together with an Examination of the Names and*

Figures Shown in the Census Report, 1882 (Allahabad: North Eastern Provinces and Oudh Government Press, 1885): "White-complexioned foreigners who called themselves by the name Arya, invaded the Indus valley via Kabul and Kashmir some four thousand years ago, [but] the blood imported by this foreign race became gradually absorbed into the indigenous, . . . so that almost all traces of the conquering race eventually disappeared. . . . The 'Aryan brother' is indeed a . . . mythical being" (3–4).

50. Many critics and historians have observed a hardening of colonial policy in India from the 1870s onward, corresponding with the rise of disciplinary race ethnology. See, especially, Uday Singh Mehta, *Liberalism and Empire: A Study in Nineteenth-Century British Liberal Thought* (Chicago: University of Chicago Press, 1999), 190–201. It is less well acknowledged that harsh administrators of the time, such as Henry Sumner Maine and James Fitzwilliam Stephen, combined the new nostalgia for Aryan caste hierarchy with stark recommendations against the spread of democracy within Europe as well. Both wrote substantial tracts against the perils of popular government at home. Maine reintroduced into contemporary jurisprudence a yearning for unwritten ancient laws, of which caste-aristocrats were once the sole depositories and administrators. See James Fitzwilliam Stephen, *Liberty, Equality, Fraternity*, ed. Stuart D. Warner (1873; repr., Liberty Fund, 1993); Henry Sumner Maine, *Popular Government* (1885; repr., Indianapolis, IN: Liberty Classics, 1976); Henry Sumner Maine, *Ancient Law* (1866; repr., New Brunswick, NJ: Transaction, 2009).

51. Indian Census Commissioner, *Census of India, 1901*, 24 vols. (Calcutta: Superintendent of Government Printing, 1902–); India Census Commissioner, *General Report on the Census of India, 1901* (London: His Majesty's Stationery Office, 1904).

52. For a history of South Asian cultural nationalism, see Christophe Jaffrelot, *The Hindu Nationalist Movement and Indian Politics* (New York: Columbia University Press, 1996). The copious literature of this movement includes Har Bilas Sarda, *Hindu Superiority: An Attempt to Determine the Position of the Hindu Race in the Scale of Nations* (Ajmer: Rajputana Printing Works, 1906); V. D. Savarkar, *Hindutva* (New Delhi: Central Hindu Yuvak Sabha, 1938); M. S. Golwakar, *We or Our Nationhood Defined* (Nagpur: Bharat Prakashan, 1939).

53. Risley, "Study of Ethnology in India," 247.

54. The influential Nazi ideologue Alfred Rosenberg hints despairingly at such recuperation in his 1930 work, *The Myth of the Twentieth Century: An Evaluation of the Spiritual-Intellectual Confrontations of Our Age* (Wentzville, MO: Invictus Books, 2011): "Every European sees Old India as a land of his dreams. . . . As a consequence, these Indian seekers preached Europe's salvation through the ideas of old India. They did not even notice that this Aryan India had . . . perished from the ideas of the later Upanishads with their endless widening of the heart. . . . [Now] Rabindranath Tagore sees the salvation of the world coming from this form of nonviolent

nationalism. Gandhi preaches constant passive resistance as a popular movement" (436).

My arguments in this section regarding the opposition between antinomian mysticism and colonial race ethnography are complicated by Sheldon Pollock, "Deep Orientalism? Notes on Sanskrit and Power beyond the Raj," in *Orientalism and the Postcolonial Predicament: Perspectives on South Asia*, ed. Carol Breckenridge and Peter Van de Veer (Philadelphia: University of Pennsylvania Press, 1993), 76–133. Compare his "From Discourse of Ritual to Discourse of Power in Sanskrit Culture," *Journal of Ritual Studies* 4 (Summer 1990): 315–45, and *The Language of the Gods in the world of Men: Sanskrit Culture and Power in Premodern India* (Berkeley and Los Angeles: University of California Press, 2006).

Pollock argues that the errors of the European Aryan hypothesis would not have been possible without prior errors of the same type within Indian tradition. There is plenty of evidence for this argument. The *Mimamsakas*, arguably the most sophisticated circle of Sanskrit intellectuals in late Vedic India, defended very stringent caste prohibitions with regard to the performance of Vedic rituals. These prohibitions were reinforced in subsequent medieval, elite *Dharmashastrik* and *Purvamimamsa* traditions. Among these, the *Manava Dharmashastra* (much translated and valorized by subsequent European scholars), recommends the strictest reprisals for unions across caste and class, and prescribes incomparably harsher punishments for the same crime when committed by so-called lowborn persons. Starting c. 400 BCE, reformist thinkers from the *Advaita*, or monist, school of Indian philosophy began to question the *Mimamsa* fetishization of ritual observances, on the grounds that what really mattered in a spiritual career was gaining the immaterial realization that the universe and all its entities were as one. Yet, they insisted that such knowledge, synonymous with liberation from all earthly suffering, could only be achieved by the high-caste Brahmin. Even the greatest and most liberal *Advaitin* master, Shankara, declared it unlikely, or at best very rare, for a non-Brahmin person to attain liberation.

But there are crucial historical circuit breakers in this narrative. There were numerous movements of revolt and resistance against Vedic elitism, which grew out of popular, or *laukika*, Hinduism with its emphasis on activities and practices associated with the profane world of unenlightened beings (*prathagjana*) and which were customarily not regarded as conducive to liberation. We have already considered dissenting Sramana traditions in the introduction. The devotional *Bhakti* movement, from 6 CE on, fed into a wide-ranging assault on hierarchies of caste, class, race, and, sometimes, gender. No less pertinent are the efforts of South Asian Buddhism, with its zero-tolerance policy on caste-hierarchy and Aryanist pretension. The burden of my argument is as follows: Early twentieth-century European racism was very likely born of a perverse historical collaboration between ancient South

Asian race/class/caste elite culture, on the one hand, and modern European race/class/caste imperial-fascist culture, on the other hand. So too, the mid-twentieth-century Western and non-Western critique of totalitarianism drew upon the favorable precedent of premodern South Asian anti-elitism, in several instances of reparative historical collaboration.

55. Christopher Isherwood, *Diaries, Volume One: 1939–1960*, ed. Katherine Buckness (London: Methuen, 1996), 84.

56. Ibid., 44.

57. Ibid., 55.

58. Cited in ibid., 83.

59. Roland Barthes, *The Neutral*, trans. Rosalind E. Krauss and Denis Hollier (New York: Columbia University Press, 2005), 12–13.

60. Rufus Jones, *A Service of Love in Wartime: American Friends Relief Work in Europe* (New York: Macmillan, 1920), xiv. The literature on interwar American pacifist practices of self is vast. Of special relevance to the uses of the gurus (especially M. K. Gandhi) at this scene are the following: A. J. Muste, *Not by Might: Christianity, the Way to Human Decency* (New York: Harper and Brothers, 1947); Richard B. Gregg, *The Power of Nonviolence* (London: James Clarke, 1937), and *Training for Peace: A Program for Peace Workers* (Philadelphia: J. B. Lippincott, 1937); Krishnalal Sridharni, *War without Violence* (Bombay: Bharatiya Vidya Bhavan, 1969), as well as *Warning to the West* (New York: Duell, Sloan and Pearce, 1942), and *The Mahatma and the World* (New York: Duell, Sloan and Pearce, 1946).

61. The politics of American interwar radical pacifism is well described in Marian Mollin, *Radical Pacifism in Modern America: Egalitarianism and Protest* (Philadelphia: University of Pennsylvania Press, 2006); Joseph K. Kosek, *Acts of Conscience: Christian Nonviolence and Modern American Democracy* (New York: Columbia University Press, 2009); and Scott H. Bennett, *Radical Pacifism: The War Resisters League and Gandhian Non-Violence in America, 1915–1936* (Syracuse, NY: Syracuse University Press, 2003).

62. A. J. Muste, cited in Mollin, *Radical Pacifism*, 20.

63. Ibid., 62.

64. Dave Dellinger, *Revolutionary Nonviolence* (Indianapolis, IN: Bobbs-Merrill, 1970), 202.

65. Fellowship of Reconciliation, *Martin Luther King and the Montgomery Story* (New York: Fellowship of Reconciliation, 1956), 13.

66. Isherwood, *Diaries*, 188. We get a sense of the tremendous CO contribution to refugee relief in the period from the annual reports of the American Friends Service Committee. See also Michael Luick-Thrams, *Out of Hitler's Reach: The Scattergood Hostel for European Refugees, 1939–43* (Iowa City, IA: Goodfellow Press, 1996). Like many pacifists, Christopher Isherwood spent a considerable portion of the war as a volunteer in refugee relief at Haverford, a classic ecumenical meeting ground from this period, where all participants (refugees and volunteers) were constantly adding to the storehouse of

Quaker, Vedantist, and Jewish spiritual practices and techniques of nonviolence.

67. See Steven J. Taylor, *World War II, Mental Institutions and Religious Objectors*
(Syracuse, NY: Syracuse University Press, 2009). Frank L. Wright's, *Out of
Sight, Out of Mind* (Philadelphia, PA: National Mental Health Foundation,
1947) is an excoriating *exposé* of interwar mental health institutions by conscientious objectors on the Selective Service scheme.

68. Dellinger, *Revolutionary Nonviolence*; for a telling account of CO prison agitation, see James Peck, *We Who Would Not Kill* (New York: Lyle Stuart, 1958),
and *Underdogs vs. Upperdogs* (New York: AmP&R Publishers, 1980).

69. James Peck, *Freedom Ride* (New York: Simon and Schuster, 1962).

70. Isherwood, *Diaries*, 117.

71. Bayard Rustin, *Time on Two Crosses: The Collected Writings of Bayard Rustin*,
ed. Devon W. Corbado and Donald Weise (San Francisco, CA: Cleis Press,
2003), 5.

72. See Max Weber, "The Nature of Charismatic Authority and Its Routinization," in *Max Weber: On Charisma and Institution Building*, ed. S. N. Eisenstadt
(Chicago: University of Chicago Press, 1968), 48–65.

73. Max Weber, *The Protestant Ethic and the Spirit of Capitalism*, trans. Talcott
Parsons (London and New York, Routledge Classics, 2001), 39.

74. Max Weber, "Politics as Vocation," in *From Max Weber: Essays in Sociology*,
ed. and trans. H. H. Gerth and C. Wright Mills (New York: Oxford University
Press, 1958), 126.

75. Max Weber, "Science as Vocation," in Gerth and Mills, *From Max Weber*, 138.

76. Ibid. 138. In the winter of 1918–1919, when Weber delivered his lectures
on vocation before the *Freistudentenschaft* circle at Munich University, his
audience included a young Jewish student of philosophy named Karl Lowith,
who would later flee Germany for a peripatetic life in exile before settling in
the United States. On the basis of this brief encounter with Weber, Lowith
would extol him in a memoir composed nearly two decades later, in 1940,
as "the one man in Germany whose words really spoke to . . . [the] Free Students," and who, had he been alive in 1933, would certainly have "interceded
on behalf of Jews who were unable to defend themselves" (*My Life in Germany
before and after 1933*, trans. Elizabeth King (London: Athlone Press, 1994), 16,
17, 18.

77. Though Weber is a sympathetic figure for our analysis, he is far from
ecumenical in his thinking. His thematic of disenchantment privileges Protestantism alone as *the* modern or secular religion that may be congenial to
democracy. This argument has its precedent, of course, in Kant's claim that
Western Christianity is the only "rational religion," in his *Religion within the
Limits of Reason Alone* (New York: Harper Torchbooks, 1960). Such arguments
are all the more objectionable in their recent iteration by Slavoj Žižek in "The
Fear of Four Words: A Modest Plea for the Hegelian Reading of Christianity,"
in *The Monstrosity of Christ: Paradox or Dialectic*, by Slavoj Žižek and John Mil-

bank, ed. Creston Davis (Cambridge, MA: MIT Press, 2009), 24–109, and also in Alain Badiou's, *Saint Paul: The Foundation of Universalism*. Taken together, this corpus altogether excises non-Western religions and spiritualities from the scene of democratization.

78. Weber, "Science as Vocation," 155. Susan Stewart gives us a lyrical meditation on the ramifications of a miniaturist sublime in *On Longing: Narratives of the Miniature, the Gigantic, the Souvenir, the Collection* (Durham, NC: Duke University Press, 1993). Consider also Arundhati Roy's nonvirtuoso god of small things, in the novel *The God of Small Things* (London: Flamingo, 1997), who can only do one thing at a time—much like Weber's scientist—and whose divinity consists in the realm of the unremarkable: platitude, bromide, cliché, commonplace, trivia.

79. Isabel Hofmeyr, *Gandhi's Printing Press: Experiments in Slow Reading* (Cambridge, MA: Harvard University Press, 2013), 33.

80. Ibid., 33–34. The phrase "maritime market of faith," is from Nile Green, *Bombay Islam: The Religious Economy of the West Indian Ocean, 1840–1915* (Cambridge: Cambridge University Press, 2011), xi.

81. There are important insights about the complexities of print-capitalism and its effects in colonial South Asia in Partha Chatterjee, *The Nation and Its Fragments: Colonial and Postcolonial Histories* (Princeton, NJ: Princeton University Press, 1993), 3–13, and Priya Joshi, *In Another Country: Colonialism, Culture, and the English Novel in India* (New York: Columbia University Press, 2002). The Ramakrishna Mission had two presses in operation by the early twentieth century. The Ramakrishna Math launched three monthly journals in its early years: *Prabuddha Bharata* in 1896, *Udbodhan* in 1899, and *Vedanta Kesari* in 1914. In 1915 it launched the Malayalam-language *Prabuddha Keralam*, and in 1921, the Tamil-language *Sri Ramakrishna Vijayam*, both monthlies as well. The Advaita Ashram press began publishing in 1905 and was responsible for the first edition of the *Complete Works of Swami Vivekananda* in 1907. Other ashrams were also scenes of prolific writing and publication. Before he left for Pondicherry, Sri Aurobindo was editing and providing the main copy for two revolutionary journals with a distinct tilt toward matters of yoga. The weekly *Bande Mataram*, launched on June 2, 1907, for a short-lived career of six months or so, was interrupted by the editor's political activities. Sri Aurobindo was interned at Alipore Jail, between May 1908 and May 1909, on charges of conspiracy in the assassination of a British Magistrate. Following his acquittal, he launched another journal, *Karmayogin: A Weekly Review of National Religion, Literature, Science, Philosophy, &C*, on June 19, 1909. He edited this journal until his departure from Calcutta in February of the following year. The multilingual Sri Aurobindo Ashram Publications Department was founded in 1934, and the ashram in its wider network saw the publication of several journals from the 1940s onward, including *The Advent, Sri Aurobindo Circle, Mother India*, and *Srinvantu*, among others. Gandhi himself took charge of many publications in his lifetime, inaugurating the

Navijivan Press in 1919. Other newsletters, journals, and magazines included *Young India* (1919–1932) and the multilingual venture *Harijan* (1933–1948). Though more muted than the others, Sri Ramana embraced publication as a mode of communication. In the early days disciples would take down his words on a slate and sometimes on the sand of ashram grounds. As disciples began to come forward in the early decades of the twentieth century with compilations of the guru's sayings and teachings, he always took care to proofread final texts himself. Among these is the *Guru Vachaka Kovai* (The garland of the guru's sayings), a transcription of Sri Ramana's verses put together by one of his earliest and foremost followers, Sri Muruganar. The print culture of Sri Ramanashramam achieved proper organization and most of its reliable output through the labors of two disciples in particular. Arthur Osborne, a British university lecturer interned during the Japanese occupation of former Siam, arrived in Tiruvannamalai on October 1945 and was responsible for the publication from October 1964 of the ashram's chief journal, *The Mountain Path*. Another Englishman, David Godman, arrived in the early 1970s upon the completion of his undergraduate studies at the University of Oxford. Godman never left Ramanashramam, where he took over the library and published several edited collections and commentaries on Sri Ramana's work. A systematic theological meditation on Sri Ramana's work became available in the 1960s through a series of talks given by Henri La Saux, a French disciple who had taken on the name Abhishiktananda. These talks were later published as *Saccidananda: A Christian Approach to Advaitic Experience* (Delhi: ISPCK, 1990). For a wonderful account of Abhishi-ktananda's work and encounter with Sri Ramana, see Susan Viswanathan, *An Ethnography of Mysticism. The Narratives of Abhishiktananda: A French Monk in India* (Shimla: Indian Institute of Advanced Study, 1998).

82. Described in Arthur Osborne, *Ramana Maharshi and the Path of Self-Knowledge: A Biography* (Tiruvannamalai: Sri Ramanashramam, 1997), 73–78.

83. Paul Brunton, *A Search in Secret India* (York Beach, ME: Samuel Weiser, 1994), 265. For negative accounts of Brunton's derived guruhood in the West, fol-lowing his encounter with Sri Ramana, see Jeffrey Masson, *My Father's Guru: A Journey through Spirituality and Disillusion* (London: Harper Collins, 1994); and Anthony Storr, *Feet of Clay: A Study of Gurus* (London: Harper Collins, 1996), 162–66.

84. Gandhi, *An Autobiography*, 16.

85. Sri Aurobindo, *Letters on Himself and the Ashram*, vol. 35 of *The Complete Works of Sri Aurobindo* (Pondicherry: Sri Aurobindo Ashram Trust, 2011), 5–6.

86. Among the many antinomian figures who are beyond the scope of this chapter a few are particularly apposite to our concerns. At the scene of fin de siècle transnational Islam, the philosopher-poet and politician Muham-mad Iqbal (1877–1938), built his vision of an independent postcolonial state for South Asian Muslims upon a bracing, neo-Hegelian, Islamic mysticism. Worked out in two poetical works, *Asrar-e-Khudi* (1915; *The Secrets of the*

Self) and *Rumuz-e-Bekhudi* (1918; *The Secrets of Selflessness*), Iqbal calls for a practice in which the ego is fortified with love, thus yoking self-interest to the interests of all others. This is at the core of his proposals for a radical Muslim democracy: "The democracy of Europe—overshadowed by socialistic agitation and anarchical fear—originated mainly in the economic regeneration of European societies. Nietzsche, however, abhors this 'rule of the herd' and, hopeless of the plebian, he bases all higher culture on the cultivation and growth of an Aristocracy of Supermen. But is the plebian so absolutely hopeless? The Democracy of Islam did not grow out of the extension of economic opportunity; it is a spiritual principle based on the assumption that every human being is a center of latent power, the possibilities of which can be developed by cultivating a certain type of character. Out of the plebian material Islam has formed men of the noblest type of life and power. Is not, then, the Democracy of early Islam an experimental refutation of the ideas of Nietzsche?" (Muhammad Iqbal, *The Secrets of the Self*, trans. Reynold A. Nicholson [London: Macmillan, 1920], n.p.).

Rich materials accrue from *dalit* antinomianism. The *avarna*, or outcaste Narayana Guru (1856–1928), built a *sadhana* of anticasteism relevant to the theme of radical democracy. He emphasized practices through which the spiritual votary would learn to view the world without discriminations of caste, class, or religion. A myth concerning B. R. Ambedkar, the caste reformer and revolutionary (and avowed rationalist), is also pertinent to the etiology of "descent." Timothy Fitzgerald, "Ambedkar, Buddhism, and the Concept of Religion," in *Untouchable: Dalits in Modern India*, ed. S. M. Michael (Boulder, CO: Lynne Reinner, 1999), 57–74, notes that the reformer was often regarded among *dalit* neo-Buddhists as a *bodhisattva*: an enlightened and compassionate being who responds without discrimination to all cries for help. The case is clarified by Chung-Fang Yu in *Kuan-yin: The Chinese Transformation of Avalokitesvara* (New York: Columbia University Press, 2001): "One of the most distinctive features of the Mahayana tradition is its call for everyone to rise to *bodhicitta* (the thought of enlightenment), and achieve enlightenment not just for oneself but for all living beings. This new aspiration is valued more highly than the earlier arhat ideal, which aims at entering nirvana upon attaining enlightenment. The career of a bodhisattva is a very long and arduous one. After making vows, one trains oneself along the bodhisattva path by practicing virtues (with giving at the head of the list), mastering meditation, and penetrating into the wisdom of emptiness (which is understood as everything being devoid of self-nature). Because bodhisattvas vow to save everyone, they remain in the world and are always accessible" (7).

87. Swami Nikhilananda and Dhan Gopal Mukerji, *Sri Ramakrishna: The Face of Silence* (Woodstock, NY: Skylight Paths, 2005), 43.

88. Jeffrey J. Kripal, *Kali's Child: The Mystical and the Erotic in the Life and Teachings of Sri Ramakrishna* (Chicago: University of Chicago Press, 1995), 199.

89. Gupta, *The Gospel of Sri Ramakrishna*, 1:30–31.

90. Ibid., 1:43.
91. The Mother, *On Thoughts and Aphorisms* (Pondicherry: Sri Aurobindo Ashram Publication Department, 1998), 119–21. Mirra Alfassa was published under the name The Mother by the Sri Aurobindo ashram publication department and was so known in the ashram community and beyond. This collection is made up of the Mother's commentaries in French during a twelve-year period, from 1958 to 1970, on Sri Aurobindo's work, *Thoughts and Aphorisms*, which was written in 1913 in the very early part of his stay in Pondicherry. The aphorism that elicits the commentary cited in the main text above is as follows: "Examine thyself without pity, then thou wilt be more charitable and pitiful to others" (118).
92. Jean Paul Sartre, *Saint Genet: Actor and Martyr*, trans. Bernard Fretchman (New York: Pantheon Books, 1963), 24.
93. Ibid., 209, 216, 209, 214. Though Sartre must have been aware of Romain Rolland's work on the gurus, given the latter's preeminence as a radical French intellectual between 1898 and 1947, *Saint Genet* only deals with Western instances of radical sainthood. It was Colin Wilson who belatedly extended Sartre's abject metaphysics to include the gurus, especially Sri Ramakrishna, in his runaway bestseller, *The Outsider* (New York: Jeremy P. Tarcher, 1956). Combining Jamesian saintly politics and Sartrean involution, Wilson's outsider defends negative metaphysics as a revolutionary pathology: "The conscious striving *not* to limit the amount of experience seen and touched; the intolerable struggle to expose sensitive areas of being to what may possibly hurt them; the attempt to see as a whole, although the instinct of self-preservation fights against the pain of the internal widening, and all the impulses of spiritual laziness build into waves of sleep with every new effort. The individual begins that long effort as an Outsider, though he may finish it as a saint" (281). See also Colin Wilson, *Religion and the Rebel* (Boston: Houghton and Mifflin, 1957).
94. Robert Pippin, "A Short History of Non-Being," *Critical Inquiry* 30, no. 2 (2004): 426.
95. Ibid., 427.
96. Saintly politics, or the *sadhana* of descent, begins its work for democracy at the moment it refuses the metaphysical *ban* on the negative—that is, its consignment to mere nonexistence. Drawing on Giorgio Agamben, *Homo Sacer: Sovereign Power and Bare Life*, trans. Daniel Heller-Roazen (Stanford, CA: Stanford University Press, 1998), all relegation of negativity to non-Being may be described as the abstract hypothesis of "bare life," concerning that figure from archaic Roman law "who may be killed and yet not sacrificed" (8); or one whose killing is unencumbered by additional semantic value and which addresses nothing beyond the event of killing itself.

Agamben's account of bare life is complicated by his view that democracy is in fact perversely premised upon the logic of bare life, because of the constitutive biopolitics of modern power, with its premium on the political uses of mere life, or life alone. (8). By this reasoning, secularized and—we might add, disenchanted—"bare life" is *the* transformative codicil of modern democracy: "If anything characterizes modern democracy as opposed to classical democracy, then it is that modern democracy presents itself from the beginning as a vindication and liberation of *zoë*, and that it is constantly trying to transform its own bare life into a way of life and to find, so to speak, the *bios* of *zoë*. Hence, too, modern democracy's specific aporia: it wants to put the freedom and happiness of men into play in the very place—"bare life"—that marked their subjection" (*Homo Sacer*, 9–10). At this point, Agamben adds, modern democracy runs into historical trouble, converging with modern totalitarianism in its restitution of bare life. In his words, "Today politics knows no value (and consequently, no nonvalue) other than life, and until the contradictions that this fact implies are dissolved, Nazism and fascism—which transformed the decision on bare life into the supreme political principle—will remain stubbornly with us" (10).

I do not at all endorse Agamben's somewhat careless account of the concurrence between democracy and fascism. While readily conceding that the narrative of *homo sacer* clarifies the procedures of totalitarianism, my case is as follows: the art or *sadhana* of descent protests antidemocracy not (as Agamben has it) simply by making a quietist and benumbed peace with the given resources or scene of mere life (as in the case of Weber's compulsory disenchantment). Rather, it seeks actively to restore sacrificial resonance to bare life (or the non-Being of negativity). It does so by reconceiving democracy as an agentive or willful self-sacrifice (falling, descent, downward ascesis, voluntary disenchantment) for the sake of solidarity with the signifiers and bearers of bare life—that is, persons and properties that have been stripped of value by historical circumstance.

97. Sri Aurobindo, *Essays in Philosophy and Yoga*, vol. 13 of *The Complete Works of Sri Aurobindo* (Pondicherry: Sri Aurobindo Ashram Trust, 1998), 98.
98. Ibid., 441.
99. Ibid., 98.
100. Sri Aurobindo, interview published in *Hindu*, 4 January 1915; cited in Heehs, *Lives of Sri Aurobindo*, 260. There are rich details on the *Arya* years elsewhere in Heehs; see especially 255–326.
101. Sri Aurobindo, *The Secret of the Vedas, with Selected Hymns*, vol. 15 of *The Complete Works of Sri Aurobindo* (Pondicherry: Sri Aurobindo Ashram Trust, 1998), 596, 593.
102. Ibid., 233–34.
103. Ibid.
104. Sri Aurobindo, *The Life Divine*, part 1, vol. 21 of *The Complete Works of Sri Aurobindo* (Pondicherry: Sri Aurobindo Ashram Trust, 2005), , 40–42.
105. Ibid., 4.
106. Sri Aurobindo's critique of Indian monism belongs to the same period as Heidegger's *existenz*-ontology. Heidegger sets out a program to recuperate

NOTES TO PAGES 83-84

monism his 1921-22 Freiburg lectures on Aristotle, during his growing
public commitments to National Socialism. In these lectures, as in the
studies *Being and Time* (1927), *Kant and the Problem of Metaphysics* (1929),
and *An Introduction to Metaphysics* (1935), he calls for a suspension of the
antinomies (spirit/matter, subject/object) authorized by Cartesian metaphysics and responsible, he claims, for alienated modern subjectivity
and the spiritual impoverishment of empirical existence. His seemingly
anodyne alternative, the tonic of an ontic-ontological accord, promises in
return for the small price of subjectivity as we know it a zen-like harmony
between individual projects and existential structures. Upon realization of this accord, the old Cartesian subject, Heidegger promises, will be
replaced by a new, improved entity, *Dasein*, which will be quite safe from
alienation, estrangement, ennui, and the more or less constant feeling of
being in exile: "Dasein's Being reveals itself as *care*; . . . no sooner has Dasein
expressed anything about itself to itself, then it has already interpreted itself
as *care (cura)*" (Martin Heidegger, *Being and Time*, trans. Richard Rojcewicz
[Bloomington: Indiana University Press, 2001], 227). Yet, for all the comfort,
affluence, gain, preciousness, and health that it experiences within the ontological *cura*, Heidegger's *Dasein* is always at risk of relapse into a debased
form of subjectivity. Having been successfully cured of its own ego, it keeps
falling into and toward the subject/ego of others. This fall into alterity
and facticity (from the surprising height of the ontological sanatorium)
Heidegger denounces as the secondary infection of affectivity: "a ruinance
of the self, in favor of the They." (*Being and Time*, 229; cf. Martin Heidegger,
*Phenomenological Interpretations of Aristotle: Initiation into Phenomenological
Research*, trans. Richard Rojcewicz [Bloomington: Indiana University Press,
2001], 97-115). Writing with all too insufficiently acknowledged elitism
and xenophobia of the descent from ontological self-care into the relational
world of "concern," "solicitude," and "empathy," Heidegger describes this
motion, vitriolically, as "subjection," "leveling down," and "averageness"
(*Being and Time*, 164, 165).
107. Sri Aurobindo, *Life Divine*, part 1, 99.
108. Sri Shankaracharya, *Viveka-Cudamani; or, Crest-Jewel of Wisdom*, trans. Mo-
hini M. Chatterji (Adyar: Theosophical Publishing House, 1999), 89, 93.
109. Sri Aurobindo, *Life Divine*, part 1, 10-11, 39.
110. Sri Aurobindo, *The Human Cycle, The Ideal of Human Unity, War and Self-
Determination*, vol. 25 of *The Complete Works of Sri Aurobindo* (Pondicherry:
Sri Aurobindo Ashram Trust, 1997), 49-50.
111. Sadananda Parivrajakacharya, *Vedanta-sara; or, An Introduction into the Vedanta Philosophy*, trans. J. R. Ballantyne (London: Christian Literature Society
for India, 1898), 50-51.
112. Sri Aurobindo, *Life Divine*, part 1, 63.
113. In his discussions of classical Western ethics, Foucault explains the concept
of *heautocracy* (in terms that evoke of the Gandhian concept of *swaraj*) as the

rule of self by self: "To form oneself as a virtuous and moderate subject in the use he makes of pleasures, the individual has to construct a relationship with the self that is of the 'domination-submission,' 'command-obedience,' 'mastery-docility,' type (and not, as will be the case in Christian spirituality, a relationship of the 'elucidation-renunciation,' 'decipherment-purification' type). This is what could be called the 'heautocratic' structure of the subject in the ethical practice of pleasure" (Michel Foucault, *The Uses of Pleasure*, vol. 2 of *The History of Sexuality*, trans. Robert Hurley [London and Harmondsworth: Penguin, 1987], 70).

114. M. K. Gandhi, *Hind Swaraj and Other Writings*, ed. Anthony J. Parel (Cambridge: Cambridge University Press, 1997), 87.
115. M. K. Gandhi, "Truth through Love," in *The Moral and Political Writings of Mahatma Gandhi*, ed., Raghavan Iyer (Oxford: Clarendon Press, 1986), 2:190.
116. M. K. Gandhi, "All About the Fast," *Harijan*, 8 July 1933; reprinted in *Moral and Political Writings*, 2:133.
117. M. K. Gandhi, "Love and Brotherhood," in *Moral and Political Writings*, 2:296.
118. Gupta, *Gospel of Sri Ramakrishna*, 1:38.
119. Ibid., 2:860.
120. Ibid.
121. Rolland, *Life of Sri Ramakrishna*, 48.
122. Ibid., 171.
123. Ibid., 183.
124. Gupta, *Gospel of Ramakrishna*, 2:948.
125. Ibid., 2:949.
126. Brunton, *Search in Secret India*, 280.
127. Viswanatha Swami, "Ecstasy of Grace," in Natarajan, *First Meetings with Ramana Maharshi*, 1.
128. See, Viswanathan, *Ethnography of Mysticism*, 63, 67.
129. See, Ramchandra Gandhi, "Is Our Heart on the Right Side?" in *Postcolonial Studies* 6, no. 1 (2003), 57.
130. Sri Ramana Maharshi, *Sri Ramana Gita*, trans. Sri Visvanatha Swami and K. Swaminathan (Tiruvannamalai: Sri Ramanashram, 1998), viii.
131. Ibid., 9.
132. Ibid.
133. This account draws on Gandhi, "Is Our Heart on the Right Side," 58.
134. Walter Keers, "Light Itself, Blazing Light," in Natarajan, *First Meetings with Ramana Maharshi*, 58.
135. Ibid., 61.
136. Sri Ramana Maharshi, *Sri Ramana Gita*, 19; A. W. Chadwick (Sadhu Arunachala), *A Sadhu's Reminiscences of Ramana Maharshi* (Tiruvannamalai: Sri Ramanashram, 1984), 97.
137. Chadwick, *Sadhu's Reminiscences*, 96; Paul Brunton and Paul Venkataramiah, *Conscious Immortality: Conversations with Sri Ramana Maharshi* (Tiruvannamalai: Sri Ramanashram, 1996), 165.

138. Arthur Koestler, *The Yogi and the Commissar and Other Essays* (London: Jonathan Cape, 1945). Koestler's yogi ethics belonged very much to the scene of transnational reparative collaboration. He insists that full realization of the yogi way requires collaboration between East and West: "Yogi-ethics . . . survives only in the East and to learn it we have to turn to the East; but we need qualified interpreters and . . . reinterpretation in the terms and symbols of Western thought" (254–55). Koestler gained his own primary information about contemporary yogis from Western interpreters, principally the writer Gerald Heard and his wider circle of pacifist comrades at Ivar Street, Hollywood. Many of these figures, including Christopher Isherwood, Aldous Huxley, Somerset Maugham, and W. H. Auden, were regular contributors to *Horizon* on the subject of the new Indian mysticism. Between 1958 and 1959, Koestler finally took a spiritual trip through India and recorded his observations in *The Lotus and the Robot* (London: HarperCollins, 1960). His *Roots of Coincidence* (London: Vintage, 1972), is another text from this period.

139. *Voices of History: Historic Recordings from the British Library Sound Archive*, 2 vol. (London: British Library, 2005).

140. See especially J. C. Bose, *Response in the Living and the Non-Living* (London: Longmans, Green, 1902), *Life Movement in Plants*, 5 vols. (London: Longmans, Green, 1918–23), and *Plant Autographs and their Revelations* (New York: Macmillan, 1927).

141. Gandhi, *The Moral and Political Writings*, 2:135, 27; Mohandas Karamchand Gandhi, *All Men Are Brothers* (Ahmadabad: Navjivan Press, 1960), 125–26.

142. Lincoln Kirstein and Beaumont Newhall, *The Photographs of Henri Cartier-Bresson* (New York: Museum of Modern Art, 1947).

143. This encounter is reported by Henri Cartier-Bresson in the Heinz Butler documentary, *Henri Cartier-Bresson: The Impassioned Eye* (Paris: Foundation Henri Cartier-Bresson, 2003).

144. Sadananda Menon, "Master of the Moment," *New Internationalist Magazine*, October 2004, n.p.

145. Henri Cartier-Bresson, "Notes by Cartier-Bresson on His Visit to Pondicherry and Sri Aurobindo Ashram" (From the archives of Magnum Photos), published in *Sri Aurobindo: Archives and Research* 14 (December 1990): 209.

146. For summary accounts of the split between amateur British and French commercial photography, see Grace Seiberling, *Amateurs, Photography and the Mid-Victorian Imagination* (Chicago: University of Chicago Press, 1986); Gus Macdonald, *Victorian Eyewitnesses: A History of Photography, 1826–1913* (New York: Viking, 1979); Michael Braive, *The Era of the Photograph: A Social History* (London: Thames and Hudson, 1966). There is a concise rendition of Walter Benjamin's objections to the market vendors and charlatans of mass or industrial photography in his 1931 essay, "A Short History of Photography," reprinted in *Screen*, 13, no. 1 (1972): 5–26.

1. Ian Hunter, "The History of Theory," *Critical Inquiry* 33 (Autumn 2006): 78–112.
2. For details about the Indian involvement in the great war, see Upendra Narayan Chakravorty, *Indian Nationalism and the First World War, 1914–1918* (Calcutta: Progressive Publishers, 1997), and S. D. Pradhan, *Indian Army in East Africa, 1914–1918* (Delhi: National Book Organisation, 1991). For an illuminating account of subaltern participation in the war, see David Omissi, ed., *Indian Voices of the Great War: Soldiers' Letters, 1914–18* (Basingstoke, UK: Macmillan, 1999). Nile Green's *Islam and the Army in Colonial India: Sepoy Religion in the Service of Empire* (Cambridge: Cambridge University Press, 2009) is a pathbreaking study of the cultural world of the Muslim soldiers of colonial India. Writing against the grain of the stereotypes regarding Muslim violence and predilection for anticolonial aggression, Green shows how Muslim soldiers (much like their Hindu and Sikh counterparts) were less the enemies of empire than its assistants. The moment we are analyzing in the present chapter concerns the transformation of these military loyalties into a flickering belief in (and commitment to) Europe's best civilizational possibilities.
3. M. K. Gandhi, cited in Chakravorty, *Indian Nationalism*, 19.
4. In a letter of June 1914 written to an English friend, Florence Winterbottom, Gandhi describes his conflicted belief that participation in the Great War may train Indians in the courageousness required for nonviolent *satyagraha*: "I am going through perhaps the severest trials of my life. I had hoped . . . to be able in India to retire from the War. Now I am in the thick of it. . . . I want to raise men to fight, to deal death to men who, for all they know, are as innocent as they. And I fancy that through this sea of blood I shall find my haven. . . . I find men are incapable through cowardice of killing. How can I preach to them the value of non-killing? And I so want them to learn the art of killing. This is all awful. But such is the situation before me. Sometimes my heart sinks within me." (Cited in Rajmohan Gandhi, *The Good Boatman: A Portrait of Gandhi* [New Delhi: Viking, 1995], 18–19). Gandhi's decision to support the war effort was opposed by many of his socialist-pacifist Western friends. The South African feminist and radical Olive Schreiner, especially, registers strong disappointment in her only extant letter to Gandhi, written on August 15, 1914: "I was struck to the heart this morning with sorrow to see that you, and that beautiful & beloved Indian poetess whom I met in London some months ago and other Indian friends had offered to serve this the English Government in this evil war in any way they might demand of you. Surely you, who would not take up arms even in the cause of your own oppressed people, cannot be willing to shed blood in this wicked cause. I had longed to meet you and Mr. Callenbach [*sic*] as friends who would under-

stand my hatred of it. I don't believe the statement in the paper can be true" (Olive Schreiner to Mohandas Gandhi, 15 August 1914, NLSA Cape Town, Special Collections, *Olive Schreiner Letters Project Transcription*, letter line numbers, 16–24).

5. Paul Fussell, *The Great War and Modern Memory* (Oxford: Oxford University Press, 2000), 314.

6. Robert Graves, *Goodbye to All That* (Harmondsworth, UK: Penguin, 2000), 7.

7. T. E. Lawrence, *Seven Pillars of Wisdom: A Triumph* (1926; repr., Harmondsworth, UK: Penguin, 1965), 21.

8. Ibid., 684.

9. E. M. Forster, *Alexandria: A History and a Guide* (1915; repr., New York: Doubleday, 1961), xvii. Wendy Moffat's sensitive biography, *A Great Unrecorded History: A New Life of E. M. Forster* (New York: Farrar, Straus and Giroux, 2010), foregrounds the dissonance between patriotism and homosexuality experienced by many others of Forster's generation. Moffat gives special attention to the fact that much of Forster's wartime cosmopolitanism was provoked by what the latter described as his "anxious but very beautiful affair" with the Egyptian tram conductor, Mohammed el Adl (cited in Moffat, *A Great Unrecorded History*, 152).

10. Santanu Das, "Introduction," in *Race, Empire and First World War Writing*, ed. Santanu Das (Cambridge: Cambridge University Press, 2011), 3–4.

11. Mulk Raj Anand, *Across the Black Waters* (1940; repr., Delhi: Vision Books, 1978), provides a revealing fictional account of an estranging yet culturally educative encounter between an Indian and East African regiment on the Western front: "As the regiment moved out of the village again after an hour's rest and refreshments, they met a platoon of stalwart black troops who wore white turbans and white tunics with red sashes, long, baggy trousers and scarlet stockings. 'Habshis,' said someone in an undertone half-suppressed by the clatter of marching feet, and there were other inquisitive whispers. 'They are sepoys like us of the Francisi Army,' said Havildar Lachman Singh. . . . 'But they have got curly hair and are jet black and not brown as we are,' young Kharku protested, his belief in the superior brown skin of his inheritance shocked by the comparison which Lachman had put them to. Lalu stared at the swarthy faces of the black troops aglow with white teeth and was greeted with smiles" (93).

12. Ibid., 14, 16.

13. Omissi, *Indian Voices*, letter no. 56, 56.

14. Ibid., letter no. 13, 32.

15. Ibid., letter no. 121, 90.

16. Ibid.

17. Ibid., letters no. 24 and 63; 38; 59.

18. Ibid., letter no. 449; 258.

19. Ibid., letter no. 119; 89.

20. Ibid., letter no. 26; 40.

21. Ibid., letter no. 25; 39.
22. Ibid., letter no. 118; 88.
23. Ibid., letter no. 115; 87.
24. Albert Memmi, *The Colonizer and the Colonized*, trans. Howard Greenfeld (Boston: Beacon Press, 1965) uses "implacable dependence" to explain decolonization as effect of the impossible contradictions in the colonizer/colonized relationship. "The colonial relationship which I had tried to define chained the colonizer and the colonized into an implacable dependence, moulded their respective characters and dictated their conduct. Just as there was an obvious logic in the reciprocal behavior of the two colonial partners, another mechanism, proceeding from the first, would lead, I believed, inexorably to the decomposition of this dependence. . . . How could the colonizer look after his workers while periodically gunning down a crowd of the colonized? How could the colonized deny himself so cruelly yet make such excessive demands?" (ix–x). It is through a twist upon Memmi's hypothesis that our argument proceeds. The contradictions that he itemizes do not merely fling colonizer and colonized apart but also, sometimes, create the conditions for a secondary reciprocity. In this instance the colonizers militate against their own worst effects by dint of their better nature, and (more surprisingly) find this project supported by the colonized in a reverse civilizing mission that holds up an ideal of European rather than non-European exemplarity as a model for self-reform. This is the path hinted at in Ashis Nandy, *The Intimate Enemy: Loss and Recovery of Self Under Colonialism* (Delhi: Oxford University Press, 1983). Nandy's concept of "intimate enmity" summons a secret if onerous ethical collaboration between Western nonplayers and their non-Western allies. The latter, he writes, "construct a West which allows them to live with the alternative West, while resisting the loving embrace of the West's dominant self" (xiv).
25. Aristotle, *Magna Moralia*, in *The Complete Works of Aristotle*, ed. Jonathan Barnes, 2 vols. Bollingen Series No. 71 (Princeton, NJ: Princeton University Press, 1995), 2:1869.
26. Theodore Adorno, *Minima Moralia: Reflections from Damaged Life*, trans. E. F. N. Jephcott (London: Verso, 2000), 16.
27. Ibid., 50.
28. Ibid., 18.
29. See Chakravorty, *Indian Nationalism*, 10–33, for an account of coercive recruitment during the Great War. David Omissi has a brief discussion of the subject in *Indian Voices*, 15–16.
30. On March 1, 1919, M. K. Gandhi had announced a nationwide *satyagraha* campaign to protest the proposed Rowlatt Act, which was designed to bring about a severe curtailment of civil and political liberties. In the course of the campaign, in an apparently inexplicable outbreak of popular violence, an English schoolteacher, Miss Mercia Sherwood, was assaulted and killed by a mob in Amritsar. In retaliation martial law was imposed in Punjab, bringing

with it a revival of punishments and forms of humiliation well rehearsed and familiar from the years of forced recruitment. It was to protest these repressive policies that the Jallianwala Bagh meeting was convened. The Congress Working Committee set up to investigate the subsequent massacre clearly felt that resentments harbored against the culture of forced recruitment contributed to the unrest in the Punjab that came to a head in April 1919. "The methods for securing recruits," the committee maintained, "travelled far beyond the line of moral and social pressure," cited in Chakravorty, *Indian Nationalism*, 26.

31. There is an engaging fictional account of the German investment in radical Islamism in John Buchan's *Greenmantle* (1916), which also recasts the Great War as a covert crusade fought between committed Muslims and Allied "Missionaries." For a historically sensationalist version of this episode, see also Peter Hopkirk, *On Secret Service East of Constantinople: The Plot to Bring Down the British Empire* (Oxford: Oxford University Press, 1995). "This book," the author writes, "tells . . . the extraordinary story of how in that war Germany sought to harness the forces of militant Islam to its cause with the help of its ally Turkey. By unleashing a Holy War against them, Wilhelm and his hawkish advisers aimed to drive the British out of India and the Russians from the Caucasus and Central Asia" (2).

32. M. K. Gandhi, *Collected Works of Mohandas Karamchand Gandhi*, 100 vols. (Delhi: Publications Division, Ministry of Information and Broadcasting, 1960–1994), 16:308. All subsequent citations of this text are abbreviated as *CWMG*). There is insightful discussion of Gandhi and the Khilafat movement in Faisal Devji, *The Impossible Indian: Gandhi and the Temptations of Violence* (London: Hurst, 2012), 67–92.

33. For a postcolonial critique of the postwar Manichaeism in anticolonial thought, see Edward Said, *Culture and Imperialism* (London: Chatto and Windus, 1993), 230–340.

34. Eleanor Roosevelt, Alexandre Bogomolov, Peng-cun Chang, René Cassin, Charles Duke, William Hodgson, Charles Malik, Hernan Santa Cruz, *Universal Declaration of Human Rights* (Bedford, MA: Applewood Books, 2001), 2.

35. See Johannes Morinsk, *The Universal Declaration of Human Rights: Origins, Drafting and Intent* (Philadelphia: University of Pennsylvania Press, 1999); Mark Mazower, *No Enchanted Palace: The End of Empire and the Ideological Origins of the United Nations* (Princeton, NJ: Princeton University Press, 2009); Roland Burke, *Decolonization and the Evolution of International Human Rights* (Philadelphia: University of Pennsylvania Press, 2010); Fabian Klose, *Human Rights in the Shadow of Colonial Violence: The Wars of Independence in Kenya and Algeria*, trans. Dona Geyer (Philadelphia: University of Pennsylvania Press, 2013).

36. See Julian Go, "Modeling States and Sovereignty: Postcolonial Constitutions in Asia and Africa," in *Making a World After Empire: The Bandung Moment and Its Political Afterlives*, ed. Christopher J. Lee (Athens: Ohio University Press, 2010), 130.

37. Samuel Moyn, *The Last Utopia: Human Rights in History* (Cambridge, MA: Belknap Press, 2010), 8. Aijaz Ahmad, in his *In Theory: Classes, Nations, Literatures* (London: Verso, 1992), argues, somewhat differently, that postwar Third-Worldist nationalism and Western antipolitics are entirely compatible projects. Ahmad is severely critical of this putative alliance, whereas (in a combined objection to Moyn and Ahmad) our case is for the positive ethical continuities across these projects.
38. Ibid., 213.
39. See Dipesh Chakrabarty, "The Legacies of Bandung: Decolonization and the Politics of Culture," in Lee, *Making a World After* Empire, 45–68
40. See Burke, *Decolonization*, 17–25.
41. See Richard Wright, *The Color Curtain: A Report on the Bandung Conference* (London: Dennis Dobson, 1956), 127.
42. George McTurnan Kahin, *The Asian-African Conference, Bandung, Indonesia, April 1955*, (1956; repr., Port Washington, NY: Kennikat Press, 1972), 39.
43. President Soekarno, cited in Wright, *Color Curtain*, 139.
44. Wright, *Color Curtain*, 170.
45. Albert Memmi, *The Colonizer and the Colonized*, trans. Howard Greenfeld (Boston: Beacon Press 1965), 63, 62.
46. Aimé Césaire, *Discourse on Colonialism*, trans. Joan Pinkham (New York: Monthly Review Press, 1972), 9, 13.
47. Memmi, *Colonizer and Colonized*, 117, 119.
48. Ibid., 127, 135, 137.
49. M. K. Gandhi, *Hind Swaraj and Other Writings*, ed. Anthony J. Parel (Cambridge: Cambridge University Press, 1997), 106.
50. Jean Paul Sartre, "Preface," in *The Wretched of the Earth*, by Frantz Fanon, trans. Constance Farrington (Harmondsworth, UK: Penguin, 1990), 24.
51. Jean Paul Sartre, "Preface," in Memmi, *Colonizer and Colonized*, xxvii–xxviii.
52. Paul Nizan, *The Watchdogs: Philosophers of the Established Order*, trans. Paul Fittingoff (New York: Monthly Review Press, 1971), 12.
53. Michel Serres with Bruno Latour, *Conversations on Science, Culture and Time*, trans. Roxanne Lapidus (Ann Arbor: University of Michigan Press, 1995), 195.
54. Jacques Derrida, "Real and Symbolic Suicides: A Dialogue with Jacques Derrida," in *Philosophy in a Time of Terror: Dialogues with Jürgen Habermas and Jacques Derrida*, ed. Giovanna Borradori (Chicago: University of Chicago Press, 2004), 94.
55. Edmund Husserl, *Phenomenology and the Crisis of Philosophy: Philosophy as Rigorous Science and Philosophy and the Crisis of European Man*, trans. Quentin Lauer (New York: Harper Torchbooks, 1965), 150.
56. See Edmund Husserl, *The Crisis of European Sciences and Transcendental Phenomenology: An Introduction to Phenomenological Philosophy*, trans. David Carr (Evanston, IL: Northwestern University Press, 1970), 5–6.
57. Husserl, *Phenomenology and the Crisis of Philosophy*, 146.

58. The phrase "lived actualization" is from James Dodd, *Crisis and Reflection: An Essay on Husserl's Crisis of the European Sciences*, (Dordrecht: Kluwer Academic Publishers, 2004), 17.
59. Husserl, *Crisis of European Sciences*, 17.
60. Ibid., 77.
61. Emmanuel Levinas, *Discovering Existence with Husserl*, trans. Richard A. Cohen and Michael B. Smith (Evanston, IL: Northwestern University Press, 1998), 61.
62. Edmund Husserl, *The Paris Lectures*, trans. Peter Koestenbaum (The Hague: Martinus Nijhoff, 1964), 35.
63. See, especially, Levinas, *Discovering Existence with Husserl*; and "Substitution" in *The Levinas Reader*, ed. Sean Hand (Oxford: Blackwell, 1994), 88–126.
64. See, Paul Ricouer, *Husserl: An Analysis of His Phenomenology*, trans. Edward G. Ballard and Lester E. Embree (Evanston, IL: Northwestern University Press, 1967).
65. Jacques Derrida's earliest published work, *Edmund Husserl's Origin of Geometry: An Introduction*, trans. John P. Levey Jr. (Lincoln: University of Nebraska Press, 1989) is a commentary upon the appendix to Husserl's *The Crisis of European Sciences and Transcendental Phenomenology*. But the critical uptake most relevant to our discussion is more palpably in evidence in works such as Jacques Derrida, "Form and Meaning: A Note on the Phenomenology of Language," in *Margins of Philosophy*, trans. Alan Bass (New York: Harvester Wheatsheaf, 1982), 155–74; and in his "'Genesis and Structure' and Phenomenology," in *Writing and Difference*, trans. Alan Bass (Chicago: University of Chicago Press, 1978), 154–68; and "Violence and Metaphysics: An Essay on the Thought of Emmanuel Levinas," in *Writing and Difference*, 79–153.
66. Jean-Paul Sartre's various uses of the Husserlian *epochē* are diffused through his greater corpus. See his *Being and Nothingness*, trans. Hazel Barnes (New York: Washington Square Press, 1956), and *Existentialism Is a Humanism*, trans. Arlette Elkaim-Sartre (New Haven, CT: Yale University Press, 2007), for the translation of reduction into the themes of willing, choosing, *dépassement*, and as the morality of freedom.
67. Alexandre Kojève, *Introduction to the Reading of Hegel: Lectures on the Phenomenology of Spirit*, trans. James H. Nichols Jr. (Ithaca, NY: Cornell University Press, 1969), 20.
68. Ibid.
69. To this recognition that humanity belongs, in a sense, to the oppressed, Fanon testifies toward the end of *The Wretched of the Earth*: "When I search for Man in the technique and style of Europe, I see only a succession of negations of man, and an avalanche of murders. The human condition, plans for mankind and collaboration between men in those tasks which increase the sum total of humanity are new problems, which demand true inventions. . . . Let us try to create the whole man, whom Europe has been incapable of bringing to triumphant birth" (242).

70. Friedrich Nietzsche, *On the Genealogy of Morals and Ecce Homo*, trans. Walter Kaufman (New York: Vintage Books, 1989), 21–22.

CHAPTER 4

1. Contemporary newspaper sources are detailed on these outbreaks, particularly with respect to civilian strikes against occupying armies in Egypt. The Southeast Asian mutinies and military insubordination in the Netherlands East Indies are well chronicled in "Secret History: Mutiny in the RAF," directed by Ian Potts (London: Laurel Productions, 1996); David Duncan, *Mutiny in the RAF: The Airforce Strikes of 1946* (London: Socialist History Society, 1999); Richard Kisch, *Days of the Good Soldier* (London: Journeyman Press, 1985); Christopher Bayly and Tim Harper, *Forgotten Wars: Freedom and Revolution in Southeast Asia* (Cambridge, MA: Belknap Press, 2010); Andrew Roadnight, "Sleeping with the Enemy: Britain, Japanese Troops and the Netherlands East Indies, 1945–1946," *History* 87, no. 286 (2002): 245–68.

2. We will review the GI mutinies toward the end of this chapter. Newspaper sources are, again, indispensable, and some salient articles include "GIs Chip in Cash for Ads to Tell Woes: GIs Air Their Feelings in Paris," *Chicago Daily Tribune*, 9 January 1946, 1–2; "GI's in Philippines Hold Fresh Rally: Batangas Group Raises Money to Further 'Go-Home" Drive,' *New York Times*, 9 January 1946, 6; Walter Lippmann: "Protest of the Troops," *Los Angeles Times*, 15 January 1946, A4; "Three Marines in Demobilization Case Confined," *Chicago Daily Tribune*, 20 February 1946, 7; "Public in U.S. Wants Troops Kept Abroad," *Los Angeles Times*, 15 September 1946, 9; "Bring Them Home!" *Chicago Daily Tribune*, 22 June 1947, 18. In 1946 Gertrude Stein published her novel about GI disaffection with militarization, *Brewsie and Willie* (New York: Random House, 1946). It is difficult to access the part played by this novel in provoking some unrest, especially in Paris, where many American soldiers flocked to the home of Stein (and Toklas) and gathered around her in clusters when she visited their camps, sharing problems and seeking her counsel. The novel was excerpted a few months prior to the mutinies; see "GI Novel Written by Gertrude Stein: She Finds the Soldiers' Minds Deadened by Their Worship Only of Efficiency," *New York Times*, 25 August 1945, 13.

3. *Bombay Chronicle*, 23 February 1946, n.p. HMIS is a now obsolete prefix from the days of the British empire for Her Majesty's Indian Ship. It was also used for naval shore establishments and buildings.

4. *Hindu*, 23 February 1946, 5.

5. These stances are summarized by Paul Rabinow, in his introduction to *Michel Foucault: Ethics*, vol. 1 of the *Essential Works of Michel Foucault, 1954–1984*, ed. Paul Rabinow, trans. Robert Hurley et al. (Harmondsworth, UK: Penguin, 2000, xxxviii–xxxix. See especially Michel Foucault, *The Uses of Pleasure*, vol. 2 of *The History of Sexuality*, trans. Robert Hurley (London: Penguin,1987), 8.

6. Exhibit A2: Letter to Commander King, File NL 9930, *Report of Board of Inquiry into the causes of the Mutiny in HMIS Talwar*, National Archives, New Delhi.
7. *Hindustan Times*, 22 February 1946, 1.
8. *Hindustan Times*, 23 February 1946, 1.
9. For figures on the interwar drop in Britain's Indian investments see Lawrence James, *Raj: The Making and Unmaking of British India* (New York: St. Martin's Press, 1997), 588–89.
10. Private sources, cited in James, *Making and Unmaking of the Raj*, 597.
11. See Stanley Wolpert, *Shameful Flight: The Last Years of the British Empire in India* (Oxford: Oxford University Press, 2006), 111.
12. Wolpert notes how, during a review of British troops in Berlin on July 21, Deputy Prime Minister Attlee received far more vociferous cheers from the soldiers than did Churchill (ibid., 89).
13. Born Fredrick Lawrence, this former Etonian had undergone a serious ideological makeover through marriage to the radical suffragist and seasoned hunger-striker Emmeline Pethick, part of whose name he had taken as his own. Herself an international, pro-Gandhian lobbyist of note, Emmeline had been weaned on radicalism in the same late-Victorian socialist circles crucial for Gandhi's early political formation. Under her guiding influence Pethick-Lawrence turned socialist, pacifist, and vegetarian by degrees, if along the respectable path of parliamentary democracy. As a member of the pragmatist and anti-utopian Labor Party, his successful career had yielded that curious paradox, a socialist baronetcy (for Peaslake, Surrey), and a facility with the language of disinvestiture and investiture so in vogue at the time.
14. The details of this juncture in Indo-British colonial history are gathered in Nicholas Mansergh, ed. *The Transfer of Power, 1942–1947* (London: Her Majesty's Stationery Office, 1970–83).
15. *Hindu*, 24 February 1946, 5.
16. Ibid.
17. *Hindu*, 27 February 1946, 6.
18. Wavell to King George VI, cited in Wolpert, *Shameful Flight*, 115.
19. Wavell to King George the VI, cited in ibid.
20. Nehru to Wavell, cited in ibid., 120.
21. See statement by Mr. Asaf Ali, *Hindu*, 24 February 1946, 5.
22. I am grateful to William Mazzarella for sharing this information from his research into Indian censorship regulations in the Maharashtra Board Archives, Mumbai, Home Dept., 5th Series, 1595/5. The actor Zohra Sehgal gives an entertaining account of postindependence cultural bans, especially concerning productions by the left-leaning Indian People's Theatre Association (IPTA), in her essay "Theatre and Activism in the 1940s," in *Crossing Boundaries*, ed. Geeti Sen (Delhi: Orient Longman, 1997): "With India in the last stages of the freedom struggle, song and play themes were radical

and left-oriented, inspiring and uniting us to action. Having joined IPTA almost as soon as I arrived in Bombay in 1945, I took an active part in these plays. In 1947, during the Interim Government when Jawaharlal Nehru was appointed vice-president, some IPTA branches were harassed by government bans which censored certain plays and called for the arrest of their perform- ers. I had recently been nominated vice-president of IPTA and wrote a most foolishly presumptuous letter to Pandit Nehru: 'I am writing to you as one vice president to another, . . .' describing the harassment and requesting his mediation. Just imagine the cheek! He wrote back in a most consider- ate manner, saying he was not aware of the harassment and would see what could be done about it. And sure enough, the aggravation stopped after some time" (33). For more on the cultural history of censorship in colonial and postcolonial South Asia, see Raminder Kaur and William Mazzarella ed., *Censorship in South Asia: Cultural Regulation from Sedition to Seduction* (Blooming- ton: Indiana University Press, 2009), and Mazzarella, *Censorium: Cinema and the Open Edge of Mass Publicity* (Durham and London: Duke University Press, 2013).

23. Aparna Bhargava Dharwadker, *Theatres of Independence: Drama, Theory, and Urban Performance in India* (Iowa City: University of Iowa Press, 2005), 46, 76, 88.

24. The 2005 production of *Kallol* is reviewed in the *Telegraph*, 5 November 2005, n.p.

25. See V. M. Bhagwatkar, *Royal Indian Navy Uprising and Indian Freedom Struggle* (Amravati: Chadwak Prakashan, 1989); Biswanath Bose, *RIN Mutiny, 1946* (New Delhi: Northern Book Centre, 1988); Dilip Kumar Das, *Revisiting Tal- war: A Study in the Royal Indian Navy Uprising of February 1946* (Delhi: Ajanta, 1993). A similar argument is made by James in *Raj*: "The cumulative effect of these mutinies was a generate a mood of despondency at the top. The weekly intelligence summary issued on 25 March bleakly admitted that the Indian army was wobbling and 'only day to day estimates of its steadiness' could now be made. All naval and air force units were no longer trustwor- thy. . . . Mainstream politicians were also discomposed by incidents which indicated their hold over the masses was by no means as assured as it had been, and might weaken further in the absence of an agreement with the British" (598).

26. Ranajit Guha, "The Prose of Counter-Insurgency," *Subaltern Studies: Writings on South Asian History and Society*, ed. Ranajit Guha, vol. 2 (Delhi: Oxford University Press, 1983), 14.

27. Ibid., 15.

28. India Office Library and Records, Letters Public and Judicial, 8/574, 120–21, cited in James, *Raj*, 595.

29. This was reported in headlines by the *Hindustan Times*, 23 February 1946: "All the city's workers were on the streets, and the disturbances became more and more widespread as the day wore on till it enveloped the entire city from

the Fort to Dadar and Mahim, a distance of 10 miles. . . . Workers of 60 mills came out. They were joined by thousands . . . from the G.I.P. and B.B. and R.C.I. railway workshops, B.E.S.T. busdrivers and conductors and students. Processions went round all over the city call upon all people to observe hartal. All traffic came to a standstill. Attempts were made to prevent the running of trains" (1).

30. See Das, *Revisiting Talwar*, 202–3.
31. A Group of Victimized R. I. N. Ratings, *The R.I.N. Strike*, ed. People's Publishing House (Delhi: People's Publishing House, 1954), 36.
32. Ibid., 5.
33. Jürgen Habermas, *The Structural Transformation of the Public Sphere*, trans. Thomas Burger with Fredrick Lawrence (Cambridge, MA: MIT Press, 1991), 127.
34. Ibid.
35. Ibid., 128.
36. This critique is developed by Seyla Behabib, "Models of Public Space: Hannah Arendt, the Liberal Tradition, and Jürgen Habermas" in *Habermas and the Public Sphere*, ed. Craig Calhoun (Cambridge, MA: MIT Press, 1992), 73–98; and Nancy Fraser, "Rethinking the Public Sphere: A Contribution to the Critique of Already Existing Democracy," in Calhoun, *Habermas and the Public Sphere*, 109–42.
37. Habermas, in *Structural Transformation*, emphasizes that the bourgeois public sphere is favorable to "a kind of social intercourse that, far from presupposing the equality of status, disregarded status altogether" (36). Thus, he insists, "The tendency replaced the celebration of rank with a tact befitting equals. The parity on whose basis alone the authority of the better argument could assert itself against that of social hierarchy and in the end carry the day meant, in the thought of the day, the parity of 'common humanity'" (ibid.).
38. An apposite definition, in the context of Habermas's foundational oeuvre, comes from Michael Warner, in his *Publics and Counterpublics* (New York: Zone Books, 2005): "The stronger modification of Habermas's analysis—one in which he has shown little interest, though it is clearly of major significance in the critical analysis of gender and sexuality—is that some publics are defined by their tension with a larger public. Their participants are marked off from persons or citizens in general. Discussion within such a public is understood to contravene the rules obtaining in the world at large, being structured by alternative dispositions or protocols, making different assumptions about what can be said or what goes without saying. This kind of public is, in effect, a counterpublic" (56).
39. Ibid., 61.
40. Ibid., 56.
41. We should note the unstable relation between the categories of subaltern and counterpublic in public sphere theory. Some thinkers take subalternity to imply marginalized groups or persons whose given social status already disqualifies them from attaining legibility within the prevailing mainstream.

Such a case is proposed in Leon de Kock, "Interview with Gayatri Chakravorty Spivak: New Nation Writers Conference in South Africa." *ARIEL: A Review of International English Literature* 23, no. 3 (1992): 29–47; and Gayatri Chakravorty Spivak, "Can the Subaltern Speak?" in *Marxism and the Interpretation of Culture*, ed. Cary Nelson and Lawrence Grossberg (Urbana: University of Illinois Press, 1988), 271–313. Yet our emphasis is on counterpublics that actively seek such disqualification/illegibility, whether or not they are deemed irrelevant to the social fabric. For discussions of this type, see Fraser, "Rethinking the Public Sphere," 123, and Warner, *Publics and Counterpublics*, 57, who alike maintain that counterpublics do not merely draw on the polemic of received identities.

42. Jacques Derrida, *The Politics of Friendship*, trans. George Collins (London: Verso, 1997), 306.

43. See Bonnie Honig, "Toward an Agonistic Feminism: Hannah Arendt and the Politics of Identity," in *Feminist Interpretations of Hannah Arendt*, ed. Bonnie Honig (University Park: Pennsylvania State University Press, 1995), 135–66. The clearest account of the performative politics being described remains Judith Butler, *Excitable Speech: A Politics of the Performative* (New York: Routledge, 1997).

44. Warner, *Publics and Counterpublics*, 59.

45. J. L. Austin, "The Meaning of a Word," in *Philosophy and Ordinary Language*, ed. Charles E. Caton (Urbana: University of Illinois Press, 1963), 7.

46. Homi Bhabha, *Locations of Culture* (London: Routledge, 1994), 94.

47. Ibid.

48. Karl Marx, *The Eighteenth Brumaire of Louis Bonaparte* (New York: International Publishers, 2004), 17.

49. A detail from the RINM archive illuminates this aspect of its constitutive liminality. Many eyewitnesses and supporters noted the multiplicity of RINM participants, each representing an important constituency for civil life and civil discussion. Yet all were baffled by one group that came into view toward the very end of the mutiny—a procession of urchins, of unknown origin and future, and quite useless to the new republic: "The procession itself had for its train a body of about 100 urchins, almost all under fifteen, who . . . rushed forward whenever a motor vehicle was sighted, shouting and yelling, and compelled all the vehicles to turn back and drive away" (*Hindu*, 26 February 1946, 7).

50. John Rawls, *A Theory of Justice*, rev. ed. (Cambridge, MA: Belknap Press, 1999), 26.

51. Bruno Latour, *Politics of Nature: How to Bring the Sciences into Democracy*, trans. Catherine Porter (Cambridge: Harvard University Press, 2004), offers the guiding proposition for this section: "Nature is the chief obstacle that has always hampered the development of public discourse" (9).

52. Michel Foucault, *Security, Territory, Population: Lectures at the College de France, 1977–1978*, ed. Michel Senellart, trans. Graham Burchell (Basingstoke, UK: Palgrave, 2007), 105.

53. Giambattista Vico, *New Science*, trans. David Marsh (Harmondsworth, UK: Penguin, 2001), 283.

54. For Marx's Vichean inheritance, see Giambattista Vico, *The Autobiography of Giambattista Vico*, trans. M. H. Fisch and T. G. Bergin (Ithaca, NY: Cornell University Press, 1944), 104; and Giorgio Tagliacozzo, ed., *Vico and Marx: Affinities and Contrasts* (Basingstoke, UK: Palgrave, 1983).

55. Marx, *Eighteenth Brumaire*, 15.

56. Karl Marx, *The People's Paper*, cited in Terry Eagleton, *Marx and Freedom* (London: Phoenix, 1997), 44.

57. This argument is eloquently rendered in Anne Middleton Wagner, *Motherstone: The Vitality of Modern British Sculpture* (New Haven, CT: Yale University Press, 2005), 15. Generationality haunts the logic of hegemony defended by many political thinkers as the crux of civil democratic society. See, especially, Antonio Gramsci, *Selections from the Prison Notebooks*, ed. and trans. Quintin Hoare and Geoffrey Nowell Smith (New York: International Publishers, 1971), for a more reliable version of the following schema. A general crime against a given society is performed by a particular group and contested by another group, which becomes synechdochal in relation to the victimized society. In time this latter group will likely undertake its own generalizable crimes and provoke the resistance of yet another lobby with counterhegemonic synechdochal potential and equally susceptible to the genetic criminality and radicalism of its dubious line of descent, on and on. Ranajit Guha, "Dominance without Hegemony and Its Historiography," in *Subaltern Studies*, ed. Ranajit Guha, vol. 6 (Delhi: Oxford University Press, 1989), 210–309, attests to the generativity at the heart of hegemony. He suggests that colonial conditions prohibit the emergence of a public sphere precisely by blocking the reproductive logic of hegemony and the conditions of antagonism on which this is premised. In lieu of a public sphere, he tells us, colonialism delivers a sterile society of civility, numbed by the practices of obedience and the institutions of order.

A neo-Hegelian take on Gramscian hegemony, thus characterized, redoubles its implicit reproductive metaphorics. For examples see, Slavoj Žižek and John Milbank, *The Monstrosity of Christ: Paradox or Dialectic*, ed. Creston Davis (Cambridge, MA: MIT Press, 2009). Žižek and Milbank argue that Hegel, following his much-touted break with traditional metaphysics, delivers a rare materialist (or singular) universalism that engages the problem of particularity without fetishizing it as alterity. He does so by showing that the universal can only ever be actualized and formalized by the *communitas*, or within the region of political/civic life—a hypothesis that he also figures, irresistibly, as the birth-event of Christian incarnation: God made man, the universal made particular. Similar arguments are offered by Alain Badiou, *Saint Paul: The Foundation of Universalism*, trans. Ray Brassier (Stanford, CA: Stanford University Press, 2003). Thinkers of this persuasion often image as constitutive the preparatory womb-likeness of the universalist ideal itself.

"The universal is an empty place," we hear from Ernesto Laclau, "a void which can be filled only by the particular" ("Identity and Hegemony: The Role of Universality in the Constitution of Political Logics," in *Contingency, Hegemony, Universality: Contemporary Dialogues on the Left*, by Judith Butler, Ernesto Laclau, and Slavoj Žižek [London: Verso, 2000], 58). Compare Slavoj Žižek: "The Universal is empty, yet precisely as such always-already filled in, that is, hegemonized by some contingent, particular content" (*The Ticklish Subject: The Absent Centre of Political Ontology* [London: Verso, 1999, 100–101). Judith Butler is perhaps alone in a defense of hegemony that scrupulously sidesteps reproductive metaphorics. She not only substitutes for the tropes of generativity the far more complex procedures of iteration but also refutes the procreative imagery of universalism in favor of particularities that stand beside/outside the universal. As she puts it, "Those who should ideally be included within any operation of the universal find themselves not only outside its terms but as the very outside without which the universal could not be formulated" (*Contingency, Hegemony, Universality*, 178).

58. Edward Said makes an influential distinction between filiative and affiliative communities in his *The World, the Text, and the Critic* (Cambridge, MA: Harvard University Press, 1983), 16–24, 111–25.

59. Judith Butler, *Antigone's Claim: Kinship between Life and Death* (New York: Columbia University Press, 2000).

60. Lee Edelman, *No Future: Queer Theory and the Death Drive* (Durham, NC: Duke University Press, 2004), 2–3.

61. Heather Love, *Feeling Backward: Loss and the Politics of Queer History* (Cambridge, MA: Harvard University Press, 2007). At his most polemical, Edelman contests the idea of the future per se as a meaningful horizon for politics, arguing that "what is queerest about us . . . is to insist . . . that the future stop here" (*No Future*, 31). As we will see at the conclusion of this chapter (à la Rawls), however, inconsequentialism does not dispense with the idea of the future so much as question its strict causativity.

62. The appeal for cultivated anachronicity, in the context of queer anti-generativity, instantly summons the familiar tropes of fin de siècle degeneration. Though votaries of this credo were as historically complex as they were diverse, some among them took the invitation to step out of natural/standard time as a badge of exceptionality. Nowhere is this more palpable than in Joris-Karl Huysmans's 1903 preface to the luxury edition of his *Against Nature*, trans. Patrick McGuinness (Harmondsworth, UK: Penguin, 2003), a classic study of a decadent, ailing aristocrat, "living alone, far from his century, among memories of more congenial times, of less base surroundings" (207–8). In his arguments against the conventions of late nineteenth-century literary naturalism, Huysmans's bid to transform the slur of sexual abnormality into a claim for special ability defaults most readily to antipathetic elitism. "Naturalism had no room," he writes "for exceptions; it thus confined itself to the portrayal of ordinary experience, striving, under

the pretext of being true to life, to create characters who came as close as possible to the average person" (205). Needless to say, such complaints against ordinariness and averageness cannot ethically equip the present discussion, which hopes to derive radical universalism out of anti-generativity, nor do they have any appeal to the theorists discussed above.

63. The phrase comes from the title of Judith Halberstam's, *The Queer Art of Failure* (Durham, NC: Duke University Press, 2011).

64. Love, *Feeling Backward*, 4; and Michael Warner, *The Trouble with Normal: Sex, Politics and the Ethics of Queer Life* (Cambridge, MA: Harvard University Press, 2000), 35–36.

65. Annamarie Jagose, *Inconsequence: Lesbian Representation and the Logic of Sexual Sequence* (Ithaca, NY: Cornell University Press, 2002), ix.

66. Between 1785 and 1797 Kant composed three related works on the subject of ethics. *Groundwork of the Metaphysics of Morals* (1785) begins the effort to identify the irreducible principles of moral obligation. These findings are repeated in the *Critique of Practical Reason* (1788), with the difference that this text brings the subject of epistemology—integral to the first critique—into the mainstay of ethics proper. The neglected *The Metaphysics of Morals* (1797), derived from the lecture notes taken by Kant's students at Königsberg, also elaborates the moral philosophy promised in the *Groundwork*.

67. Immanuel Kant, *Groundwork of the Metaphysics of Morals*, trans. and ed. Mary Gregor (Cambridge: Cambridge University Press, 2003), 7.

68. Ibid.

69. Ibid.

70. Immanuel Kant, *The Metaphysics of Morals*, trans. and ed. Mary Gregor (Cambridge: Cambridge University Press, 1996), 127–28; emphasis in original.

71. See Kant, *Groundwork*: "Freedom and the will's own lawgiving are both autonomy and hence reciprocal concepts, and for this very reason one cannot be used to explain the other or to furnish a ground for it but can at most be used only for the logical purpose of reducing apparently different representations of the same object to one single concept (as different fractions of equal value are reduced to their lowest expression)" (55–56).

72. Ibid., 38, 39.

73. As Kant says, "The will determines itself immediately" (ibid., 50).

74. The case against legal precedent is made cogently in Kant, *Metaphysics of Morals*: "All that ethics teaches us is that if the incentive which juridical lawgiving connects with that duty, namely, external constraint, were absent, the idea of duty by itself would be sufficient as an incentive" (21).

75. This is a consistent theme in Kant's ethical oeuvre. See, *Groundwork*: "Imitation has no place at all in matters of morality" (21); and *Metaphysics of Morals*: "Reason commands how men are to act even though no examples of this could be found" (10).

76. Kant, *Metaphysics of Morals*, 148.

77. Kant, *Groundwork*, 8.

78. Kant, *Metaphysics of Morals*, 196.
79. Peter Brown, *The Body and Society: Men, Women, and Sexual Renunciation in Early Christianity* (New York: Columbia University Press, 2008).
80. This tendency among early Christian celibates is highlighted in Eusebius, *The Church History*, trans. Paul L. Maier (Grand Rapids, MI: Kregel, 2007). An exemplary account of celibacy as a mode of moral immaculacy or self-perfection appears in Origen, *On First Principles*, trans. G. W. Butterworth (New York: Harper Torchbooks, 1966). There is a clearer case for celibacy as a practice of self-reduction in St. John Chrysostom, *On Wealth and Poverty*, trans. Catharine P. Roth (New York: St. Vladimir's Seminary Press, 1981); St. John Chrysostom, *On Marriage and Family Life*, trans. Catharine P. Roth (New York: St. Vladimir's Seminary Press, 1997); St. Gregory of Nyssa, "On Virginity," in *The Fathers of the Church: St Gregory Ascetical Works*, trans. Virginia Woods Callahan (Washington, DC: Catholic University of America Press, 1967). See also Peter Brown, *Poverty and Leadership in the Later Roman Empire*, the Menahem Stern Jerusalem Lectures (Hanover, NH: University Press of New England, 2002).
81. John Stuart Mill, *Utilitarianism* (London: Longmans, Green, Reader, and Dyer, 1871), 3.
82. G. W. F. Hegel, *The Encyclopedia Logic*, pt. 1 of the *Encyclopedia of Philosophical Sciences*, trans. T. F. Geraets, W. A. Suchting, and H. S. Harris (Indianapolis, IN: Hackett, 1991, 82.
83. Mary Gregor, "Introduction," in Kant, *Groundwork*, vii.
84. A. G. Henderson, "A Sketch of Kant's Life and Work," in *On the Philosophy of Kant and a Sketch of Kant's Life and Work*, by Robert Adamson and A. G. Henderson (London: Routledge/Thoemmes Press, 1993), 3.
85. Manfred Kuehn, *Kant: A Biography* (Cambridge: Cambridge University Press, 2001), 119.
86. Hamann to Kant, cited in Kuehn, *Kant: A Biography*, 119.
87. See Whitney Davis, "Winkelmann Divided: Mourning the Death of Art History," in *Gay and Lesbian Studies in Art History*, ed. Whitney Davis (Binghamton, NY: Haworth Press, 1994), 141–60.
88. Eric O. Clarke, "Kant's Kiss: Reflections on the Philosophy of Lifestyle," *boundary 2* 38, no. 2 (2011): 196.
89. In his *Metaphysics of Morals* Kant insists that ethics requires a disposition and way of life: "not only the concept of virtue but also how to put into practice and cultivate the *capacity for* as well as the will to virtue" (169; emphasis in original).
90. The primary sources for the biographical paraphrase in the main discussion are E. A. Ch. Wasianski, *Immanuel Kant in seinen Letzten Lebensjahren*, vol. 3 of *Über Immanuel Kant*, ed. Ludwig Ernst Borowski (Königsberg: Freidrich Nicolovius, 1804); and Thomas De Quincey, "The Last Days of Immanuel Kant," in *The Last Days of Immanuel Kant and Other Writings*, vol. 3 of *De Quincey's Works* (Edinburgh: Adam and Charles Black, 1862), 99–166. These are

supplemented with other biographical matter in Kuehn, *Kant: A Biography*, 100–143; William Wallace, *Kant*, ed., William Knight (Edinburgh: William Blackwood and Sons, 1932). Eric Clarke's "Kant's Kiss" draws on many of these materials.

91. De Quincey, "Last Days of Immanuel Kant," 119.

92. Immanuel Kant, *Anthropology from a Pragmatic Point of View*, trans. and ed. Robert B. Loudon (Cambridge: Cambridge University Press, 2006), 142–43. Michel Foucault's complementary doctoral thesis on Kant's *Anthropology* is published as *Introduction to Kant's Anthropology*, ed. Roberto Nigro, trans. Kate Briggs and Roberto Nigro (Cambridge, MA: Semiotext(e), 2008).

93. Michel Foucault, "What Is Enlightenment," in *The Foucault Reader: An Introduction to Foucault's Thought*, ed. Paul Rabinow (Harmondsworth, UK: Penguin, 1991), 50.

94. John Kaye, *Kaye's and Malleson's History of the Indian Mutiny of 1857–1858*, ed. Colonel Malleson, C.S.I., vol. 1, Cabinet Edition (London: W. H. Allen, 1888), 148, 147. The consolidated edition cited here combines John Kaye's two initiatory volumes, *History of the Sepoy War in India,1857–1858*, along with three additional volumes by Colonel Malleson.

95. Jawaharlal Nehru, *The Discovery of India* (Bombay: Asia Publishing House, 1973), 323.

96. Karl Marx and Frederick Engels, *The First Indian War of Independence, 1857–1859* (Moscow: Foreign Languages Publishing House, 1959), 145.

97. On the subject of the British imperial security regime in Asia, see James Hevia, *The Imperial Security State: British Colonial Knowledge and Empire-Building in Asia* (Cambridge: Cambridge University Press, 2012).

98. Kaye, *History of the Indian Mutiny*, 146.

99. Ibid., 146.

100. Ibid., 440–41, 251.

101. Ibid., 236.

102. Ibid., 254.

103. Ibid., 435.

104. David Omissi discusses colonial applications of the martial race theory in *The Sepoy and the Raj: The Indian Army, 1860–1940* (London: MacMillan, 1994), 10–23. See also Michael Barthorp and Jeffrey Burn, *Indian Infantry Regiments, 1860–1914* (Oxford: Osprey, 1979).

105. J. M. Wikely, *Handbooks for the Indian Army: Punjabi Musalmans* (Calcutta: Office of the Superintendent, Government Printing, 1915), 49.

106. Major Holland-Pryor, *Mappillas or Moplahs* (Calcutta: Office of the Superintendent, Government Printing, 1904), 11.

107. Sri George Macmunn, *The Martial Races of India* (London: Marston, 1933), 1, v.

108. Compare Wikely, *Punjabi Musalmans*, 2; Major Morris, *Handbooks for the Indian Army: Gurkhas* (Delhi: Government of India, 1933), preface, n.p.

109. Wikely, *Punjabi Musalmans*, 35.

110. Morris, *Gurkhas*, 39, 52.

111. Wikely, *Punjabi Musalmans*, 87, 107.
112. Major R. T. I. Ridgeway, *Handbooks for the Indian Army: Pathans* (Calcutta: Office of the Superintendent, Government Printing, 1910), 227.
113. Morris, *Gurkhas*, 126, 146.
114. Ridgeway, *Pathans*, 179.
115. See Omissi, *Sepoy and the Raj*, 27.
116. John Masters, *Bugles and a Tiger: A Personal Adventure* (London: Michael Joseph, 1957) 95; cited in Omissi, *Sepoy and the Raj*, 27.
117. Wikely, *Punjabi Musalmans*, 23–24.
118. *R. I. N. Strike*, 32.
119. *Inquiry of RIN Commission, 1946*, Draft Report, S. No. 14, 16–17, RIN Mutiny Papers, National Archives, Delhi.
120. Ibid., S. No. 4, Part III, 1149.
121. Ibid., Bombay Witnesses, vol. 1, 37.
122. Ibid., 6.
123. Ibid., 84.
124. Ibid., 41.
125. Ibid., 38.
126. Ibid., 170.
127. Ibid., Draft Report, S. No. 6, Part III, 1141.
128. Ibid., Delhi Proceedings, vol. 3, 603, 604–605.
129. Ibid., Draft Report, S. No. 4, Part I, 49.
130. Ibid., Delhi Proceedings, vol. 3, 598.
131. Ibid., Bombay Witnesses, vol. 1, 255. Lizzie Collingham, *The Taste of Food: World War II and the Battle for Food* (New York: Penguin Press, 2012), describes the significant improvement made in colonial army food rations after 1943 to prepare Indian troops for a push into Burma and Southeast Asia. In her words, "An Indian army catering corps was formed and the field service ration was improved. Mutton, carefully labeled as *halal* for the Muslims and *jhatka* for the Hindus and Sikhs, was introduced. Fresh vegetables, fruits and marmite, rich in vitamin B, were added to the menu. An emergency ration pack suitable for use by any Indian no matter what caste was developed, containing a chocolate bar fortified with vitamins which provided 1,350 calories. A twenty-four hour operational 2,700-calorie ration contained biscuits, chocolate, cheese, a tin of sardines, sugar, milk powder, tea and salt. Eight-man composite ration packs provide a hearty 4,400 calories and incorporated tins of mutton" (413–14).
132. *Inquiry of RIN Commission, 1946*, Bombay Witnesses, vol. 1, 53.
133. Ibid., 91, 119.
134. Ibid., Draft Report, S. No. 12, 93; 117.
135. Ibid., Draft Report, S. No. 14, 6.
136. Ibid., Bombay Witnesses, vol. 1, 127.
137. See *Hindustan Times*, 18 February 1946, 1.
138. *New York Times*, 17 February 1946, 14.

139. *Inquiry of RIN Commission, 1946*, Delhi Proceedings, vol. 2, 85.

140. James Bonar, *Malthus and His Work* (New York: Harper and Brothers, 1885), 177.

141. Ibid., 181.

142. Amartya Sen, *Poverty and Famines: An Essay on Entitlement and Deprivation* (Oxford: Oxford University Press, 1982). For similar insights into Malthusian symbolic reproduction, see Frances Ferguson, "Malthus, Godwin, Words-worth, and the Spirit of Solitude," in her *Solitude and the Sublime: Romanticism and the Aesthetics of Individuation* (New York: Routledge, 1992), 114–28.

143. This evidence is persuasively garnered in Lizzie Collingham, *Taste of Food* .

144. There is a pathbreaking expose of the British policies that lead to devastating famine conditions in South Asia in Madhushree Mukerjee, *Churchill's Secret War: The British Empire and the Ravaging of India during World War II* (New York: Basic Books, 2010).

145. "The Things We Forgot to Remember," BBC Radio 4, 7 January 2008; cited in Collingham, *Taste of Food*, 145.

146. How interesting it is to learn that the RINM surrender in late February was haunted by the stray rumor—and rumor it surely was—that British reinforcement troops were prepared to reemploy scorched-earth tactics and blow up portions of greater Bombay so as to maintain imperial command over the city and its native armed forces. We have this on the testimony of the mutineer Madan Singh: "There is another crucial point to be recalled to-day. You see, next to the Castle Barracks there was an 'iron gate' closer to the town half of Bombay. It was cleverly wired to the system so that in the event of an enemy trying to capture Bombay, a press of the switch would blow up the whole of Greater Bombay. This was the scorched earth policy of the then British government" (Reeta Sharma, "Hero's Honor for Royal Mutineer," *Tribune*, 25 February 1999, n.p.).

147. In Lyotard's words, 'The plaintiff lodges his or her complaint before the tribunal, the accused argues in such a way as to show the inanity of the ac-cusation. Litigation takes place. I would like to call a *differend* the case where the plaintiff is divested of the means to argue. . . . A case of differend between two parties takes place when the 'regulation' of the conflict that opposes them is done in the idiom of one of the parties while the wrong suffered by the other is not signified in that idiom" (Jean-François Lyotard, *The Differend: Phrases in Dispute*, trans. Georges Van Den Abbeele [Minneapolis: University of Minnesota Press, 1988], 9).

148. *Inquiry of RIN Commission, 1946*, Delhi Proceedings, vol. 3, 667.

149. Ibid., Draft Report, S. No. 14, 229.

150. Ibid., 292.

151. *R. I. N. Strike*, 55.

152. Bhagwatkar, *Royal Indian Navy Uprising*, 77.

153. Bhabha, *Location of Culture*, 219.

154. Ibid., 235.

155. Ibid., 217.

156. *New York Times*, 23 February 1946, 14.
157. See *New York Times*, 5 January 1946, 1.
158. *Time*, 4 February 1946, 18.
159. *New York Times*, 21 February 1946, 14.
160. *New York Times*, 20 January 1946, 32. See also Erwin Marquit, "The Demobilization Movement of January 1946," *Nature, Society and Thought* 15, no. 1 (2002): 5–40.
161. *New York Times*, 13 January 1946, E3.
162. *New York Times*, 8 January 1946, 22: "The men demonstrating in Manila and Le Havre are reverting without warrant to a civilian status. . . . What they have done is indefensible, and they should be made to understand this."
163. *New York Times*, 10 January,1946, 4.
164. *New York Times*, 20 February, 1946, 27.

EPILOGUE

1. The tension between conventional life and ethical life is a recurring theme in Foucault's work. It is germane to his final lectures on cynicism. In his words, "What in fact does 'alter the value of the currency' (*parakharattein to nomisma*) mean? . . . I would just like to point out that what should be stressed first of all with this theme of 'change, alter the value of the currency' is the connection—indicated by the word itself—between currency and custom, rule, law. *Nomisma* is currency; *nomos* is the law. To change the value of the currency is also to adopt a certain standpoint toward rule, or law. . . . The Cynics do not change the metal itself of this coin. But . . . by going to the extreme consequence . . . they reveal a life which is precisely the opposite of what was traditionally recognized as the true life" (Michel Foucault, *The Courage of Truth*, vol. 2 of *The Government of Self and Others, Lectures at the College de France, 1983–1984*, ed., Fredric Gros, trans. Graham Burchell [Basingstoke, UK: Palgrave Macmillan, 2011], 227).
2. M. K. Gandhi, *Hind Swaraj and Other Writings*, ed. Anthony J. Parel (Cambridge: Cambridge University Press, 1997), 84.
3. Edmund Husserl, *The Crisis of European Sciences and Transcendental Phenomenology: An Introduction to Phenomenological Philosophy*, trans. David Carr (Evanston, IL: Northwestern University Press, 1970), 151.
4. For a rich discussion of Sri Aurobindo's metrical commitments, see Tamara Chin, "Anti-Colonial Metrics: Homeric Time in an Indian Prison, ca. 1909," *English Literary History* (forthcoming, 2013).
5. Sri Aurobindo, *Letters on Poetry and Art* (Pondicherry: Sri Aurobindo Ashram Trust, 2004), vol. 27 of *The Complete Works of Sri Aurobindo* (Pondicherry: Sri Aurobindo Ashram Trust, 2011), 121.
6. Ibid., 121; see also Sri Aurobindo, *The Future Poetry*, vol. 26 of *The Complete Works of Sri Aurobindo* (Pondicherry: Sri Aurobindo Ashram Trust, 2011), 38.
7. Gandhi, *Hind Swaraj*, 88.

8. Ibid., 89.
9. Ibid., 90.
10. Ibid., 89-90.
11. I am building this analysis on the recommendations in favor of the subjunctive mode in Raymond Williams, "Forms of English Fiction in 1848," in his *Writing and Society* (London: Verso), 150-65.
12. Michel de Certeau, *The Practice of Everyday Life*, trans. Steven Rendall (Berkeley and Los Angeles: University of California Press, 1984), 9, 12-13.
13. Ibid., 13.
14. Hadot, cited in Arnold Davidson, "Introduction: Pierre Hadot and the Spiritual Phenomenon of Ancient Philosophy," in Pierre Hadot, *Philosophy as a Way of Life: Spiritual Exercises from Socrates to Foucault*, ed. Arnold Davidson, trans. Michael Chase (Oxford: Blackwell, 1995), 9, 8, 17. See also Pierre Hadot, *The Present Alone Is Our Happiness: Conversations with Jeannie Carlier and Arnold J. Davidson*, trans. Marc Djaballah and Michael Chase (Stanford, CA: Stanford University Press, 2011). In an evolving project, Toril Moi also defends OLP as a spur toward the quotidian creative freedom that comes from giving up on expert or dominant ways of seeing. See Toril Moi, "'They practice their trades in different worlds': Concepts in Poststructuralism and Ordinary Language Philosophy," *New Literary History* 40, no. 4 (2009): 801-24.
15. Certeau, *Practice of Everyday Life*, 13.
16. Raymond Williams illuminates this scene indirectly in "Cambridge English, Past and Present," and "Beyond Cambridge English," both in Williams, *Writing and Society*, 177-91, 212-26.
17. The historical circumstances and disciplinary consequences for English studies, of the Newbolt Report of 1921 are documented in Chris Baldick, *The Social Mission of English Criticism, 1848-1932* (Oxford: Clarendon Press, 1983), 86-108. The literature on the cultural elitisms engendered by Cambridge English and its heirs is voluminous. For select examples, see Sneja Gunew ed., *Feminist Knowledge: Critique and Construct* (London: Routledge, 1990); W. V. Spanos, "The Apollonian Investment of Modern Humanist Education: The Examples of Matthew Arnold, Irving Babbit, and I. A. Richards," *Cultural Critique* 1 (Autumn 1985): 7-71; John Frow, "The Social Production of Knowledge and the Discipline of English," *Meanjin* 29, no. 2 (1990): 353-67; David Lloyd, "Arnold, Ferguson, Schiller: Aesthetic Culture and the Politics of Aesthetics," *Cultural Critique* 2 (Winter 1985-1986): 137-69; Dipesh Chakrabarty, "Postcoloniality and the Artifice of History: Who Speaks for "Indian" Pasts?" *Representations* 37 (Winter 1992): 1-26; Rey Chow, *Writing Diaspora: Tactics of Intervention in Contemporary Cultural Studies* (Bloomington: Indiana University Press, 1993).
18. F. R. Leavis, *The Living Principle: English as a Discipline of Thought* (Chicago: Elephant Paperbacks, 1998), 9.
19. Ibid., 10.

20. F. R. Leavis, "Memories of Wittgenstein," in *The Critic as Anti-Philosopher: Essays and Papers by F. R. Leavis*, ed. G. Singh (Chicago: Elephant Paperbacks, 1998), 129–45.
21. F. R. Leavis, *Living Principle*, 57.
22. P. F. Strawson, "Intellectual Autobiography of P. F. Strawson," in *The Philosophy of P. F. Strawson*, ed. Lewis Edwin Hahn (Chicago: Open Court, 1998), 19.
23. See ibid., 10; see also G. J. Warnock's translation of a roundtable discussion at Royaumont following Austin's talk, "Performative-Constative," in *Philosophy and Ordinary Language*, ed. Charles E. Caton (Urbana: University of Illinois Press, 1963), 22–54.
24. This is a constant theme in Stanley Cavell, *Must We Mean What We Say?* rev. ed. (Cambridge: Cambridge University Press, 2002).
25. Michael Dummett's politics in this regard are strikingly on display in his *Of Immigration and Refugees* (London: Routledge, 2001). Strawson's Indian students and interlocutors include the philosophers Arindam Chakrabarty, Ramchandra Gandhi, and Roop Rekha Verma. Strawson visited India twice between 1975 and 1980, giving lectures, reading papers, and participating in discussions in Delhi, Lucknow, Santiniketan, and Calcutta.
26. Gilbert Ryle, *The Concept of Mind: 60th Anniversary Edition* (London: Routledge, 2009), 255.
27. Gilbert Ryle, "Ordinary Language," in Caton, *Philosophy and Ordinary Language*, 108.
28. J. L. Austin, "Performative-Constative," in Caton, *Philosophy and Ordinary Language*, 42.
29. Michael Dummett, in *Origins of Analytical Philosophy* (Cambridge, MA: Harvard University Press, 1993), is eloquent on this theme: "The disadvantage of this approach lies in its unsystematic nature. This for Wittgenstein was a merit, . . . [but] Wittgenstein leaves us in the dark about whether his program can be executed: it is another disadvantage for the repudiation of system that it leaves us with no way of judging, in advance of complete success, whether a strategy is likely to be unsuccessful" (20).
30. See Cavell, *Must We Mean What We Say?* 42.
31. Ludwig Wittgenstein, *Philosophical Investigations*, trans. G. E. M. Anscombe, 2nd ed. (Oxford: Basil Blackwell, 1988), 46, 48.
32. Hadot's interest in and engagement with Wittgenstein's work is yet more evidence for the rare internationalism of OLP. This connection is well documented in Pierre Force, "The Teeth of Time: Pierre Hadot on Meaning and Misunderstanding in the History of Ideas," *History and Theory* 50 (February 2011): 10–40. See also Pierre Hadot, "What Is Ethics," in Hadot, *Present Alone Is Our Happiness*, 175–85.
33. Phillipa Foot, *Virtues and Vices* (Oxford: Clarendon Press, 2002), xiv (emphasis in original).
34. J. L. Austin, "Performative-Constative," 15.
35. P. F. Strawson, "On Referring," in Caton, *Philosophy and Ordinary Language*, 183.

36. Austin, "Performative-Constative": "There's a whole lot of things to be considered and weighed up: . . . the situation of the speaker, his purpose in speaking, his hearer, questions of precision, etc." (33).
37. See Cavell, *Must We Mean What We Say?* 33.
38. See R. Rhees, "Can There Be a Private Language?" in Caton, *Philosophy and Ordinary Language*, 91.
39. Ramchandra Gandhi, *The Availability of Religious Ideas* (London: Macmillan, 1976), is apposite here: "In addressing you I seek, solicit, a communicative response from you, I do not merely causally interact with you. And I cannot solicit a communicative response from you—thereby in some decisive sense leaving it to you to respond or not—without exhibiting minimal care for you (I may of course be unaware of all this)" (5–6).
40. For a cogent account of logical positivism and the verification principle, see Alfred Jules Ayer, *Language, Truth and Logic* (New York: Dover, 1952).
41. The double influence on OLP of Frege and Husserl is amply tracked by Michael Dummet in *Origins of Analytical Philosophy*.
42. Gilbert Ryle, *On Thinking*, ed. Konstantin Kolenda (Oxford: Wiley-Blackwell, 1979), 85.
43. J. L. Austin, "The Meaning of a Word," in Caton, *Philosophy and Ordinary Language*, 15. Austin's full-scale assault on the tyranny of the fact in theories of meaning is fully documented in his *Sense and Sensibilia*, reconstructed by G. J. Warnock from the manuscript notes (Oxford: Clarendon Press, 1962). Jacques Derrida, in a famous critique of Austin, finds the latter's antipositivism wholly inconsistent with his putative antimetaphysics, thus drawing attention to, while rejecting, OLP's innovative counterfactualism (in the sense in which the term is being canvassed in the main discussion above). See Derrida, "Signature, Event, Context," in *Margins of Philosophy*, by Jacques Derrida, trans. Alan Bass (New York: Harvester Wheatsheaf, 1982): "And if it is alleged that ordinary language, or the ordinary circumstances of language, excludes citationality or general iterability, does it not signify that the 'ordinariness' in question, the thing and the notion, harbors a lure, the teleological lure of consciousness whose motivations, indestructible necessity, and systematic effects remain to be analyzed? Especially since this essential absence of intention for the actuality of the statement, this structural unconscious, if you will, prohibits the saturation of a context. For a context to be exhaustively determinable, in the sense demanded by Austin, it at least would be necessary for the conscious intention to be totally present and actually transparent for itself and others, since it is a determining focal point for the context. The concept of or quest for the 'context' therefore seems to suffer here from the same theoretical and motivated uncertainty as the concept of the 'ordinary,' from the same metaphysical origins: an ethical and teleological discourse of consciousness" (327).
44. Wittgenstein, *Philosophical Investigations*, 20.
45. Strawson, "On Referring," 176.

46. Cavell, *Must We Mean What We Say?* xxxiv.
47. Dummett, in *Origins of Analytical Philosophy*, has a telling phenomenological gloss on the attitude under discussion: "Every mental act must have a noema, and hence have the quality of being directed towards an object: but it is no more problematic that there should be a noema that misses its mark, so that no external object corresponds to it, than that a linguistic expression should have a sense that fails to supply it . . . with any actual objective reference. A delusive perception is therefore no longer a problem: it possesses the feature of intentionality as well as does a veridical one, but simply happens to lack any actual object" (74).
48. Wittgenstein, *Philosophical Investigations*, 42.
49. Wittgenstein speaks for OLP at large in his objections to the pursuit of originality in philosophical endeavor: "It is . . . of the essence of our investigation that we do not seek to learn anything new by it" (*Philosophical Investigations*, 42).
50. I am referencing Derrida's objections to Austin from his "Signature, Event, Context": "Could a performative statement succeed if its formulation did not repeat a 'coded' or iterable statement, in other words if the expressions I use to open a meeting, launch a ship or a marriage were not identifiable in a way as a 'citation'" (326).
51. Judith Butler, *Excitable Speech: A Politics of the Performative* (New York: Routledge, 1997), 15.
52. Ibid.
53. Leavis writes disparagingly of Wittgenstein's admiration for Empson in his "Memories of Wittgenstein," 144–45.
54. William Empson, *Seven Types of Ambiguity* (New York: New Directions, 1966), 240.
55. Ibid., 245.
56. See Ramchandra Gandhi, "Hoping and Wishing," in Gandhi, *Availability of Religious Ideas*, 42–52.
57. See Gilbert Ryle, *Collected Papers*, vol. 2 of his *Collected Essays, 1929–1968* (London: Routledge, 2009), 456, 211, 204. Compare Wittgenstein, *Philosophical Investigations*: "We see a complicated network of similarities overlapping and criss-crossing. . . . I can think of no better expression to characterize these similarities than 'family resemblances'" (32).
58. Wittgenstein is apposite again: "Is an indistinct photograph a picture of a person at all? Is it even always an advantage to replace an indistinct picture by a sharp one? Isn't the indistinct one often exactly what we need?" (*Philosophical Investigations*, 34).

Index

Abhishiktananda (Henri La Saux), 198n81
Adorno, Theodor, 102–3, 153, 154
Advaita school, 82–83, 194n54
Against Nature (Huysman), 217n62
Agamben, Giorgio, 53, 54, 200n96
ahimsa (nonviolence), 18, 28, 33, 109, 136, 149, 154–57, 159–60
Alden, Percy, 8, 12
Alfassa, Mirra (later, Mirra Richards), 79, 80–81, 200n91; The Mother of Sri Aurobindo Ashram, 200n94
Ali, Muhammed, 104–5
Ali, Shaukat, 104–5
Althusser, Louis, 94, 113–14
Ambedkar, B. R., 26, 199n86
American Friends Service Committee (AFSC), 72
American GIs, 147–48, 211n2
analytic philosophy. *See* OLP (ordinary-language philosophy)
Anand, Mulk Raj, 206n11
Anderson, Amanda, 167
animal rights, 147–48, 168n6
Anscombe, G. E. M., 158
Anthropological Society of London, 66
anticolonialism. *See* counterpublics; moral imperfectionism; mutineers; Royal Indian Navy Mutiny (RINM)
Anti-Dühring (Engels), 45
anti-generativity, 27, 122, 145–46, 217n62
Antigone, 128

antimaterialism: in the belle époque, 25, 35–36, 35–37, 181n30; derivations of, 51–53; historical context of, 30–31; as metaphysics, 46–47; syndicalism, 31, 32, 40, 44, 50–51, 178n7; Tawney on, 34, 52; women of Bermondsey, 42–43, 151. *See also* asceticism; labor unrest; *philophusikia; phusikaphobia;* Sorel, George
antipositivism, 93, 159, 226n43
anti-Semitism, 52, 111
aparigraha (nonpossession), 33–34
Arendt, Hannah, 5, 45, 51, 54, 124
Aristotle, 53, 102, 187n99
Arya (journal), 80–81, 82
Aryanism: ascent, 69, 81–82; encounter with Dravidian/Dasyu, 81–82; eugenics, 68–69, 192n48, 192n49; European, 26, 66, 69, 194n54; originary hierarchy of, 66, 68–69, 80–81, 192n48; origins of, 57–58, 68; racial and social domination, 26, 68, 192n48; redefinition of term by Sri Aurobindo, 80–82; Vedas, 81, 194n54
Aryan Path, The (theosophical journal), 20
ascent, science of: caste hierarchy, 26–27, 68–69, 192n48; opposition to, 80–81; race ethnology, 26, 56, 66–69, 192n46, 192n48, 192n49; totalitarianism, 3, 5, 15–16, 29, 30, 82, 150, 157

Sabarmati Ashram, 26, 61, 70
sacrifice, 27, 71–74, 84, 94, 100–102, 107, 151, 195n66
sadhana, 64–65, 78, 85, 89–90, 151, 199n86, 200n96
Said, Edward, 63–64, 74, 114, 128, 217n58
the saint, 55–56, 200n93
Saint Genet (Sartre), 79, 200n93
Salt, Henry, 168n6
Salter, William MacIntyre, 173n77
samadhi, 78, 85
Samuel, Herbert, 12
Sartre, Jean-Paul, 79–80, 94, 109, 114, 200n93, 210n66
Sassoon, Siegfried, 95
savyasachi, 17–18
Sayre, Farrand, 175n108
scarcity, 100, 102, 108
Schmitt, Carl, 15–16, 51
Schreiner, Olive, 205n4
Schumpeter, Joseph, 6–7, 9
scorched-earth policies, 143–44, 222n146
Scott, John W., 41
Search in Secret India, A (Brunton), 77
Secret of the Veda, The (Sri Aurobindo), 81, 82
Sehgal, Zohra, 212n22
self-: forgetfulness, 125; improvement, 10, 14, 15, 19; limitation, 52–53; love, 129; mastery, 84; perpetuation, 129–31, 145, 174n94; reduction, 34, 76, 138, 141–44, 151; ruination, 2, 27, 82, 151; rule, 10, 14–15, 19, 202n113; sacrifice, 19–20, 43–44, 52–53, 71–74, 76, 84, 195n66, 202n113
the self: *askesis*, 1–2, 168n4; contagious self, 89–90; disaggregation of, 155; ego, 71–72, 83–84, 85, 90–92, 129; *heautocracy*, 202n113; *zakia* (guarding oneself), 137
Sen, Amartya, 143, 222n142
Sen, Keshub Cunder, 188n8
sepoy (sipahi) mutiny, 27, 119–20, 133–34, 135, 213n22
sepoys, 97–100, 133, 135
Serres, Michel, 110
Sevagram commune, 26, 61
sexuality, 70–71, 214n38
sexual reproduction, 128, 129, 142–45, 222n142
shame (concept), 15
Shaw, Bernard, 31, 169n13

Sickness of An Acquisitive Society, The (Tawney), 183n49
sipahi (Sepoy) mutiny, 27, 119–20, 133–34, 135, 213n22
slavery, 81–82, 114, 192n46
Sloterdijk, Peter, 174n95, 188n5
Smillie, Robert, 38
sophists, 176n119
Sorel, George: on academic philosophy, 184n63; Henri Bergson's influence on, 47, 50–51, 185n68; on limits of materiality, 50–51; "man of exemplary properties," 32–33; metaphysics of, 45–46; syndicalism, 31, 32, 37, 40, 44, 50–51, 178n7; on wealth accumulation in the belle époque, 37; on work, 51
soul force (Gandhi), 156
South Africa, 8–9, 18–19, 26
South Wales coal fields, 40
Sramanas, 24, 176n113
Sri Aurobindo: *Advaita Vedanta*, 82–83; *Arya* (journal), 80–81, 82; on beauty, 155; Cartier-Bresson's photographs of, 91; critique of Indian monism, 201n106; on the disaggregation of self, 155; as guru, 61; Mirra Alfasa and, 79, 200n91, 200n94; publications of, 80–83, 197n81; reinterpretation of the Vedas, 81–82; on totalitarianism, 82; on the value of creative writing, 155; during World War I, 81–82
Sri Muruganar, 198n81
Sri Ramakrishna: ashram of, 61; Chicago Parliament of Religions (1893), 58; engagement with the world, 78; Isherwood on, 70; Max Müller, 57; on the non-ego of ontology, 85, 88; path to radical spiritual perfection (*nirvikalpa samadhi*) taught to, 78, 85; Vivekananda, 58–60, 72, 86, 89, 188n8, 197n81; William James on, 57, 77; writings of, 77, 197n81
Sri Ramana: Cartier-Bresson's photographs of, 90–91; death of, 90–91; detachment, as characteristic of, 86–87; followers of, 61–62, 87–88; as guru, 61, 87–88; heart credo of, 87–88; Isherwood on, 70; *mukti* (liberation), 87; publications of, 77, 198n81; yoga of the heart, 87
Sri Ramanashramam, 198n81
Sri Sri Ramakrishna Kathamrita (Sri Ramakrishna), 77, 85